**Lockheed, Atlanta,
and the Struggle for
Racial Integration**

Lockheed, Atlanta, and the Struggle for Racial Integration

RANDALL L. PATTON

The University of Georgia Press
ATHENS

Paperback edition, 2021
© 2019 by the University of Georgia Press
Athens, Georgia 30602
www.ugapress.org
All rights reserved
Designed by Kaelin Chappell Broaddus
Set in 10.25/13.5 Minion Pro by
Classic City Composition, LLC

Most University of Georgia Press titles are
available from popular e-book vendors.

Printed digitally

The Library of Congress has cataloged the hardcover edition of this book as follows:

Names: Patton, Randall L., 1958– author.
Title: Lockheed, Atlanta, and the struggle for racial integration / Randall L. Patton.
Description: Athens, Georgia : The University of Georgia Press, [2019] | Includes
    bibliographical references and index.
Identifiers: LCCN 2019010726 | ISBN 9780820355146 (hardcover) |
    ISBN 9780820355153 (ebook)
Subjects: LCSH: Affirmative action programs—Georgia—History—20th century. |
    Lockheed-Georgia Company—History. | Lockheed Aeronautical Systems Company.
    Georgia Division—History. | Public-private sector cooperation—United States—
    History—20th century. | Civil rights movements—United States—History—20th
    century.
Classification: LCC HF5549.5.A34 P37 2019 | DDC 331.13/30975823109045—dc23 LC record
    available at https://lccn.loc.gov/2019010726

Paperback ISBN 978-0-8203-6172-7

For Hugh Gordon and Harry Hudson . . .

CONTENTS

Acknowledgments ix

A Note on the Company Name xi

Introduction 1

CHAPTER 1 "Economic Necessity and Governmental Pressures"
Lockheed and Equal Employment Opportunity before Georgia 15

CHAPTER 2 "Lockheed Will Live in the Southern Tradition"
Lockheed Comes to Georgia, 1951–1954 35

CHAPTER 3 "Progress to Be Permanent Had to Be Gradual"
Gradualism and Its Discontents, 1954–1960 58

CHAPTER 4 "A Problem That Was Already Here"
The Early Plans for Progress Era, 1961–1964 76

CHAPTER 5 "Build the People"
The Era of Uncertainty, 1965–1970 101

CHAPTER 6 "The Competitive Economic Advantages of Having an Excellent Minority Hiring Record"
The Banks Case and Its Aftermath, 1966–1972 122

CHAPTER 7 "Atlanta Will Be a Problem"
Lockheed-Georgia and the MEA, the NAB, the CETA, and the Equal Employment Conundrum, 1973–1982 142

Conclusion 163

Epilogue 173

Appendix. Representative Documents 181

Notes 189

Bibliography 207

Index 215

ACKNOWLEDGMENTS

I thank a number of people for their help in bringing this project to fruition. Several colleagues at Kennesaw State University were patient enough to serve as informal sounding boards for ideas. In particular, LeeAnn Lands, David Parker, Susan Rouse, and Brian Wills helped me talk through options and vent frustrations.

In 2011, I helped organize a conference at my university on Integrating the Workplace. That conference helped me understand the broader significance of Lockheed-Georgia and allowed an opportunity to discuss employment desegregation with some of the leading authorities. I deeply appreciated sharing ideas with participants, attendees, and co-organizers of that conference, especially Joseph Abel, Terry Anderson, Jennifer Delton, Flora Devine, Frank Dobbin, Rebecca Hill, Robert A. Pratt, David Roediger, Robert S. Smith, Johannes Steffens, Steve Usselman, Seneca Vaught, and Gavin Wright. Lockheed Martin's Brian Johnstone was instrumental in helping us organize that conference.

The director and staff of the Kennesaw State University Archives provided aid in the research for the manuscript. Archives director Tamara Livingston and former digital archivist Anne Graham went above and beyond the call of duty in dealing with the acquisition and organization of a complex manuscript collection. Anne and current digital archivist Alissa Helms digitized resources that greatly facilitated this work, including the Hudson manuscript, many interviews associated with the Gordon collection, and a number of photographs and documents. And Joyellen Freeman, curator of special collections, was always helpful. Thank you to all the archives staff.

Lockheed Martin and corporate historian Jeff Rhodes graciously granted permission to use some images from the *Lockheed Southern Star*. That permission implies no endorsement of any of the author's interpretations or assertions. This project is an independent scholarly study and received no financial support from Lockheed Martin.

My emeritus colleague Thomas A. Scott provided important background and context with his own research on the history of Lockheed-Georgia's home, Cobb County. In addition to his work, Tom has been a good friend and a thoughtful adviser.

Mick Gusinde-Duffy at that University of Georgia Press expressed early confidence in the project. His advice and counsel have been crucial. Bethany Snead, who guided the book through the publication process, has been kind, helpful, and wise—as usual. She deserves a medal for putting up with this technochallenged author through yet another manuscript. Jon Davies of the University of Georgia Press also was very helpful. Copy editor Ellen Goldlust improved the manuscript immensely; her help is greatly appreciated.

The comments provided by the manuscript's anonymous readers at both the proposal and draft stages improved the manuscript significantly. I thank them for their patience, close reading, and constructive critiques, and I have attempted to implement most of their suggestions. Any errors or shortcomings, however, are solely my responsibility.

To Hugh Gordon and Harry Hudson, I extend special posthumous thanks. Gordon became convinced that there was a story to tell about him and Lockheed. Though we often differed over precisely how to tell that story, he and I came to share a commitment to the project. Hudson wrote a rare, thoughtful memoir of his working life that served as a critical resource for this study. Harry's son, Harry Hudson Jr., graciously donated a copy of his father's memoir to the KSU Archives. I often tell the story of how he went looking for his father's manuscript in the attic after the subject had come up in a phone interview we were conducting. Without Hugh, Harry, and Harry Jr., this project would not have been possible or even conceivable.

My family—wife, Karen; sons, Randall and Matthew; daughter-in-law, Lisy; and nieces and nephews and grandnieces and grandnephews—helped keep me centered.

A NOTE ON THE COMPANY NAME

From January 6, 1951, to July 19, 1961, the subsidiary/division based at Air Force Plant 6 was Lockheed Aircraft–Georgia Division. From July 20, 1961, to September 2, 1987, the official name was Lockheed-Georgia Company. The Marietta subsidiary/division was informally known as Lockheed-Georgia throughout the 1951–87 period, and that designation has been used throughout the book. Since January 27, 2000, the Georgia location has been part of Lockheed Martin Aeronautics Company.

Lockheed Martin Aeronautics Company granted permission to use some photographs from the Lockheed-Georgia newsletter, the *Lockheed Southern Star*. The company neither sponsored nor reviewed this manuscript, and this permission implies no endorsement of the interpretations contained herein.

Lockheed, Atlanta, and the Struggle for Racial Integration

INTRODUCTION

Hugh Gordon, a white former personnel executive, sat down for an interview with Reginald Kemp, a black former aircraft manufacturing experimental technician. Each was a retiree from Lockheed Aircraft's Georgia division, headquartered in Marietta. Gordon was researching the integration of the workplace at Lockheed and in the South, a struggle in which both he and Kemp had been foot soldiers. Gordon was surprised to learn that he and Kemp shared the same "hire-in date" at Lockheed—May 14, 1951. "At that time, employment was less than 3,000 and only a small area of the massive B-1 factory building was lighted and in use for an aircraft assembly line," he recalled. He and Kemp "seemed to have a difference of opinion as to the location of the Employment Office." The two men got into a conversation about "head houses." Access to the main Lockheed-Georgia facility, Air Force Plant 6, then as now, was via tunnels. The structure at the entrance to each tunnel was referred to as a head house.

> Head House #3 was one of five large employee tunnel entrances in the B-1 building, which at 2,000 by 1,000 feet was said to [be] the largest aircraft building in the free world. On Head House #3 there was a large "Employment" sign with a smaller sign which read, "Through these doors pass the greatest aircraft team in the world."
>
> The security turnstiles were removed and replaced with recruiter desks. Reginald and I discussed where we were hired. He said he was hired in Head House #4. That puzzled me, and I was about to contradict him. He saw that, and we both laughed when he said, "You were in the *white* Head House." Head Houses 1, 2, 4, and 5 were only open and manned by security guards at shift change. Unskilled job applicants were told to report to Head House #4 at appointed times. Reginald and a small group of black applicants stood and waited until a factory supervisor came out and looked over the group. Then he pointed to several and said, "Follow me." Reginald said he was big and strong and that was clearly what the supervisor was looking for.[1]

The anecdote reveals much about race and employment in the mid-twentieth-century U.S. South. Gordon, a southern white college graduate who had grown up in Norfolk, Virginia, had been instructed to report to Head House 3. Kemp reported as instructed and was hired in materials handling. Semiskilled, skilled, professional, and management jobs were generally reserved for whites, except in businesses that were owned by African Americans and/or served the black community. Even decades later, Gordon reflexively missed the racial overtones of the hiring process in the early days at Lockheed, though he had spent much of his professional career engaged in efforts to overcome the legacies of segregation and white supremacy. Gordon left behind a cache of records from his career in personnel at Lockheed. He also spent much of his late retirement years interviewing Reginald Kemp and others and collecting records from former colleagues. The collection of Gordon's papers, the interviews he conducted with others, oral history interviews of him, and the items he acquired from others form the Gordon, Kruse, Wentzel Collection in Kennesaw State University's Archives. This collection, in turn, provided the major resource for this project.

Gordon was a veteran of World War II, while Kemp had taken a leave from his Lockheed job to serve in Korea. Gordon became a commissioned officer and flew fifty-three night combat missions in the Southwest Pacific in a P-61 Black Widow Night Fighter. He received numerous decorations, including the Distinguished Flying Cross for downing two enemy bombers and turning away two others attacking General Douglas McArthur's massive invasion fleet that landed on the Philippine island of Luzon. After his bloody combat experiences in the stalemate of Korea, Kemp returned to the United States and processed out of the army. When he and a group of his soldier friends stopped in South Carolina for a bite to eat on their way home, they were not allowed to enter the restaurant; instead, their food was passed to them through a small window. Kemp, like many black veterans of World War II and Korea, noted the irony of risking his life for his country abroad only to return home to a segregated society in which he was treated as a second-class citizen or worse.

Harry Hudson, an African American World War II veteran who spent a career at Lockheed between 1952 and 1988, left behind an unpublished memoir of his working life when he passed away in 2003. Hudson's eldest son, Harry Jr., discovered the manuscript in his attic and donated a copy to the Kennesaw State University Archives. In 2015, he and the author published an edited version of the manuscript as *Working for Equality*. The Hudson manuscript also served as a major resource for this study. Hudson was well aware of his status as a racial pioneer. As he wrote in the preface to the manuscript, "If there is any social significance to this narrative it will have to be the gradual reduction of discrimination over the years ... and the economic uplift that an organization such as Lockheed provided for the community." In this study, I have cited the original archival manuscript.

A few other critical resources made this book possible. The *Lockheed Southern Star*, a slickly produced company publication, was useful in examining how racial issues were—and often were not—handled in management's communications with workers and workers' communications with one another. The *Atlanta Daily World*, the city's dominant African American newspaper, provided a wealth of material covering race and employment issues at Lockheed and generally. Records from a major early discrimination lawsuit, *Banks et al. v. Lockheed*, found in the NAACP Legal Defense Fund papers, provided a crucial addition to the section on the 1960s and early 1970s. The affidavits filed by thirty-six complainants in 1961, contained in the Joseph Kruse Papers within the Gordon, Kruse, Wentzel Collection, allowed a more detailed look at shop-floor interactions than would otherwise have been possible. Supplementing these sources were a number of formal oral histories and less formal interviews (the latter conducted by Hugh Gordon).

Through these and other resources, this study examines the role of Lockheed personnel in bridging the color line in employment in the 1950s and crafting the business response to the civil rights movement in the arena of employment opportunity, following that corporate involvement through the 1970s and early 1980s.

Jennifer Delton (*Racial Integration in Corporate America, 1940–1990*) and Frank Dobbin (*Inventing Equal Opportunity*) study the broad emergence of race, the dialogue around equal employment, and affirmative action policies through organizational records; Dobbin also studies aggregate Equal Employment Opportunity Commission data. These works include sometimes extended discussions of individual companies. General studies of equal employment and affirmative action are numerous. Some of the best include Nancy MacLean (*Freedom Is Not Enough: The Opening of the American Workplace*) and Terry Anderson (*The Pursuit of Fairness: A History of Affirmative Action*). Gavin Wright (*Sharing the Prize*) examines the economic impact of the civil rights revolution in the American South, finding generally positive outcomes—or at least more positive than generally acknowledged—thereby complicating a near truism that the movement integrated public accommodations and voting but fell short in the economic arena.

Philip Rubio (*A History of Affirmative Action, 1619–2000*) sketches the outlines of the origins and operation of what might be called affirmative action for whites or white privilege, elaborating on the construction of the structures of racial discrimination in the broad sweep of U.S. history. Ira Katznelson (*When Affirmative Action Was White*) presents a case for the New Deal era as a hothouse for the creation of policies that at least in the short term widened rather than narrowed the opportunity gap between the races. Philip Skrentny (*The Ironies of Affirmative Action*) writes thoughtfully on the meaning of affirmative action and what he views as the ironic course of its implementation often as a pragmatic shortcut to racial justice. Timothy Minchin and John Salmond (*After the Dream*) survey the landscape of civil rights struggles in the wake of the Voting Rights Act, focusing significant attention on employment and economic opportunity.

A few useful studies of single firms or industries have appeared in recent years. Robert S. Smith (*Race, Labor, and Civil Rights*) and Steve Watkins (*The Black O*) have written excellent studies of racial policies at two large firms—Duke Power and Shoney's, respectively. David Hamilton Golland (*Constructing Affirmative Action*) uncovers the rich history of the desegregation of the construction trades.

This book differs from these works in the depth of coverage it provides for a single, critical firm—Lockheed's Georgia division—over an extended period, 1951–80. The author is not aware of any comparable study of a single corporation. Corporations generally do not offer open access to personnel records and confidential data on the racial makeup of their workforces. EEO-1 forms, which since 1966 have collected workplace racial and gender data, are available for study only with the proviso that individual firms not be identified in any published study. The Hugh Gordon Papers, the Hudson manuscript, and legal records together create an unusual window into this firm's experience with race. This study provides a detailed look at the internal workings of a major corporation dealing with the desegregation of its workforce in the critical years between 1950 and 1980.

Though Lockheed's Georgia division was located outside Atlanta, Marietta and Cobb County had long been perceived as part of the Atlanta metropolitan area, and Lockheed-Georgia was lodged firmly within the regional economy. The first official definition of the Atlanta Metropolitan Area came in February 1949, when the U.S. Census Bureau included Fulton, Cobb, and DeKalb Counties. In June 1953, 5,743 Lockheed-Georgia workers resided in Cobb (4,007 within the Marietta city limits), while another 3,209 commuted (often in carpools) from Fulton. Those from Fulton included 3,025 from the city of Atlanta, among them African American employees Harry Hudson, John Patterson, Alfred "Tup" Holmes, and Willie Elkins, all of whom played leading roles in integrating the plant.[2]

This book traces the local story of workplace desegregation through the eyes of Hugh Gordon, Harry Hudson, and some of their colleagues. It is a narrative history that connects local events with national narratives of civil rights reform, affirmative action, the role of government and public-private partnerships, and the business reaction to state intervention in employment generally in the late 1970s and early 1980s.

The story told here is a selective one. It is largely a male story, reflecting the dominant policy narratives and cultural tropes of the era. Political leaders and policy wonks from Robert Kennedy to Daniel Patrick Moynihan and corporate training managers such as Lockheed's Robert Hudson emphasized their conception of breadwinners and the dissolution of black family life. Management in Gordon's era was overwhelmingly—indeed, nearly universally—male, particularly on the higher rungs of the corporate ladder. This book tells the story of employment in this period from the perspective of discrimination against African Americans, though the story of employment in this period could—and should—be told from many other perspectives as well. And most (though not all) African American workers mentioned in this study were members of the black middle class from the Atlanta area. The complicated dynamic of race and class is not the primary focus here, though it is touched on lightly at a few points, including in the CETA story.

The literature on civil rights is massive, but the scholarship on the economic impact of the movement is somewhat more limited. Delton and Dobbin have done pioneering work on the public-private partnerships and on Gordon and other personnel professionals who were involved in equal employment efforts through the 1980s. Delton has helped begin to unravel the false or at least oversimplified dichotomy between voluntary and compulsory efforts to combat employment discrimination. She also highlights the role of corporate management in advancing civil rights in the workplace.[3]

Dobbin, a Harvard sociologist, excavates and highlights the role of human resources professionals in developing corporate affirmative action and equal employment policies. The weakness of the U.S. national state, he argues, left the field of defining the meaning of *equal employment* and how it might be achieved largely to the private sector. "Fair employment laws led to more extensive corporate responses in the United States than elsewhere," Dobbin writes, "precisely because no federal authority could establish a simple litmus test for compliance." In this environment, HR professionals (referred to as *personnel managers* in Gordon's day) began to function as members of a social movement. "The role of the personnel profession in defining equal opportunity is the part of this story that has been least well documented," according to Dobbin, whose groundbreaking work illustrates the role of the personnel profession in defining equal employment and constructing practices and policies to achieve it, for good and ill. Dobbin's influential *Inventing Equal Opportunity* highlights the work of Gordon and Lockheed-Georgia: "The foot soldiers of equal opportunity were to be found not on the streets of Selma, but in the personnel office at Lockheed's Marietta, Georgia, plant."[4]

This volume focuses on what Philip Skrentny describes as the pragmatic aspect of affirmative action, constructing a historical narrative of the evolution of affirmative action in private-sector employment and the ways in which managers and workers shaped corporate practices. The setting for the Lockheed-Georgia story is the culture of segregation and white supremacy outlined by Philip J. Rubio and Ira Katznelson. Particularly in the early part of the period under study, African American demands for jobs and training clashed with the existing institutions and cultural norms that Georgia native and Lockheed plant manager James Carmichael termed the "southern tradition."[5]

Kevin Stainback and Donald Tomaskovic-Devey provide a skeletal framework within which to situate the Lockheed narrative. They collated and interpreted a vast amount of data for EEO-1 reports in their 2012 book, *Documenting Desegregation: Racial and Gender Segregation in Private-Sector Employment since the Civil Rights Act*. The Civil Rights Act of 1964 created the Equal Employment Opportunity Commission, which began its operations in July 1965, and required companies covered by the act to file annual reports on the employment of minorities beginning in 1966. The raw data from these reports are a gold mine for historians and social scientists, with a couple of caveats. Scholars may access the data only if they agree not to identify particular firms. This author chose not to delve into such data: given the firm-specific nature of this project, having detailed knowledge of Lockheed's performance that could not be used (or, ethically speaking, even hinted at) would have made writing all the more difficult. In addition, the EEO-1 data begin only in 1966, and the majority of this study takes place before that date. A number of scholars have previously made use of EEO-1 reports, including Dobbin.

The analytical framework developed by Stainback and Tomaskovic-Devey provides critical statistical background and context for the Lockheed story. They organized the historical experience of workplace desegregation into four periods. The Civil Rights Act—more specifically, the initial EEO-1 reports filed in 1966—served as the beginning point for measuring racial and gender desegregation. The authors characterize the pre-1966 workplace as effectively totally segregated: "Before the Civil Rights Act of 1964, both racial and gender employment segregation and inequality were deeply institutionalized in U.S. workplaces." The prevailing baseline assumption across the United States was "that white males would hold authority over others and that women of all races and nonwhites of all genders would tend to hold lower-rewarded and subordinate positions."[6]

The work of Delton, Wright, MacLean, and Anderson acknowledges the racial and gender hierarchies that dominated the U.S. economy in the 1940s and 1950s. The long civil rights movement included the threatened 1941 march on Washington that pushed President Franklin Delano Roosevelt to issue Executive Order 8802, initiating a process of pressure and response that stretched from FDR to JFK's Executive Order 10925. The Roosevelt, Truman, Eisenhower, and Kennedy administrations took action to promote equal employment opportunity among federal contractors.[7] Chapters 1–4 of this book examine the Lockheed experience during the era of near-total segregation. Though overall employment gains for African Americans were minimal, at least some progress, however halting and painful, occurred in breaking down the barriers to equal employment.

Stainback and Tomaskovic-Devey draw on organizational theory to hypothesize that large organizations (such as Lockheed) exist "to regulate and stabilize behavior" and thus resist change. For corporations to significantly alter employment practices, the authors argue, "both motivation (spurred by either leadership or coercion) and an alternative model of behavior and practice are typically required." They posit that two factors make change within the workplace possible: "*environmental uncertainty* associated with social movements and political pressure" and "the institutionalization of models of equal opportunity compliance and regulatory oversight." This book identifies both coercion and leadership—indeed, the interaction of various levels of coercion with management leadership—as motivating factors in the Lockheed case. In responding to pressure from government, social movements, and internal actors, Lockheed management played a large role in developing and "institutionalizing" the apparatus of equal employment oversight and compliance. But the appropriate environmental pressures were not sufficient to produce significant change. "The central assumption" of *Documenting Desegregation* is "that the primary actors in the process of employment desegregation are within workplaces."

This book also documents efforts by workers and managers to pressure Lockheed-Georgia to live up to the rising expectations established by executive orders and legislation.[8]

The remaining three historical periods identified in Stainback and Tomaskovic-Devey's volume form the superstructure within which Lockheed managers and workers acted. The authors label the period 1964–72 "the age of uncertainty," when although the federal government imposed dramatic legal changes, "almost no regulatory, legal, or even human resource capacity to monitor or coerce change" existed. Companies and the new Equal Employment Opportunity Commission struggled to define the new order. Social movement pressure continued and intensified in the employment arena during this period. After historic victories in the spheres of public accommodations and voting rights, the civil rights movement pressed forward toward other long-standing goals such as equal employment opportunity. The urban unrest of the late 1960s prodded the government and the private sector toward greater action to address economic grievances. Lockheed-Georgia workers implemented legal action, suing the company in 1966 under the Civil Rights Act. In this period of uncertainty, African American male workers nationally and at Lockheed-Georgia experienced relatively rapid employment gains.[9]

The third phase of EEO history is "the short regulatory decade," 1973–80, when a number of legislative fixes, executive orders, and regulatory interpretations had codified and strengthened the hand of the Equal Employment Opportunity Commission and the Office of Federal Contract Compliance. Black men's gains from the previous period continued, though at a somewhat reduced pace, while white women advanced more rapidly. African American women, however, found their employment opportunities severely limited in both eras.[10] At Lockheed, this period coincided with severe challenges that included a dramatic reduction in overall site employment (from more than thirty thousand to around ten thousand). But the new regulatory environment continued to influence the company and its Georgia location, evidenced by the emergence of equal employment progress as a factor in the awarding of new federal contracts.

The fourth and final era delineated by Stainback and Tomaskovic-Devey was the long period between 1980 and 2005. The regulatory environment weakened with the advent of the Reagan administration. The appointment of affirmative action opponent and future Supreme Court justice Clarence Thomas as head of the Equal Employment Opportunity Commission and the new administration's generally pro-business, antiregulatory stance combined with the waning of social movements to alter the external environment for firms. "Black employment desegregation stalled, and white women's gains in the workplace continued on a positive, if not as rapid, trajectory," the authors conclude. "During this period, the women's and civil right movements diverge, and we see a marked decline in civil rights movement activity even as women's movement organizations continue to grow in both size and influence." Since 1980, EEO data show, workers have even seen racial resegregation in some industries.[11] Because the internal sources for Lockheed-Georgia run out during this era, it is treated mainly in the volume's conclusion, which is based largely on published sources.

The broad outline sketched in *Documenting Desegregation* forms the context for this book's story of the struggle for equal employment at Lockheed-Georgia. Chapter 1 introduces Lockheed Aircraft and briefly examines the company's experience with employment desegregation during World War II. The company had no connection to the Atlanta area in this period; all its manufacturing facilities and subsidiaries were located in California. But in 1941, labor markets, especially in skilled trades such as aircraft manufacture, were as segregated in Burbank as in Marietta. The chapter traces Lockheed's response to President Roosevelt's Executive Order 8802, which prohibited discrimination by federal contractors and established the Fair Employment Practices Committee to oversee implementation. Though the remainder of the book focuses on Lockheed's Georgia branch, critical managerial personnel—James Lydon, Eugene Mattison, and others—moved from Burbank to Marietta in the early 1950s, bringing their experience in Lockheed's first corporate efforts at opening jobs to African Americans.

Chapter 2 details the encounter between Lockheed management and Georgia's "southern traditions." Lockheed moved into a massive aircraft manufacturing facility built by the federal government and operated by Bell Aircraft, a Buffalo, New York, firm, during World War II. Air Force Plant 6 produced Boeing's B-29 bomber through a contract with the government before being shuttered with the close of the war. Lockheed reopened the plant in 1951 to help meet surging government demand during the Korean War and hired James V. Carmichael to serve as general manager, the same position he had held in 1944–45, the final year of Bell's tenure at the plant. Carmichael, the local face of Lockheed, worked closely with Lydon, who moved from the California division and became director of industrial relations at Lockheed-Georgia. Carmichael and Lydon managed the Georgia plant's response to protests from the Atlanta NAACP chapter and President Harry S. Truman's Executive Order 10308 on employment discrimination. Though racial discrimination in employment was a national problem, Lockheed managers were convinced that desegregation presented special problems in the South. Chapter 2 also introduces Harry Hudson, one of a small group of highly educated men who seemed to have been recruited as the first real candidates for black advancement into the lower levels of management. Hudson and the others in his group were trained to work on the aft section of B-47 Stratojet bombers (again, a Boeing design under contract). In late 1953, Hudson became the first African American supervisor at Lockheed-Georgia, but work crews remained strictly segregated. After John F. Kennedy became president and issued Executive Order 10925, African American workers began filing complaints, and their affidavits, along with contemporary interviews conducted with the petitioners, offer a rare window into the shop-floor experiences and the struggle to change the culture of segregation.

Chapter 3 traces the experiences of Hudson and other African American workers through the remainder of the 1950s. Lockheed's workforce expanded with a new contract for the C-130 Hercules transport plane, various models of which remained a staple of Lockheed's Georgia branch for decades. The company hired a somewhat larger number of black workers specifically for work on the C-130 and began a slow process of integrating work crews. Hudson managed his segregated crew until 1959, when he was selected as the first African American to supervise an integrated crew. In the meantime, the number of African American production workers surged to around six hundred. Frustrated with what appeared to be excessive elementary training, nearly nonexistent opportunities for advanced training, and virtually no avenues for advancement, many of these workers organized to protest. Locked into a segregated local union, black workers were forced to pursue these grievances outside the normal channels. The Truman and Eisenhower administrations' executive orders contained no real enforcement mechanisms, and the International Association of Machinists seemed intent on preserving white access to skilled jobs. Yet the mere existence of federal mandates and occasional inspections, along with public pressure from organizations such as the NAACP and the Urban League, seems to have created a space within which such protests could receive a hearing and perhaps nudge the company to take limited action. By 1960, however, black progress seemed to have halted, settling in at a level that African American workers viewed as little more than tokenism. Moreover, future prospects seemed dim. The initial large military demand for the C-130 had been sated, and the plane's future seemed limited.

Chapter 4 turns to a new phase of the struggle for equal employment opportunity. In 1961, Lockheed-Georgia received a huge contract for a new aircraft, the C-141 Starlifter. The contract not only promised employment growth but coincided with Kennedy's executive order, which for the first time required that government contractors take "affirmative action" to guarantee a nondiscriminatory workplace. Executive Order 10925 also included language that permitted the President's Committee on Equal Employment Opportunity (PCEEO) to cancel contracts for recalcitrant firms. Almost immediately after Kennedy's executive order, thirty-six African American workers filed complaints alleging that Lockheed-Georgia continued to operate on a Jim Crow basis. The complaints threatened the C-141 contract and set the stage for negotiations that led to the formation of Plans for Progress. This initiative, the brainchild of Atlanta attorney Robert Troutman, consisted of a campaign to convince federal contractors (initially) and other firms (later) to develop and sign their own versions of Lockheed's initial affirmative action plan. Mattison, who replaced Lydon as director of industrial relations at the Marietta plant, defended the facility's record by arguing that the problem (a culture of segregation) was "already here." Mattison and his protégé, Gordon, helped develop plans to try to change that culture.

Chapter 5 focuses on Lockheed's efforts to comply with the new Civil Rights Act. Gordon compiled reports for upper management on Lockheed's progress in equal employment opportunity and responded to managers' and supervisors' charges that the company was favoring black workers. The training department developed a racial awareness training program for managers and supervisors, Build the People, that explicitly characterized Lockheed's EEO policies as an act of social responsibility. This chapter offers a detailed examination of the Build the People manual and the response of Lockheed's EEO point man, Gordon.

In the late 1960s and early 1970s, Lockheed faced a major lawsuit from African American employees and increasing pressure from the Equal Employment Opportunity Commission and the Office of Federal Contract Compliance. Black protest again emerged, adding to the pressure from the lawsuit and the Equal Employment Opportunity Commission. Chapter 6 details Lockheed's management response to these challenges. Mattison and Gordon drew lessons from North American Rockwell's victory over Lockheed in the contest for the space shuttle contract, concluding that North American had leveraged its affirmative action efforts to its advantage: EEO had become a factor in the award of major contracts. Lockheed settled the Banks case in the midst of a cost overrun scandal involving the new C5-A transport plane as well as massive job cuts. Lockheed management fought a rearguard action to try to preserve some black job gains in the midst of the cutbacks.

Chapter 7 traces Gordon's outside activities on behalf of Lockheed in the EEO arena. In 1965, Gordon formed the Atlanta area Voluntary Merit Employers Association (MEA) as part of a Plans for Progress initiative. MEA focused on convincing area firms to voluntarily develop affirmative action plans, make good-faith efforts to hire and promote African Americans (and later women) into "breakthrough jobs"—that is, jobs not previously held by members of underrepresented groups. Beginning in 1968, Gordon also served as Lockheed's lead representative to the National Alliance of Businessmen (NAB), a public-private partnership that constituted the Johnson administration's response to the ongoing urban crisis. NAB received federal funds for job training and training wage subsidies. These funds were disbursed by local NAB "metros" under contracts with private firms. NAB's main mission was to move beyond "breakthrough jobs" (which many saw as tokenism) and attack joblessness among specific groups of "hard-core" unemployed, including "ex-offenders," "disadvantaged youth," Vietnam veterans, and minorities (categories that overlapped considerably). Gordon formed the NAB Atlanta metro and traveled the Southeast, helping other cities form affiliated metros.

In 1973, Congress enacted the Comprehensive Employment and Training Act (CETA), which sought to consolidate many of the federal government's existing job training programs, increase the funding for such training, and assign responsibility for managing the training funds to local "prime sponsors" (generally city or state governments). With the 1975 recession, however, Congress allowed sponsors to use CETA funds to create public-service employment jobs as a countercyclical measure to fight unemployment. In the case of Atlanta, the advent of CETA coincided with the election of the city's first African American mayor, Maynard Jackson, in 1973. Private sector NAB representatives welcomed federal funding for training under the auspices of business, as in NAB metros, but generally opposed government control of similar job training funds. Gordon and his NAB colleagues also strongly opposed CETA's public-service-employment provisions. NAB's national leadership, including Lockheed-Georgia's president, Robert Ormsby, lobbied the Carter administration for reforms that would guarantee NAB and the private sector a dominant role in allocating CETA training funds. NAB leaders charged Gordon with putting together a team of experts and drafting revisions to CETA. The process, detailed in this chapter, revealed the growing distrust between the white business community and Atlanta's new black leadership and had implications for national policy.

Though CETA has been the subject of a number of econometric analyses, little has been written about the largest public works program since the Great Depression. A deep dive into the legislative and community-by-community history of CETA lies beyond the scope of this volume. This brief treatment of the topic focuses on Gordon's role as a Lockheed representative to various external organizations broadly related to equal employment opportunity. But the intersection of emerging black political power, the business community's pushback against the public sector (the neoliberal turn), and the fate of the "hard-core" unemployed represented by the CETA story and its context deserve greater scholarly attention.

The Jackson administration eventually made its own uneasy partnership with Atlanta's business community, restoring with some modifications the partnership between the downtown business elite and city government described by Clarence Stone. Manning Marable and Glenn Eskew have made the case that the civil rights movement met only severely limited success or outright failure in the economic sphere. The black middle class accepted "upward mobility within the very centers of corporate power," in Marable's phrase, and abandoned a broader vision of economic transformation and redistribution. This civil rights movement narrative tracks well with the argument that U.S. (and, indeed, western) corporate leaders initiated a fierce assault against the increasingly restive social movements that had emerged during the 1960s, the tumult Immanuel Wallerstein has dubbed the revolutions of 1968.[12]

Wright, in contrast, argues that the civil rights movement and its associated government policies have had a positive impact, noting the significance (within limits and motivated in large part by fear of more stringent regulations) of the corporate approach. But Wright's analysis and Marable's and Eskew's more pessimistic views are not necessarily mutually exclusive.

When Gordon's papers run out in the 1980s, the partial window into Lockheed's internal affairs closes. The volume's brief conclusion sketches Lockheed's post-1980s EEO history and summarizes some of the broader implications. Just as Barack Obama's 2008 election did not herald the elimination of racial discrimination in America, Lee Rhyant's 2000 selection as the first African American general manager of what had become Lockheed Martin's Georgia division certainly did not initiate a postracial era in employment at the company. Yet it would be a mistake to dismiss either of these events. Though the social transformation sought by the mainstream civil rights movement, the student movement, and the women's movement proved elusive, and progress in racial desegregation stalled and economic inequality drifted back toward pre–New Deal levels, particularly after 1980, Georgians and southerners, black and white, found that their economic fortunes had changed for the better. The struggle at Lockheed played a role in opening job opportunities, training, and higher incomes to African Americans in the Atlanta region.

CHAPTER 1

"Economic Necessity and Governmental Pressures"
LOCKHEED AND EQUAL EMPLOYMENT OPPORTUNITY BEFORE GEORGIA

In 1998, Walter Boyne, a former director of the National Air and Space Museum, published a detailed company-sponsored history of Lockheed. Boyne's narrative briefly addressed the company's experience with desegregation in Georgia, strongly implying that all events occurred after 1961. Boyne mentioned not at all the desegregation of the firm's California facilities during World War II or the company's experience with the "Training within Industry" program. The bulk of the book, as expected, focused on Lockheed's development of new aircraft and overall financial performance. But *Beyond the Horizons* offered just hints of top management's thinking on race and the Georgia division. Boyne had access to all unclassified company records and materials, though he did not cite specific sources or include notes. Boyne's description of management's policy on segregation in Marietta included a characterization of chair Robert Gross's instructions to Dan Haughton: "marching orders" to see that the company "complied with new federal laws promoting integration." But no laws existed until 1964, so Boyne may have been referring to executive orders. According to Boyne, Haughton "passed on the instructions" to project engineer W. A. "Dick" Pulver and his crew, who "brought desegregation about indirectly and with subtlety." Boyne made no reference to the C-141 contract dispute or the "Plan for Progress" signed by Robert Gross's brother and business partner, Courtlandt Gross, in May 1961, instead observing that *White* and *Colored* signs disappeared quietly from restrooms and drinking fountains, with paper cups appearing at water fountains. Cafeterias closed, replaced by food carts. This approach worked, he contended, "not immediately, but over time." Black employment gradually increased, and "black supervisors became increasingly common." While change did take time, the company's efforts were "sustained . . . and successful."[1] Moreover, Boyne made no mention of the pre-1961 history of desegregation at either Lockheed's California facilities or its Georgia division.

Lockheed Martin's 2013 corporate history, *Innovation with Purpose*, offered scarcely more details, focusing on the 1961 C-141 contract crisis and the emergence of Plans for Progress. The more recent history acknowledged—barely—early World War II efforts to desegregate the aircraft industry, noting that, "Before World War II, only five Lockheed employees were women. By June 1943, that number had exploded to nearly 35,000. Women and African Americans did their part to defend the country and proved their worth in the workplace." Left unstated was the fact that prior to Executive Order 8802, neither Lockheed's California workforce nor those of other aircraft manufacturers in most of the nation had any African Americans. The 2013 volume also made no mention of any of Lockheed's pre-1961 desegregation efforts in Georgia.[2]

Lockheed's corporate histories principally told the story of the firm's contributions to aviation and national defense and its financial ups and downs. But Lockheed played a central role in desegregating the U.S. aircraft industry and American manufacturing in general. The company and its management personnel actively shaped and reshaped the business community's response to the civil rights movement and its demand for expanded employment opportunities for African Americans. From the firm's experiences with FDR's Fair Employment Practices Committee during World War II through its decision to reopen a mothballed facility in the heart of segregated Dixie in the early 1950s to its participation in the quasi-voluntary Plans for Progress initiative in the 1960s, the company was an early desegregation leader among major U.S. corporations. Lockheed-Georgia almost certainly led firms in the Deep South in promoting a more racially diversified workforce during the 1950s and 1960s, though that leadership unquestionably had its limitations. During and after the 1960s, Lockheed personnel stood at the heart of efforts to develop public-private partnerships to address equal employment opportunity. The company actively promoted the idea that corporations had a responsibility to address social problems and that social responsibility could be combined with efficiency in business operations. During the 1970s, Lockheed's representatives to regional and national employment organizations pulled back from support for programs they deemed counterproductive to promoting private-sector growth and autonomy and played a role in reshaping the business community's response to state intervention in the economy.

Lockheed Martin is the current corporate identity of a pair of pioneer firms in American aviation. Allan and Malcolm Loughead, innovative mechanics with a passion for the newfound technology of flight, founded the Alco Hydro-Aeroplane Company in 1912, at about the same time that Glenn L. Martin founded his eponymous company. The Loughead brothers' firm went through several incarnations, with the brothers eventually settling on Lockheed—a phonetic spelling of the family name—for the firm in 1926. Lockheed Aircraft remained the company's moniker until 1995, when it merged with Martin to form Lockheed Martin.

The Loughead brothers had some success during the World War I years but struggled financially until their firm developed the Vega in 1927, just six months after Charles Lindbergh's historic transatlantic flight demonstrated the viability of long-distance air travel. The Lockheed Vega, a six-passenger plane designed without the familiar struts that helped support wings on early aircraft, hit the market at the same time as the Lindbergh-induced flight boom. Lindbergh himself flew the Vega in a series of flights crafted to test potential commercial airline routes, and sales took off. The Vega quickly became a cultural icon. In 1932, when Amelia Earhart became the first woman to fly solo across the Atlantic, she piloted a bright red Vega 5B; the previous year, Wiley Post had flown his modified Vega 5C around the world. Both planes are familiar sights today at the Smithsonian Air and Space Museum in Washington, D.C.[3]

The emerging popularity of aviation generally and the success of the Vega specifically made Lockheed, with a growing cash income and little accumulated debt, a takeover target. In 1929, a group of Detroit automobile industry executives and investors approached Allan Loughead's investors with a deal they could not refuse, purchasing the firm out from under its founder. Lockheed's assets and brands were merged into the Detroit Aircraft Corporation, something like "a General Motors of the air." The timing was, however, not auspicious. The October 1929 stock market crash and the ensuing Great Depression sank Detroit Aircraft, and Lockheed's assets went on the bankruptcy auction block in early 1932.[4]

Robert Gross led the group of investors who purchased Lockheed's assets and went on to serve as the CEO of a reorganized Lockheed Aircraft from 1934 to 1956, presiding over the company's expansion into Georgia. Gross could not fly a plane and had no technical background in aviation. He came to the emerging industry from the investment side. Gross graduated from Harvard in 1919 and began his business career as a runner for an investment banking firm. He developed an interest in the profit potential of aircraft manufacturing and specialized in aviation-related investments.

Gross had an eye for talent and skill, which led him to hire engineers Hal Hibbard and Kelly Johnson, who helped develop the Lockheed Electra, an all-metal, twin-engine transport plane, in 1934.[5] For the remainder of the twentieth century, transport aircraft provided Lockheed with its bread and butter.

The new plane helped secure the company's future, but high development costs left the company with a $500,000 loss in 1934. Gross negotiated a $200,000 loan from the Reconstruction Finance Corporation, a government-sponsored nonprofit geared toward helping keep firms afloat during the Great Depression. Though Lockheed established a larger civilian market presence than many other aircraft manufacturers in the 1930s, Gross's company benefited early from federal subsidies.[6]

While Gross welcomed government support via the loan, he viewed other New Deal policies pursued by President Franklin Delano Roosevelt and the federal government with considerable anxiety. The passage of pro-labor legislation such as the National Labor Relations Act (Wagner Act) in 1935 made it easier to organize workers. The mainstream American labor movement also fractured into two branches. The American Federation of Labor (AFL) and its member unions, including the International Association of Machinists (IAM), represented the more conservative wing of the labor movement, devoted to founder Samuel Gompers's vision of pure and simple unionism that pursued a higher material standard of living for (mostly skilled) workers. The insurgent Congress of Industrial Organizations (CIO), made up of unions that had broken away from the AFL as well as new industrial unions such as the United Automobile Workers, symbolized a new emphasis on organizing across craft lines to promote industrial and social democracy.

Business leaders opposed unionization of any kind, but after 1935, many came to accept the inevitability of union organization under the New Deal legal-political framework. Forced to this conclusion, some business leaders chose to negotiate with AFL unions as a way of avoiding organization by the CIO. Business leaders were joined by many civil rights organizations in their skepticism about the Wagner Act and its protections for labor unions. Trade unions had long been bastions of racial privilege in the United States. The two most important and influential organizations representing African American interests—the National Association for the Advancement of Colored People (NAACP) and the National Urban League—strongly opposed passage of the act. Civil rights leaders feared that the new law would empower unions strong enough to negotiate contracts that excluded black workers from employment, training, and advancement opportunities. W. E. B. Du Bois, writing in the NAACP's influential magazine, *The Crisis*, declared that the AFL was "not a labor movement." Rather, he argued, "it is a monopoly of skilled laborers, who joined the capitalists in exploiting the masses of labor whenever and wherever they can."[7]

The entire aircraft industry faced a vigorous union organizing effort in early 1937, with Gross deftly playing the two major federations against one another. Historian Wayne Biddle observes that Gross recognized the AFL-affiliated IAM "before the more radical" CIO-affiliated United Automobile Workers "could gain a foothold" among Lockheed workers. Gross insisted that most Lockheed workers did "not really want any union," but the workers recognized that they needed some sort of organization "with which to combat this infectious spread of radicalism that is sweeping the country." In addition, Lockheed granted a 6 percent wage increase and time and a half for overtime, giving the firm the highest pay rates in the industry. Gross's efforts were rewarded with relative labor peace for the remainder of 1937 while most of his California competitors faced intermittent strikes during prolonged organizing campaigns.[8]

The Atlanta-born IAM was among the most conservative of AFL unions and was particularly infamous among civil rights activists as a defender of white supremacy. Until the mid-1940s, the machinists' union's initiation ritual required new members to declare, "I will never propose for membership in this association any other than a competent white candidate." Joseph Abel argues that IAM locals sometimes diverged from the seemingly strict requirement for racial separation. In Texas's aircraft manufacturing industry during World War II, for example, local union leaders found that pursuing grievances of black workers along with those of whites helped solidify the union's position against intransigent management. By the end of the war, nearly half the delegates to the IAM convention supported elimination of the all-white provision from the ritual. For all that, however, gains by black workers in Texas during the war proved transitory as demobilization cut deeply into the ranks of aircraft workers.[9]

Even as new industries such as aircraft manufacturing emerged in the 1920s and 1930s, entrenched attitudes, regional business patterns, and racially segmented labor markets limited opportunity for African American workers throughout the nation and especially in the South. The burgeoning demands of the war era began improving the prospects and bottom lines of aircraft manufacturers as early as 1936. Congress began to change some of its contracting requirements and boosted payments to manufacturers to guarantee production. "More importantly," according to Jacob Vander Meulen, "in 1938, warplane exports soared, providing a profitable safety valve for the industry." For example, Lockheed signed a $25 million contract to provide two hundred Hudson MK1s (a modified version of the Super Electra), to the British government in 1938. Such contracts led to rapid growth of production and the labor force. Lockheed employed only 334 people in 1934, but by the end of 1938, the company's workforce had topped 3,000. Full U.S. rearmament and then entry into the war led to even further growth for Lockheed and the industry. The Hudson contract and, more important, the development of the P-38 for the U.S. Army Air Corps, put Lockheed into a "frenzy of activity." Employment ballooned to 17,000 by the end of 1940 and peaked at 91,000 in 1943.[10]

As Lockheed's labor needs mushroomed, R. Randall Irwin, the company's first director of industrial relations, managed efforts to hire qualified workers. A Lockheed company publication referred to Irwin as "a one-man industrial relations, public relations, and publicity staff." Irwin had joined Gross and corporate secretary Cyril Chappellet on Lockheed's management team as publicity director in 1933. The following year, Irwin proposed publication of a newsletter, the *Lockheed Star*, which became a key component of company efforts to build a sense of community among its workers.[11]

Irwin's legacy at Lockheed included much more than publicity. Beginning with the company's 1938 growth spurt, Irwin assumed responsibility for the pioneering training efforts. After signing the British government contract, the company intensified its recruitment and hiring of engineers and skilled workers. The demand associated with the international tensions of the late 1930s and the attendant military buildups in the United States, Britain, and elsewhere offered rich potential markets for Lockheed and the relatively new aircraft industry, but not enough experienced aircraft engineers and workers existed. Irwin led Lockheed's initiatives to address the personnel problem.

Lockheed's drive to find or train qualified personnel received a boost from the federal government. In 1937, as the world drifted toward war, Congress passed the Fitzgerald Act to encourage the revival of apprenticeships as a path to skilled employment. A 1940 congressional research report argued that the move toward mechanization and mass production in the early twentieth century had made skilled workers a smaller proportion of the workforce, and employers preferred hiring skilled workers away from competitors over investing in training programs. Trade unions had also played a role in the decline of apprenticeships, limiting access to the trade and thus propping up wages (though the author of the report labeled this the least important of the three main causes of the decline).

By the mid-1930s, many industry and government officials had recognized the narrowing of the paths toward skilled work even as significant numbers of skilled laborers remained necessary not only in older industries but also in newer industries such as aircraft manufacturing that renewed and reshaped the demand for skilled workers. Machines and their tenders could not build airplanes. The Fitzgerald Act, along with amendments to the Fair Labor Standards Act (1938), allowed the secretary of labor wide discretion in waiving wage and hour regulations to promote and encourage apprenticeships. The aircraft industry "was singled out for particular attention" in a confidential report for President Roosevelt that called for upgrading the quality and quantity of skilled mechanics in the interest of "national defense."[12]

As a result, by mid-1940, the Labor Department's federal apprenticeship committee had "aided three major aircraft manufacturers" in developing new standards and training programs. Lockheed's Irwin helped craft what appears to have been the first of these arrangements when he negotiated a training agreement with the federal government and the Burbank, California, school system. Under the agreement, a hundred young men between the ages of eighteen and twenty-three would work at Lockheed's Burbank plant for thirty-six hours per week in addition to spending four hours at a local high school, where they would receive "class instruction on the theoretical side of the trade." The apprentices would gain experience in a wide array of aircraft-related skills—"machine, metal, and woodwork, pattern-making, blueprint reading," among others—to avoid overemphasis on any one skill. The apprentices would be paid for forty hours of work per week, with wages beginning at forty-three cents per hour and rising to eighty cents an hour by the end of the four-year program.[13] This program set the tone for Lockheed's emphasis on training, a corporate priority that remained intact through the 1950s and 1960s.

The aircraft industry, like many other industries requiring significant amounts of skilled labor, simply did not hire African Americans for production work in the pre–World War II years. The NAACP's labor secretary, Herbert Hill, reported that aircraft executives provided what he labeled "typical responses" to his inquiries: in 1940, the industrial relations director of Vultee Aircraft had flatly admitted to Hill, "I regret to say that it is not the policy of this company to employ people other than of the Caucasian race; consequently we are not in a position to offer your people employment at this time." The following year, the president of North American Aviation said that although "we are in complete sympathy with the Negroes, it is against company policy to employ them as aircraft workers or mechanics"; however, "there will be some jobs as janitors for Negroes." Discrimination was not only legal but "typical."[14] Lockheed executives appear to have refrained from such public statements, but the company followed a similar policy.

The explosive growth of jobs in war industries generated rising expectations. Civil rights organizations, including the National Urban League and the NAACP, worked to convince President Roosevelt to act decisively to prohibit discrimination in employment. After much discussion and debate within FDR's inner circle, the president issued Executive Order 8802 in June 1941, using the language of the struggle to preserve democracy to justify banning racial discrimination among defense contractors. The order asserted that the "full participation in the national defense program by all citizens of the United States, regardless of race, creed, color, or national origin" was essential for maintaining "workers' morale" and "national unity" for the defense of "the democratic way of life." The order also established the Fair Employment Practices Committee (FEPC) within the Office of Production Management to investigate complaints of discrimination and "take appropriate steps to redress grievances which it finds to be valid."[15]

The FEPC, however, had no specific enforcement powers for redressing grievances. The committee relied on working through existing agencies and above all persuasion, achieving tangible results. Economist William J. Collins argues that the FEPC opened up jobs for African Americans, principally by publicly identifying and shaming firms that discriminated. The FEPC "accelerated the pace of black economic advancement" by "(1) providing advice on how to integrate the workplace, (2) giving managers a ready excuse for hiring blacks if white workers objected, (3) threatening to bring more powerful government agencies into the fray on the side of the FEPC, and/or (4) publicly embarrassing firms and unions that refused to hire blacks." Collins also sharply differentiates the FEPC's work in the South from its experiences in the northern states. The committee's work was difficult everywhere but encountered intransigence in the South. The region's history of de jure segregation and disfranchisement of black voters coupled with its deeply segregated labor markets made the FEPC's work nearly impossible. But outside Dixie, the FEPC experienced at least some success.[16]

Robert C. Weaver, a Harvard-educated economist and member of FDR's "black cabinet," coordinated a number of studies of African American employment opportunities before, during, and after World War II. An activist scholar who spent most of his career working for various federal and New York State agencies, Weaver combined research with advocacy. In

1966, he became the first African American appointed to a cabinet-level position, when President Lyndon Baines Johnson appointed him to serve as the first secretary of the Department of Housing and Urban Development. "Perhaps the most significant, and certainly the earliest, example of a sound approach to the integration of Negroes in aircraft production," Weaver observed in a 1945 article, "occurred at the Lockheed-Vega Plant in Southern California." Although Lockheed had previously employed no black workers, the company responded quickly to FDR's executive order, developing a comprehensive plan underpinned by four "fundamental principles": "(a) the company proceeded after it had developed a comprehensive plan for dealing with this matter; (b) management instilled a feeling of cooperation and a sense of responsibility for the success of the plan in all executives and supervisors; (c) management was positive and firm in its statement and approaches to the problem; (d) from the outset management was committed to a policy of selecting carefully the workers who were to pioneer the way for Negro employment."[17]

Chappellet sent an August 1941 memo to all executives and supervisors announcing the new policy of nondiscrimination and "outlining the reasons" for it, along with a copy of FDR's Executive Order 8802, which would be posted on bulletin boards throughout plant facilities "for the information of all employees." Chappellet's memo frankly acknowledged that although Lockheed and its subsidiary, Vega, had "never had any discriminatory policies with regard to race, color, or creed, it is, nevertheless, a fact that no Negroes are now in the employ of either company." After "full consideration" and in the interest of "cooperating fully with the Federal Government in the national defense program," Lockheed would devote "special effort" to compliance with the order. Chappellet also expressed top management's "earnest hope that the subject will not be made an issue for excessive discussion"—in essence announcing that the matter was not open for debate. He was certain "that it will not become an issue if all employees in positions of authority lend their full interest to this program." "When and where a member of the colored race is employed," he declared, "it will be with full consideration of his personality, character, aptitudes and skill, so that he should be given full opportunity to adjust himself to his job and associates. If all supervisors do their part, I am sure that the problems involved in the employment of Negroes will be handled effectively." Finally, Chappellet expressed the commitment of Lockheed's top executives to a program of active recruitment, hiring, training, and advancement of black workers and made clear that management personnel were expected to make the program work.[18]

Lockheed's house newsletter, the *Lockheed-Vega Star*, announced on August 15, 1941, that the company would be hiring black workers. The article accompanying the announcement contained a direct quotation from Chappellet's memorandum to management and a quotation from "a similar communication" sent to the IAM lodge representing Lockheed-Vega workers. The company then set about hiring its first African Americans.[19]

The FEPC held a series of public hearings in the fall of 1941 to assess compliance with the executive order. Hearings were held in Los Angeles on October 20–21, garnering extensive coverage in the *California Eagle*, a local African American newspaper and a longtime champion of employment opportunity for blacks. Reporter John Kinoch surveyed conditions in the area's aircraft plants, offering his audience an overview of employment conditions. The survey indicated haphazard progress in the first months following the order. Douglas Aircraft had become the first to hire blacks for skilled positions, but as of October 1941, the company employed only nine African Americans. North American Aviation, whose president had brazenly stated his company's racially discriminatory policy just months earlier, also had announced that it would comply with the executive order, although according to Kinoch, the company currently employed "something less than 10 Negroes ... as janitors." Kinoch declared Lockheed "the bright spot of local aircraft employment," with twenty African Americans working at skilled jobs.[20]

Lockheed hired its first black worker in California plants in August 1941. In a letter written to Weaver around the end of the summer, Irwin lauded his company's efforts, citing "the progress we have made in employing Negroes since our statement of policy a few weeks ago." Lockheed had hired thirty-one African Americans, twenty-two of them in "mechanical work." By the end of 1942, Lockheed employed about a thousand African Americans, and that number had grown to twenty-five hundred as of March 1943. Many of these new employees held skilled and semiskilled production jobs. Nevertheless, African Americans accounted for only a tiny fraction of Lockheed's employees, whose numbers peaked at ninety-four thousand in 1943 before falling to sixty-three thousand the following year as efficiency improved.[21]

Lockheed continued its relatively open approach to desegregation through World War II. In a July 1943 *Lockheed Star* article, "Democracy at Work," Irwin placed FDR's executive order on a par with the Declaration of Independence and Lincoln's Emancipation Proclamation in the pantheon of American history. The United States had "experienced 80 years of wars and peace before another president issued a document aimed to give all races an equal opportunity to live under liberty and pursue happiness." Lockheed and Vega had determined to "comply fully" with the order, making "a special effort to train and employ Negroes 'in capacities commensurate with their individual skills and aptitudes.'" Those words were quoted from an April 1941 memorandum authored by Sidney Hillman, a labor leader and associate director of the Office of Production Management, to all defense contractors. Writing even before Roosevelt issued the executive order, Hillman urged defense contractors to refrain from discrimination and to use all available labor without regard to race; however, his phrasing left room for some local interpretation. Irwin's article announced that Lockheed had now hired three thousand African American workers and had experienced only a "few difficulties," most of which had resulted from "lack of understanding." Irwin declared proudly, "It can now be said that Negroes have taken their places as full-fledged producers of Lockheed and Vega war planes, which are going forth to fight for freedom of all nations and races everywhere. . . . On this Independence Day, Lockheed and Vega will stand as an outstanding symbol of Democracy at Work."[22] Irwin thus endorsed the promotion of democracy at home and abroad and linked that struggle to the success of Lockheed aircraft production.

The Urban League's journal, *Opportunity*, also offered high praise for Lockheed's desegregation efforts in the fall of 1944. Los Angeles Urban League executive director Floyd Covington profiled Reginald L. Jones, one of the new Lockheed employees and a man whose background was so typical of the African American middle class that Covington termed it "trite." Jones had "spent five years as a waiter on the dining cars of the Southern Pacific Railroad" before working for seven years for a black-owned insurance company. After earning a degree from the College of Commerce at the University of California at Berkeley, Jones had accepted a job as a warehouseman with Lockheed in November 1941, moving up to become a general clerk in the fall of 1942. By December 1942, Jones had moved to the personnel department as a clerk, and over the next year, he rose from personnel assistant to personnel technician and finally to personnel representative, rapidly climbing the corporate ladder. According to a congratulatory note from a plant superintendent, Jones's promotions had been "justly deserved because of the grand job you have done at this plant in provoking harmony between the two races and because of the handling of certain cases, the results of which were gratifying to all concerned." Irwin echoed those sentiments in another congratulatory note, observing that Jones had earned "a large share of the credit for the harmonious relations between the white and Negro employees at Lockheed." Though Covington did not say so explicitly, Jones appears to have been largely responsible for recruiting black workers and helping managers work through any factory floor issues that emerged from desegregation. In essence, he seems to have served as an intermediary between new black workers and white workers and managers. Covington summed up Jones's story as that of "another American who had 'Crashed the Color Line'" but followed that phrase with a sentence that captured the tension often embedded within the experience of African American corporate employees: "Without reference to race as such, he does his job and does it well."[23]

Based in large part on the Lockheed experience, Robert Weaver concluded that his study of the aircraft industry during World War II "illustrated clearly that when economic necessity and governmental pressures require the introduction of minorities into new types of work, it can be achieved." Activist government policy combined with a tight labor market (itself perhaps manipulated by the government) could overcome systemic racial discrimination to open job training and employment opportunities. Beyond government policy and high levels of employment, the most important factor "in effecting relaxations in the color caste system in employment" was "the strategic position of management."[24]

In October 1944, Irwin presented a brief overview of Lockheed's experiences in hiring African American workers at a Howard University conference on the Postwar Industrial Outlook for Negroes. By this time, Irwin had left Lockheed to become director for industrial relations research for the Aeronautical Chamber of Commerce of America, and he told his audience that the prewar aircraft industry had employed virtually no African Americans as a consequence of the highly technical nature of aircraft work: most firms had preferred to hire workers with one or two years of extended technical training in junior colleges or aeronautical schools, and those educational opportunities simply had not been available to African Americans. Thus, according to Irwin, there was "practically no supply of skilled Negroes" available for aircraft work, and companies did not maintain extensive internal training departments. In addition, he contended, blacks simply did not apply for aircraft work. "For a five year period," Irwin observed, "not one Negro applied at the factory with which I was most familiar."[25]

But spurred by the demands of war, "changes in the nature of aircraft production made it possible to employ relatively untrained and unskilled persons." Though he did not mention the program by name, Irwin was clearly referring to a major public-private partnership with which he had been intimately involved, Training within Industry. The brainchild of Channing

Dooley, a champion of government-business partnerships in industrial training since World War I, Training within Industry was a massive effort to teach managers and supervisors how to train production workers and included a focus on breaking down complex jobs into component parts. The new approach attempted to blend the best of the scientific management approach with techniques developed by the newer human relations approach to personnel. The program was established as an advisory committee to the War Manpower Commission. Irwin played a key role in introducing the program to Lockheed and served on the TWI National Advisory Council. "On the production lines—assembly work and fabrication—we learned how to break the job processes down so that relatively few hours or days or, at first, weeks of training were needed instead of the one to two or three years that previously had been required," Irwin recalled.[26] In his view, the new production and training methods enabled the employment of lower-skilled black workers.

As job opportunities rapidly increased in 1940 and early 1941, more African Americans began applying for such jobs. Aircraft executives "began realizing that here was a large untapped source of production man-hours." Lockheed and other firms, Irwin insisted, "began to seek ways and means of utilizing it." Lockheed's "management held several meetings to discuss the problem as to how Negroes could be integrated into the working forces." Management's "greatest concern" was "the attitude of the employees who were already in the plants," not only in the South but across the country as a whole. Fortunately, like a bolt from the blue, "the Executive Order of June 25, 1941, . . . provided a basis of action." FDR's action, however, enabled company executives to explain to workers that integration was happening as a result of a government mandate and that they had no choice but to comply.[27]

In his talk, Irwin also outlined the steps Lockheed had taken to introduce black workers, a process that closely matched Weaver's description but added the vetting of African Americans "for character, attitude, and adaptability" in consultation with the Urban League and other "local Negro groups." Both managers and new black employees received a sort of orientation:

> Before [African American workers] were placed in the factory the supervisors in those particular groups to which they were assigned were talked to by top management and informed of the company policy, and their cooperation was earnestly solicited. The results were more than satisfactory. At the same time, the new Negro employees were talked to, were informed

that there had not been Negroes employed in the factory before and that the success of the company's program would depend upon the manner in which they adapted themselves to the social and working conditions within the plant.[28]

Irwin did not elaborate on the content of these sessions. Later in his presentation, however, he related stories that offered clues to the traits desired among black applicants and employees.

"One failure" occurred when an applicant underwent all the usual tests and was found to have an "undesirable temperament." As a result of the company's "eagerness to extend the employment of Negroes we waived the temperament test results and employed him," but the new hire "considered every position to which he was assigned far beneath his dignity, ability, and skill." He was "entirely unwilling to do the work that was handed to him and to qualify for promotion." In the end, the man "walked off the job . . . and charged the company with discrimination." The employee no doubt would have offered a different version of events, but Irwin's deployment of the story in this setting indicated that the racial views of white management personnel remained strongly influenced by stereotypical notions of black attitudes.[29]

Irwin also presented a contrasting example. One contented black employee had written a letter in which he noted "the courtesy of my fellow white employees." He "still marvel[ed] at the fact that, with the thousands here, I have met with no insult, either open or veiled." The man cited the "stimulating" psychological benefits of "being given equal opportunity and the same chances of advancement alongside one's fellow white Americans, when one is a Negro." Interracial industrial work at Lockheed had encouraged the worker to "believe that industrial democracy is possible in America." Irwin declared that these two employees had each "got out of his opportunity just about what he expected and what he put into the job in his relations with other employees." In other words, workers' experiences depended primarily on their individual behaviors and attitudes. Moreover, Irwin stated, Lockheed employed both white and black counselors to help employees work through these issues, implying a therapeutic approach by the company.[30]

Irwin concluded by quoting from the personnel report on another African American worker, Smokey Whitfield. Other black workers "go to Smokey with their troubles. Being a good workman, he is in an ideal position for being on the ground floor of any friction that might arise." Moreover, "supervision recognizes Smokey as being a great aid to them in working out the problems of the Negro employees that might arise from time to time." Smokey was quoted as insisting that "peace and harmony prevail among the Negroes in the Production Department." In response to tales of some African American workers who had been let go or quit, Smokey declared, "It is a good thing that we got rid of some of them. There are still quite a few the company could get along very well without." Whitfield was the quintessential "good Negro," calm, levelheaded, hardworking, and established as an informal leader among his peers.[31]

That such less enlightened attitudes survived is unsurprising, and it is of course impossible to verify that Irwin was citing genuine sentiments expressed by employees (or to assess those employees' motivations for expressing those sentiments). Nevertheless, Lockheed played a leadership role in breaking down racial barriers to industrial employment during World War II, drawing justifiable praise from scholars and activists. Lockheed served as perhaps the best example of Weaver's insistence that management commitment and planning could crack the walls of employment segregation. The aircraft industry "also illustrated that, given economic necessity, relaxations in traditional bars to Negro employment are most easily and extensively achieved in industrial centers outside the South, where the color caste system is least firmly entrenched." While employment segregation was a national rather than merely regional problem, Weaver found that plants in the South proved tougher to penetrate. For example, in 1941, the industrial relations manager at Vultee Aircraft's plant in Nashville, Tennessee, told the city's NAACP chapter, "We do not now believe it advisable to include colored people with our regular working force. We may at a later date be in a position to add some colored people in minor capacities, such as porters and cleaners." By the spring of 1942, the plant employed twenty African Americans as janitors but none in production jobs. "The picture in Southern aircraft plants is uniformly bad," Weaver wrote in 1945, though he found that the Bell Aircraft–operated plant in Marietta was among "the least bad."[32]

According to historian Tom Scott, the U.S. government's wartime "decision to build a bomber plant" near Marietta, in rural Cobb County, "was the result of fortuitous circumstances and the hard work of visionary local statesmen determined to lead the area out of the Great Depression." During the 1930s, a nascent coalition pressed for greater industrial development and outside investment in the county. Prominent members of the coalition included James V. Carmichael, an attorney and businessman who went on to serve as the local management face of both Bell and Lockheed; General Lucius Clay; and Mayor Rip Blair. Carmichael and his colleagues opposed the race-baiting associated with the Eugene Talmadge faction in Georgia politics and "saw a positive role for government [at the local, state, and national levels] in improving education, building a modern infrastructure, and actively recruiting" outside industry.[33]

As the country geared up for war in 1941, Marietta's coalition garnered federal support first for the construction of Rickenbacker Field, a modern airstrip. After the U.S. entry into the war in December, the army sought to increase production of the massive Boeing-designed B-29 bomber. The long production runs required for the new planes—indeed for all aircraft during World War II—necessitated that Boeing license its plans to other manufacturers to meet the military's demand. Cobb's boosters then convinced Bell to agree to operate a federally constructed plant, and it soon became one of the largest aircraft manufacturing facilities in the world.[34]

By late 1944, Government Aircraft Plant 6 employed more than twenty-eight thousand workers, including about two thousand African Americans, who worked in separate buildings from their white counterparts. About twelve hundred of these black workers were employed in janitorial, loading, material handling, and other traditionally black jobs, but the remainder had received training that enabled them to move into semiskilled and skilled manufacturing work, though they remained segregated. Bell, like Vultee and North American, had initially refused to hire black workers for any jobs beyond unskilled labor but eventually gave in to pressure from the FEPC and the Atlanta Urban League, producing a rare southern victory for African American laborers. Nevertheless, the company "was so effective in its segregationist policy that few white workers were aware that blacks performed skilled jobs." Blacks accounted for 16 percent of Cobb County's population but just 7 percent of the workforce at the plant. In addition, strict departmental segregation drastically curtailed black workers' chances for advancement and promotion. Carmichael negotiated an agreement with the FEPC to open more training opportunities to black workers, but as demand for aircraft began to wane by the end of 1944, the facility began to reduce its total employment.[35] The factory then closed in January 1946.

By the end of the war, the U.S. government had purchased more than ten thousand of Lockheed's P-38 planes alone, but Robert Gross and his aircraft industry colleagues understood that the wave of production and profits had crested even before the conflict had ended. Late in the war, Gross observed, "We must recognize that we shall probably never again during this war be able to make the money that we made in the years 1942 and 1943." Gross's assessment proved correct. In 1944, at its production high point, Lockheed delivered almost six thousand aircraft. Deliveries fell below three thousand the following year before cratering to just 465 in 1946, when Lockheed employed just seventeen thousand workers. Even at that, the 1946 aircraft deliveries and employment numbers represented significant improvements over the company's prewar position. The government's support of the aircraft industry had helped revolutionize production, management, training, and personnel relations, while the war had also offered evidence for Weaver's contention that government policy combined with high demand could begin to reshape labor markets to a much greater degree than either of those phenomena alone. As William Hartung, a project director at the Center for International Policy and author of a critical history of Lockheed and the military-industrial complex, observes, "The military buildup for World War II resulted in an aircraft industry that was on a whole different scale from the struggling, on-again-off-again business that companies like Lockheed struggled with in the early to mid-1930s." Yet the withdrawal of massive military demand threatened to burst the industry's balloon.[36]

For a time, Lockheed and the rest of the aircraft industry struggled to adjust to the new reality. Gross emerged as a key supporter of the creation of a permanent close relationship between government and defense-related industries. In this advocacy, Gross promoted both his view of the perilous international situation that would become the Cold War and his company's narrow economic interests, with the two largely coinciding. As Hartung observes, "This practice of equating the aircraft industry's interests with the national interest was to serve Lockheed and its rivals well in the decades to come." The convergence also turned Gross into a devotee of at least a measure of economic planning. He believed that "he and his colleagues could successfully lobby for a policy of peacetime government subsidies for the aerospace industry, even if it did not compare to the levels of government business achieved during World War II."[37]

At an August 1945 hearing, Gross urged Congress to help the aircraft industry maintain the productive base it had developed during the war with a variety of aid measures. Gross's colleague Donald Douglas bitterly complained that "after telling industry to drop everything and concentrate on war production ... Government should not, now that the war is over, say to industry ... you're on your own." The public and congressional mood, however, favored reductions in defense expenditures, and while military contracts through the late 1940s far exceeded prewar levels, they fell far short of Gross's desires. After a burst of postwar Wall Street optimism, Lockheed stock began slumping, dropping by two-thirds by early 1947.[38]

Gross continued to press his case, testifying about the future of the aircraft industry before a Senate committee in May 1946. He echoed other executives in making a pragmatic case for maintaining the industrial base, including aircraft production, in the interest of innovation. The Lockheed chair called for the creation of a board composed of "disinterested, farsighted, public-spirited Americans that will get for their country an air power that is adequate, continuous, and permanent, and thus in so doing it will secure for a world that certainly needs it, peace, but peace with justice."[39]

"We have always had the ambition to make the business pay, just on the basis of commercial and private type airplanes," Gross told a business audience that same year, but "in spite of my personal feelings on the subject, the aircraft industry needs substantial Government support." By 1947, Lockheed faced ruin when Trans World Airlines canceled a contract for Constellation transport aircraft: according to Gross, "If we can liquidate our inventory we wind up '47 with $50 million in cash. If we can't sell our inventory, we are through." For help, Gross turned to the newly created U.S. Air Force, which purchased ten cargo planes, enabling Lockheed to avoid bankruptcy, although the company still declared a $9 million loss for 1947. For the rest of the decade, the company survived by selling reconnaissance and fighter planes to the military. Not until the Korean War, however, did the cost-conscious U.S. Congress adopt Gross's ideas and move toward permanent mobilization. The advent of the Cold War created an environment within which economic planning and long-term massive public investment became palatable to both Congress and Gross and his business colleagues.[40]

That environment also created conditions that favored African American civil rights, even in the heart of the segregated South—at least to some extent. But advocates of equal employment opportunity continued to face daunting challenges. A National Association of Manufacturers survey of more than twenty-one hundred white business owners and white- and blue-collar workers found that 65 percent of respondents favored segregated workplaces, while 68 percent "said white jobs should not be opened to Negroes." Among managers, white-collar workers, and owners, 74 percent opposed moving blacks into traditionally white jobs. Though racial exclusion was less popular in the Northeast and among blue-collar workers, people in all parts of the country and in all sorts of jobs were "inclined to discriminate and segregate." Support for workplace segregation was strongest in the South.[41]

Structural barriers to African American advancement also were stronger—or at least more openly acknowledged—in the South. African American workers confronted a vicious cycle. The South's segregated labor markets had constricted economic opportunities for African Americans and in turn contributed to prevailing ideas about the limited potential of black workers. These ideas then buttressed the region's unwillingness to devote money to the parts of its segregated school system that served African Americans, which received even fewer resources than the underfunded schools for whites. The lack of educational opportunities then prevented African Americans from expanding their access to labor markets. Divergence in schooling paralleled and reinforced divergence in the labor market and ultimately shored up the racial hierarchy.

Even when southern states responded to challenges to segregation in the 1930s by reluctantly increasing appropriations for black schools, the new funds were devoted largely to expanding traditional offerings. The concept of "Negro jobs" had become deeply ingrained, with even sympathetic reformers falling prey to the idea. New York railroad entrepreneur and philanthropist William H. Baldwin Jr. had observed in 1899, "It is a crime for any teacher, white or black, to educate the Negro for positions which are not open to him." Three decades later, when the Rosenwald Fund conducted surveys to demonstrate a need for black high schools, attitudes had changed little: "In place after place the response indicated that there were no black jobs for which a high school education would be useful." The South's labor markets had been shaped from their inception by attitudes about race and the class interests of plantation owners. Landlords had little interest in paying higher taxes to improve education for black sharecroppers and tenant farmers. Planters frequently believed that education had a deleterious effect on black workers: according to a 1905 report by North Carolina's labor commissioner, "nine of ten farmers opposed compulsory education for blacks because 'educated Negroes in nearly all cases become valueless as farm laborers.'" Such attitudes and the power of those who held them led to inadequate funding for black schools and widely held biases against hiring blacks for skilled and managerial jobs. Labor economist Herbert Northrup, historian Robert Margo, and economist Donald Dewey attested to the continued rigidity of segregated labor markets as late as the mid-1950s, with Northrop noting, "If anything, by 1950, segregation of job facilities had become more rigid."[42]

African Americans had recorded many gains at Lockheed and other firms during the World War II years. However, demobilization and rapid technological advancements caused much of that progress to melt away. In the absence of full employment pressure and a national emergency, those gains would probably be much more difficult to reproduce and extend, particularly when Lockheed reopened what had now become known as Air Force Plant 6 in Marietta at the height of the Korean War.

CHAPTER 2

"Lockheed Will Live in the Southern Tradition"
LOCKHEED COMES TO GEORGIA, 1951-1954

"The walls of prejudice are falling," the president of Tuskegee Institute announced in November 1951. Speaking to more than five hundred members of the Career Conference on the campus of his institution, Frederick Douglass Patterson suggested that the South was "in the process of change from an economy of scarcity and exploitation" to "an economy of expansion and individual human development." The key manifestation of this transition, he declared, was "the extension of educational opportunity to all of the South's citizens." Patterson was referring to efforts by many southern states to narrow the gap in funding for school systems for whites and blacks, a strategy that sought in part to defend continued racial separation, as well as to the general increase in funding for higher education around the country.[1]

Another conference speaker, Joseph Bird, college relations director for RCA, insisted that fair employment practices also were making headway: "Racial prejudice is becoming less and less a barrier to employment of Negroes in American business," he declared, citing his firm; one of the nation's leading military contractors, Lockheed; and a few other large national companies. Patterson no doubt had in mind Lockheed's main California plants, which had been pacesetters in labor market desegregation during World War II and continued to draw praise from civil rights organizations. Lockheed had reopened the mothballed World War II facility in Marietta, Georgia, earlier that year, but black employment there did not yet indicate any significant change from southern tradition.[2]

While some walls may have been falling, many African Americans had lost ground since World War II. The collapse of southern agricultural employment, meager though it had been, had helped push tens of thousands off the land and into northern cities in what became known as the Great Migration. Wartime jobs had provided relief and improvement, but many of those opportunities had disappeared after 1945. Gavin Wright observes that the economic lot of many black southerners actually worsened in the first decade and a half after World War II. The GI Bill exemplified the trend. Lack of adequate facilities and the local control and administration of the bill's programs limited its effectiveness for African Americans in the South. The region's black colleges were few, small, underfunded, and unable to accommodate the rapid influx of potential students. Fewer still offered any postbaccalaureate programs; none offered advanced degrees in engineering. The disparate impact of the GI Bill helped account for a "widening ... gap" between blacks and whites, as whites took advantage of available educational opportunities that were unavailable to blacks. The Social Security program did not cover agricultural workers, domestic workers, or people who worked at home—occupations dominated by African Americans. Until the mid-1950s, 65 percent of African Americans nationwide fell outside the law's coverage; in many areas of the South, the proportion was closer to 80 percent. The same categories of workers were also originally exempted from the Fair Labor Standards Act, which established a minimum wage, mandated a forty-hour workweek with overtime pay, and offered other protections. Ira Katznelson argues that these and similar policies and practices shaped an era "when affirmative action was white."[3]

The Urban League reported in June 1954 that "the economic status of Southern Negroes [had] improved," although "the vast majority" were still "restricted to low-paying, unskilled jobs." Professional and white-collar jobs for blacks in the South were "almost non-existent," while "supervisory and management jobs [were] rarely given to Negroes except in enterprises operated by Negroes [and] for them." In 1950, black family incomes averaged a mere $1,869 per year, just 54 percent of the average white family income of $3,445. Individual African American workers earned only 52 percent as much as whites nationwide, and according to the Urban League, "the picture in the South was even worse." Two of the region's rare bright spots were Western Electric's communications equipment plants in North Carolina and Lockheed's Georgia plant.[4]

But in September 1951, after Lockheed reopened the facility, general manager James V. Carmichael announced, "Lockheed will live in the southern tradition." Walls would not be falling in Marietta: "We will employ colored people according to their ability but they will not be mixed on the assembly line with whites." Both the *Atlanta Constitution*, the largest-circulation newspaper in the South, and the *Atlanta Daily World*, the nation's first successful African American daily, covered Carmichael's address. For the *Daily World*, the story merited front-page placement, while the *Constitution* relegated the story to page 6. The African American paper used the phrase *southern tradition* in its headline, while the *Constitution* intoned, "Segregation carried out at Lockheed." Both papers reported the substance of Carmichael's remarks and featured the same extended quotation.[5]

As these parallel stories indicate, even moderate black and white leaders viewed the issue of equal employment through different lenses. Ralph McGill, the *Constitution*'s editor-in-chief, had long advocated the improvement and amelioration of the conditions of segregation for African Americans and critiqued the inequality that characterized the South's "separate but equal" economy, society, and polity. Yet at least until the *Brown* decision in 1954, McGill nominally supported legal segregation. In this attitude, McGill had much in common with Carmichael. The *Constitution*'s story on Carmichael's address observed that a defense plant in Augusta had recently issued "specific directives . . . outlawing segregation" and noted that government directives "discouraged" segregation, but the paper cast no direct doubt on the propriety of Carmichael's assertions.[6] And the *Constitution* represented the views of moderate white urban and suburban southerners.

A headline that assured readers that segregation would be maintained at the Lockheed plant, placed discreetly within the paper rather than jumping out from page 1, would probably have reassured the paper's readers, as would Carmichael's characterization of the aspirations of black residents of Atlanta and its suburbs. "All the colored people want," Carmichael insisted, "was the opportunity to earn a living for themselves and their children, the opportunity to get an education for their children, and the right to be citizens." Carmichael declared that he had talked to middle- and working-class blacks and their leaders and "that is all they want here in the South."[7]

For its part, the *Atlanta Daily World* was becoming one of the country's most conservative African American papers, generally aligned with the moderate wing of the Republican Party. C. A. Scott, the *World*'s longtime publisher, backed civil rights but urged caution and restraint, especially as the movement gained steam after 1955. The *World* endorsed the Republican presidential candidate, Richard Nixon, in 1960, drawing widespread criticism from other African American newspapers such as the *Chicago Defender*, and discouraged sit-ins and other more activist protests in favor of negotiations to end segregation in downtown Atlanta stores in the early 1960s. But the *Daily World* also displayed a skepticism born of long experience with the coded language of the segregated South. In response to Carmichael's characterization of what "the colored people want," the paper pointed out that he had "apparently ignore[d] the government's policy relating to defense contracts."[8]

The view of many local African Americans was perhaps best expressed by Harry Hudson, a pioneer in crossing the racial divide at Lockheed-Georgia. Hudson had heard via "the grapevine" that Carmichael had "made the statement ... that as long as he was manager of the facility, no 'niggers' would ever hold a higher position than that of a janitor." Such private statements, rumored or actual, buttressed the prevailing view that Lockheed was not seriously interested in desegregating its Georgia workforce. Hudson believed that Carmichael's public statements were "strictly propaganda" and that Carmichael understood that he would at least have to make some token effort at integration to satisfy "the powers that be in Washington."[9]

Carmichael played a central role in both public and behind-the-scenes negotiations over race and employment in the early years at Lockheed-Georgia. The company in-house Georgia newsletter, the *Southern Star*, began weaving a narrative about history, patriotism, duty, enterprise, and labor with its inaugural issue on March 29, 1951. Carmichael, who embodied the plant's history in Marietta, informed employees that the facility's initial task would "be to take a number of B-29s out of mothballs" and refurbish them for action in Korea and elsewhere in a dangerous new world. "Some of them," Carmichael observed, "may be the very ones that came off these efficient assembly lines in the memorable years 1942 to 1945." Carmichael had managed the facility for Bell Aircraft during World War II, and he knew that he would not be the only Bell veteran in the reconstituted workforce. For those who remembered the World War II experience, Carmichael told fellow employees that he "share[d] the pride ... that we as individuals have again been called upon to do a patriotic and exciting service to our country." He connected the old struggle to the new Cold War and its hot manifestation, the Korean War: "The roar of each plane as it comes alive under your hands will thrust us farther away from the danger of chaotic war." He continued, "Georgia workers made an outstanding record in the last war," and he was certain that "we will do as well or better in this second command performance."[10] At least within the company, he hoped to rekindle some of the esprit de corps that World War II had engendered but that had subsequently withered.

The front page of the initial issue of the *Southern Star* carried two other items of long-term significance. Carmichael sought to encourage workers to believe that unlike the fleeting Bell experience, Lockheed planned to remain in Georgia for the long haul: "The modification of the B-29s may be only a warm-up of the plant.... Plans for the production of a current military plane are in discussion with the Air Force at this time." In addition, a story headlined "Labor Negotiations Begin with IAM" revealed that Lockheed would grant recognition to the machinists' union without going through an election, having already opened negotiations with the International Association of Machinists. Management reminded workers, however, that Georgia's right-to-work law made union membership voluntary and required the modification of certain clauses in the contract for Burbank and other Lockheed facilities.[11] Lockheed's efforts to secure semipermanent work for the Georgia division and maintain relations with the IAM shaped the contours of desegregation policy at the plant for more than two decades.

The *Southern Star* also began profiling top officials of Lockheed's new Georgia division. The series opened with a biographical piece on Carmichael that detailed the Marietta attorney's struggle to recover from being struck by an automobile at the age of sixteen. Though seriously injured, Carmichael recovered but was left with permanent damage that limited his mobility. In 1933, after "trad[ing] in his wheelchair for a cane," he received a law degree from Emory University. He quickly established a successful legal practice and was elected to the state legislature in 1936. Carmichael participated in the negotiations that resulted in the construction of Government Aircraft Plant 6 in Cobb County in 1942 and served as the general manager of the facility for Bell Aircraft during World War II, when it produced 668 B-29 Superfortresses.[12] While overseeing Bell's Georgia operation, Carmichael had also served as Governor Ellis Arnall's executive director of the state revenue department and "helped write a new state constitution." The piece thus overtly connected Carmichael with the Constitution of 1945's abolition of the poll tax, one of a trio of basic measures that southern states had used to disfranchise African Americans over the preceding half century. Also in 1945, federal court decisions had invalidated Georgia's whites-only Democratic primary. Arnall, unlike former governor Eugene Talmadge, Georgia's most vocal supporter of the segregationist order, had refused to engage in any sort of legal maneuvering to save the white primary. With the popular Arnall ineligible for reelection in 1946, the state's anti-Talmadge faction had settled on Carmichael as the standard-bearer for Georgia's racial moderates, urban business leaders, middle-class professionals, and many supporters of FDR and the New

Deal. According to *Southern Star* editor Betty Chandler, Carmichael's "bold campaign slighted none of the hot issues and earned national attention." However, although Carmichael received the most votes, amassing "the largest popular vote ever given any candidate for governor in Georgia," Georgia's peculiar county unit system meant that Talmadge won the election. Thereafter, Chandler wrote, "Carmichael grinned [the election] off, congratulated the winner, and took a job as assistant to the president of Scripto, the world's top producer of mechanical pens and pencils."[13]

Talmadge's death in December 1946, prior to his inauguration, threw Georgia into political chaos as various factions wrangled over who should assume office in his stead. Carmichael refused to insert himself into the scramble, declaring that he would neither seek nor accept the governorship under current circumstances. In a statement that cast light on his entire career, he told the *Atlanta Constitution*, "I feel that Georgia needs and must have a few years of political peace if she is to progress industrially, agriculturally, and economically."[14]

Carmichael was a key player in Georgia's emerging business-oriented development coalition. Perhaps the most important single leader in that coalition, Coca-Cola's Robert Woodruff, sought Carmichael as a replacement to oversee the day-to-day operations of what had become by the early 1950s the leading Georgia-based multinational corporation. Carmichael declined, citing his lifelong health problems, and devoted himself to promoting the Atlanta area's economic development. As Tom Scott, the leading historian of postwar economic development in Cobb County, observes, Carmichael urged Georgians to "embrace change" and "advocated a meritocracy in which talented individuals would be honored for their achievement in bringing the South into an era of prosperity, power, and cultural influence." In a 1950 commencement address at Emory University, Carmichael declared, "I sicken of these people who are always waving the Confederate Flag and telling us what a glorious heritage the South has. No one denies this heritage, but too many of our people want to keep on living on who they are and where they came from."[15]

Carmichael's selection to head Lockheed-Georgia's operations thus reflected not only his experience as the manager of a large aircraft plant facing pressure to keep up with war demands but also his reputation as a racial moderate, and his appointment sent a positive signal to groups such as the Urban League. Carmichael's public record contrasted sharply with the views of Eugene Talmadge's son, Herman, who had won the governorship in 1948 by espousing a white supremacist agenda, promising vigorous opposition to federal civil rights legislation, and threatening to close public schools rather than integrate. In short, as the state's political leadership lined up to defend the segregationist order, Carmichael's pro-business stance sent a very different message.[16]

Although the Talmadge administration and its successors did not interfere with or publicly criticize any of Lockheed's efforts at desegregation but did engage in many of the same massive resistance tactics pursued by other southern states. Talmadge's successor, Marvin Griffin, traveled to Little Rock, Arkansas, in 1957 to offer moral support for Orval Faubus's defiance of the federal courts and opposition to desegregation at Central High School. Ernest Vandiver, who followed Griffin, campaigned on the slogan "No, not one"—meaning not one African American child in a white school.

However, Carmichael's September 1951 remarks provoked a firestorm of criticism from civil rights organizations, particularly the NAACP. In an attempt to quell the brewing controversy, representatives of the group's Atlanta chapter met with Carmichael in early November 1951 "to secure an explanation" for Carmichael's statements about continued segregation on the production floor, an "apparent violation" of President Truman's February 2, 1951, Executive Order 10210, which had declared that "there shall be no discrimination in any act performed hereunder against any person on the ground of race, creed, color or national origin, and all contracts hereunder shall contain a provision that the contractor and any subcontractors thereunder shall not so discriminate."[17]

Carmichael assured the NAACP committee that "his plans contemplate no discrimination," the *Daily World* reported, and recent newspaper accounts had suffered from a "misplacement of emphasis." The public announcement about living in "the southern tradition," Carmichael said, was "produced by rumors and misrepresentations of policies among employees" and could hamper the plant's main goal of maximum production for the war effort by threatening to disrupt "harmonious labor relations." At some point between September and November, Carmichael "had closed down the plant, called all workers together in one place," and clarified for them Lockheed's policy of "maximum training and use of labor at all levels of employment." Carmichael said that he had "secured what he believes is a sympathetic understanding from all workers" and maintained that "there will be no discrimination" and "that Negro applicants would be welcomed for any job for which they are qualified or can be trained to fill."[18]

Nevertheless, Carmichael stood by his commitment to segregated assembly lines. And his choice of wording—"any job for which they are qualified or can be trained"—offered room for interpretation. Were black workers simply unqualified and untrainable for some jobs? Given his emphasis on "southern tradition," some observers certainly would answer in the affirmative, as Hudson and others well understood.

The fifty-five hundred employees Carmichael addressed would have included few African Americans, none of them working directly in production or management. According to a January 1952 memorandum, Lockheed employed "467 . . . Negroes who work as janitors, utility workers, material sorters, paper balers, [and] parts cleaners"—traditional jobs for African Americans within white-owned and -managed enterprises.[19]

Two months earlier, the *Daily World* had reported that Carmichael "promised to include Negro staff members in their Personnel and labor divisions" and "study policies" of other firms engaged in desegregation efforts. Lockheed officials told NAACP representatives that they would "possibly visit" International Harvester's Memphis, Tennessee, plant and General Motors' New Orleans facility, "where complete integration of workers has reportedly been initiated.[20]

International Harvester in particular was well known for its efforts to promote equal employment opportunity. The nation's leading manufacturer of agricultural equipment, Harvester employed more than ninety thousand people at more than twenty plants. Its mechanical cotton picker had revolutionized cotton agriculture, drastically reducing the amount of human labor required and helping to push African Americans off southern farms after World War II. In this light, Jennifer Delton notes, perhaps "it was appropriate that the company had an active antidiscrimination program."[21]

Harvester had integrated its plants in Evanston, Illinois; Louisville, Kentucky; and Memphis by following a three-step process developed and implemented by its recently retired industrial relations specialist Sarah Southall: "(1) study and analysis of the local situation; (2) careful selection of qualified Negroes; and (3) cooperation with employees and union officials." The first step involved "many meetings with white community leaders" and "likely employees" in which company officials explained that Harvester had no crusading agenda to revolutionize local customs or promote the dreaded "social equality." Nevertheless, Harvester's "white employees in these plants still rebelled when blacks were upgraded into skilled positions." White workers staged four wildcat strikes to protest "Negro upgrading" between 1948 and 1953, and other actions were threatened. Integration may have proceeded, but the progress was far from smooth and steady.[22]

International Harvester also developed a training program for supervisors that included instruction on the company's antidiscrimination policies and "emphasized the hard-nosed economic, practical, and patriotic realities that necessitated the policy: the need for the most qualified people, the expense of segregation, the right of all Americans to earn a living so they were not a burden on taxpayers." Supervisors were also presented with case studies of difficult racial situations. The program did not include appeals to morality or ethics, and the company tried to present the program as just one among many training activities, reflecting the view, widely shared at the time, that racial integration was best accomplished quietly.[23]

This approach bore the influence of the human relations strategy advocated by Southall and Harvester CEO Fowler McCormick, and Lockheed followed the same basic plan, although it is not clear whether Lockheed officials ever consulted with International Harvester's managers. And Lockheed unquestionably adopted a less detailed approach. It (like most other corporations) did not institute such training for supervisors until the late 1960s, and there is no evidence that company officials met with locals to discuss such matters prior to or during the first few years of operating the Marietta plant. Only after Carmichael's "southern tradition" address created a public relations problem did he and Lockheed's division industrial relations director meet with African American leaders represented by the Urban League, and these meetings were not public knowledge. Moreover, no evidence indicates that the company conducted orientation meetings with white or black employees.

Atlanta civil rights leaders remained wary of Lockheed's promises and remained completely opposed to any attempt to desegregate employment while maintaining segregation on the factory floor and ancillary facilities. Anticipating that Lockheed would continue to resist full integration until federal pressure required it, they began to lay the groundwork for just such a campaign. In November 1951, NAACP leaders urged "large numbers of Negroes" to "apply for jobs at all levels in all skills" as the company ramped up hiring, explaining that a "number of discriminations must be successfully proven before any successful attack can be made on the policies outlined by Mr. Carmichael."[24]

Later in the month, Atlanta NAACP chapter president C. L. Harper and the chair of the branch's Military and War Mobilization Committee, C. W. Greenlea, rejected Carmichael's offer of jobs for black workers within a segregated framework, informing him that the NAACP "cannot commit itself to a policy of segregation in any field of activity." Appealing to Cold War sentiment, Harper and Greenlea declared that by allowing "discrimination in employment," the United States would "give our enemies a cold war [propaganda] weapon more powerful than guns, planes, or battleships."[25]

In early December, Harper and Greenlea wrote to Robert E. Gross, Lockheed's president and CEO, that Carmichael had "raised the question as to whether the President's Executive Order No. 10210 was contained in Lockheed's 'definitive contract' with the government," since the January 1951 contract predated the order.[26] By reiterating that Lockheed would not discriminate yet raising the possibility that the federal government's non-discrimination policy did not apply, Carmichael probably sought to paint his company in the best light—and insulate it from legal challenges that it was not doing enough.

In late January 1952, Carmichael and other Lockheed personnel officials, including James P. Lydon, met with representatives of the Atlanta Urban League, among them chapter president Grace Towns Hamilton. It is not clear who suggested the idea for the meeting, but the Urban League had a long-established reputation for working behind the scenes with local power brokers to open up opportunities for African Americans. Lockheed officials and most other business leaders preferred to work with the Urban League over the NAACP and other civil rights groups.

Lydon, a native of Buffalo, New York, and a Notre Dame graduate, had already spent fifteen years working in labor relations with Lockheed. After moving from California to Marietta in 1951 to become director of industrial relations for the Georgia plant, Lydon, like other newcomers, was somewhat surprised by the rigid local segregation practices, although he would certainly have been well aware of the exclusion of black workers from Lockheed's West Coast plants a decade earlier.[27]

Carmichael opened the meeting by trying to dampen expectations for job growth in Marietta since "there had been some cutbacks in scheduled plane production by Washington." Carmichael attributed the cutbacks to "fears of overproduction" as the Korean War appeared to be winding down. Carmichael acknowledged that although blacks made up more than a quarter of the seventeen-hundred-man production force, none of those men performed skilled or supervisory work. According to Carmichael, "the employment of Negroes in skilled and technical jobs would be resented by other plant personnel," and he thought "it would seem advisable to utilize skilled and technical Negro personnel as supervisors of future Negro employees."[28] That is, the segregated framework would remain in place. Though the NAACP had flatly rejected this approach, the Urban League was willing to negotiate the details of such a deal.

Carmichael and Lydon outlined a plan to begin hiring, training, and using African American workers in semiskilled and skilled positions in the refitting of B-29s (now being phased out) as well as in the construction of the rear assembly of the Boeing B-47 jet bomber. In both cases, black workers would work on separate assembly lines, separated from white workers by large containers.[29] This was something of a step up from the arrangement that had been in place when Bell Aircraft (and Carmichael) operated the facility during World War II. At that time, the handful of skilled African American employees completed their piecework in separate buildings and the small subassemblies were subsequently moved to the main building for inclusion into the final assembly.

When Urban League representatives raised "questions of recruiting and placement of Negro workers," Carmichael "admitted his concern about these problems." He asked participants to "give thought to the advisability of Lockheed establishing a separate Negro Employment office." Attendees also discussed how to train the 550 or so African Americans that Lockheed anticipated hiring. Carmichael seemed to suggest that they would spend the bulk of 1952 on "in-plant training," since the company could not follow its general practice of contracting with local white schools to provide classes. Lockheed also agreed to provide the Urban League with detailed information about the skills required and to recognize the "Employment Opportunities Committee of Urban League . . . as the official agency in developing minority employment policies."[30]

As Lockheed continued to ponder the way forward, Julius Thomas, director of industrial relations for the National Urban League, conducted "a survey of employment opportunities" for African Americans in firms nationwide that had or were believed to have defense contracts, presenting his findings to the President's Committee on Government Contract Compliance in July 1952. The National Urban League identified several general categories of discrimination that testified to the lack of skilled and managerial employment opportunities for black Americans: "employs Negroes only for unskilled jobs"; "Negroes not hired for technical or clerical jobs"; "Negroes not accepted for training programs conducted by the company." Somewhat less common, though still present, were companies that "refuse[d] to hire Negroes in any capacity."[31]

According to the report, discrimination could be found across the country. Arizona's Motorola Research Laboratories refused to hire black workers in any capacity, as did Indiana's Anaconda Wire and Cable and Container Corporation of America. The nearly one thousand workers at the International Shoe Factory of Springfield, Illinois, included no blacks, nor did Minnesota's Land O' Lakes Creamery. A Cleveland, Ohio, business leader declared, "If I don't want to work next to a Negro, none of my employees should have to, either." Many more firms employed black workers in limited numbers and capacities and restricted them to unskilled and nonsupervisory positions. Ohio's B. F. Goodrich accepted no African Americans in company training programs, while Firestone employed no African Americans in production jobs and only a few as janitors.[32]

The survey included fewer southern firms because they were less likely to have defense contracts, (though the number was growing rapidly), but the results there were similar. Five Kentucky firms employed black workers only in unskilled jobs, as did B. F. Goodrich Chemical and Reynolds Metals. National Carbide's workforce of 550 included 80 African Americans, all but 1 of them in unskilled jobs. The lone black professional was employed in the personnel department, presumably to deal with the black workers.[33]

The aircraft industry loomed large in the survey. Consolidated Vultee Aircraft (formed by the merger between Vultee Aircraft and Consolidated Air and known as Convair) and Bell Aircraft facilities in Texas employed "Negroes in unskilled but not skilled production jobs" and refused "to employ Negroes for technical and clerical jobs" or "accept Negroes in training programs." Some California aircraft plants had moved at least partly away from older attitudes about race and skilled labor, but Douglas Aircraft, North American Aviation, Northrop Aircraft, and General Electric's aviation division refused "to employ Negroes in technical and clerical jobs." In addition, GE's California aviation plants did not "accept Negroes in training programs" and did not hire blacks for skilled production work.[34]

Lockheed-California was conspicuously absent from the survey, possibly because it was significantly ahead of others on minority hiring. However, the Urban League survey criticized Lockheed-Georgia for limiting black workers to unskilled jobs in the production area, noting that "promises have been made that Negroes will be upgraded into semi-skilled jobs" but that "they will be maintained in segregated areas."[35]

By the summer of 1952, Lockheed had apparently begun to follow through on those promises, at least to some extent, by hiring Morehouse College graduate Robert S. Kennon to recruit black workers. According to Hugh Gordon, who had been hired nearly a year earlier, "I think somewhere up the line," management decided "we're going to hire this black guy to do the recruitment in southwest Atlanta." Kennon "didn't have an office, and when he came into the plant he needed somewhere to hang his hat." Gordon's manager asked him if he would mind "when Ken comes in, can he put something in your desk?" Gordon replied, "'Sure.' So we had the first integrated desk in the South!" But Gordon "didn't see him much because he was out doing his thing."[36]

In the spring of 1953, Kennon's recruiting mission took him to his alma mater, where he joined representatives from R. J. Reynolds, General Cable, American Bakeries, and Ford as well as professionals, educators, and government officials to talk with students about job opportunities. With Kennon's employment and recruiting activities at historically black colleges, Lockheed fulfilled part of its promise to the Urban League, and despite the limitations of the company's efforts, it was well ahead of other Georgia-based firms.[37]

One of Kennon's recruits was Harry Hudson, another Morehouse College graduate who co-owned an Auburn Avenue service station. Kennon pulled his car into the Hudsons' service station on Sunday afternoon, August 10, 1952, and struck up a conversation with Hudson, asking whether he would like to work for Lockheed. According to Kennon, "Lockheed was looking for Negroes with mechanical ability and a college degree." Hudson became one of ten "Super Negroes" hired at the same time in 1952 as part of Lockheed's deal with the Atlanta Urban League. All had attended college, and five had graduated, though the jobs for which they were hired did not require college, and white workers who held only high school diplomas routinely were hired for these positions. At the time, however, as Hudson noted, "a degree from a black college was considered equal to a diploma from a white high school." White workers did not appreciate the presence of Hudson and his fellows in the plant, but he nevertheless felt enormous pride: to him it seemed like "the thirteenth wonder of the world . . . the largest aircraft manufacturing plant in the world [with] seventy-six acres under one roof, air-conditioned, and twenty-seven miles of neon lights." Becoming part of something so big made Hudson feel that he was "somebody. After all, [I] was now employed at the Bomber Plant," as the facility had been known since the war.[38]

Race and its consequences were never far from the surface, however. On his first visit to the plant, Hudson and the men hired with him were introduced to Lloyd DeWester, their white supervisor. "We did not know," Hudson recalled, "that he was the only manager that would take the first colored department. . . . No other manager would accept the responsibility." Hudson and his fellows developed an excellent working relationship with DeWester, a foreman from the California division, as they spent ten weeks in training, learning to read blueprints, understand hydraulics, use basic aircraft manufacturing tools and equipment, and do more complicated math. Instructors and higher management constantly reminded Hudson and his colleagues that such intensive training cost the company about $10,000 per worker and predicted "that we would never make it through three weeks," let alone the full ten-week training.[39]

But they did. When they finished, DeWester took the men to meet their new supervisor. While they were waiting for him to arrive, a "good ole boy" drove up on a cart and stopped: "He had never seen Negroes in a skilled production area before. He cut the engine, . . . got comfortable and stared and stared." The new supervisor, too, was taken aback by the sight of his crew. According to Hudson, "If you have ever seen a young child on his first visit to the zoo, then that was the expression on the man's face."[40]

Hudson's crew began work in a segregated area of the plant on subassembly jigs, drilling rivet holes. The men measured carefully and took great care with their work, but inspectors marked virtually every hole drilled by Hudson and his crew as "out of tolerance." After two weeks of such scrutiny, "the inspector called us together and told us that he had been instructed by upper management to reject everything that he could of our workmanship to prove that 'niggers' were unsuited for skilled labor and could not be trained to do so." The inspector told them "he was a moral and Christian man and his conscience would not let him go on with this farce," and he asked that the men not tell anyone about the conversation because it could cost him his job. Going forward, however, the African Americans' rejection rate was "far below the plant average."[41]

In December 1952, Hudson's crew, along with other black workers recruited over the preceding three months, moved up from subassemblies to a major assembly—the aft section of the fuselage for the B-47. Several weeks later, Hudson moved to another project, an experiment in constructing the B-47's nose section. Lockheed had initially purchased the section from another firm, Temco, and attached it to the remainder of the fuselage; however, Hudson and his crew were "informed that if we could produce a top quality nose within budget and on schedule," Lockheed-Georgia "would be awarded the contract from Temco and [our] unit would complete the manufacture of the fuselage." After overcoming various technical difficulties, the African American crew won the contract for the company, and in the process, Hudson earned a promotion to "lead man," an hourly classification just below the salaried management position of supervisor. In June 1953, Hudson garnered another—albeit unofficial—promotion, overseeing a crew of fifteen: it seemed, however, "that no one knew there was an acting supervisor (Negro, that is) on the graveyard shift in the plant."[42]

By the end of the year, the progress of Hudson and his colleagues was garnering notice. The *Atlanta Daily World* reported that "more than 400 Negroes are being trained to produce two sections of the B-47 Stratojet" and that Lockheed anticipated bringing its number of African American employees to about thirteen hundred over the next twelve months. Publicity director Lee Rogers emphasized the value of Lockheed's training programs in "raising the economic potential of the workers in this section" and estimating that such specialized technical training would cost as much as $600 in tuition alone at a private technical school. Moreover, as Rogers noted, workers received $1.55 per hour while in the training program (near the top in U.S. hourly manufacturing earnings at the time and more than twice the $0.75 minimum wage), and when they finished, they could leave Lockheed and take their additional human capital with them, allowing them to "get higher paying jobs elsewhere."[43]

Company officials acknowledged that the "educational achievements of Negro workers"—all of whom were high school graduates and three-quarters of whom had two years of college or more—were "much higher than those of white workers." Only a "serious lack of skilled Negro workers" in the Atlanta area prevented Lockheed from hiring more African Americans, and the company intended to hire and train "all we can find" for production positions. Lee Rogers insisted that the program sought to train and employ black workers for worthwhile positions and not "just to put colored people on the payroll."[44]

As Lockheed-Georgia implemented its limited desegregation plan, the black press prodded the company by noting the distinction between the California and Georgia divisions on the race issue. Columnist and poet Beatrice Murphy highlighted what she characterized as a good record of equal opportunity employment by Lockheed in California in a February 1953 piece for *Afro Magazine*. During a visit to a California plant, she observed "colored secretaries, colored engineers, and colored men and women working side by side with white men and women on the assembly line in various shops." About thirty-three hundred of the facility's thirty-five thousand employees were African American, as were roughly two hundred of the twenty-five hundred engineers. However, Lockheed's "California representatives make it clear that they cannot speak for the personnel policies of the Marietta plant," which "works independently."[45]

According to Hudson, African American workers at Lockheed-Georgia fared somewhat better after Dan Haughton became general manager in late 1952. Haughton, an Alabama native and graduate of the University of Alabama, had joined Lockheed in 1939 as a systems analyst, absorbing as much information as he could and making himself indispensable.

He rose rapidly through the company ranks, serving as an assistant to the vice president of Vega during World War II and as president of two other subsidiaries after the war. In 1951, Haughton was named assistant general manager of the Georgia division under Carmichael (though Haughton probably called most of the shots) before moving up to vice president and general manager, when Carmichael returned to managing the Scripto Pen company in Atlanta. Like Carmichael, "Uncle Dan," as Hudson and virtually everyone else called Haughton, was a native southerner and graduate of a major southern state university, but unlike Carmichael, Haughton had nearly two decades of experience in the aircraft industry. Hudson and other employees viewed Haughton most favorably among Lockheed's Georgia and national leaders during this period, lauding his interest in individual workers and his fairness.[46]

Haughton outlined the company's labor relations philosophy at a December 1954 conference. The *Atlanta Daily World* encapsulated that philosophy under the headline "Says People, Not Machine, Key to Industrial Success." Haughton emphasized Lockheed's efforts to "maintain confidence and team spirit," which included the "fine house organ," the *Southern Star*, "weekly staff meetings, mass assemblies," and "assemblies each Christmas." The company sent letters to employees' homes on important matters and gave all workers company financial statements. These strategies, as well as the company's family days (picnics with games and plant tours) and recreational programs, reflected the three principles that guided the company's labor relations approach: management must "respect the dignity and integrity of all men," keep the anxiety level within the plant as low and "free from worry as possible," and "foster feeling of friendship, common purposes, good will, and pride of work."[47]

Haughton understood that many of the white managers who had transferred from California were troubled by the overt racism they observed, including not just *White* and *Colored* signs on drinking fountains and restrooms but Ku Klux Klan members in full regalia passing out anti-Catholic literature along local Highway 41. Haughton told the California transplants that they would "have to put up with it at least for a while. It should go away. . . . We are a military organization here." The conception of Lockheed as a military organization not only reflected the company's dependence on the Defense Department but also implied that officials saw the company as covered by Truman's 1948 order to desegregate the military.[48]

Hudson became a key resource in Lockheed's effort to recruit and train more African American workers. After the firm received the B-47 nose section contract, Hudson "was asked to recommend everybody that

I thought capable of doing aircraft work." Hudson initially supplied about thirty names of associates with mechanical ability, general knowledge, and manual dexterity, and "all were hired." For the next four years, Hudson received regular requests for more suggestions, ultimately providing what Pamela Laird calls "pull" and creating a network that helped improve black representation within the company.[49]

In early September 1953, Lockheed's superintendent of assembly, Clint Weinke, asked Hudson to take a two-hour test, "as a formality only," to see if he had "the ability to be a supervisor." After Hudson earned "one of the highest marks" on the test, he received a supervisor's badge—and instructions not to put it on until the following Monday morning. At that point, according to Weinke, Hudson should turn in his hourly badge and "don't say a damn word to anyone until they notice the new badge and then say, 'damn right, I [am] a supervisor now.'" The promotion gave Hudson responsibility for twenty African Americans working on the B-47 bomber and earned him a raise from eighty-six to ninety-six dollars a week as well as a number of "surprised expressions" and a front-page article in which the *Atlanta Daily World* celebrated "the first member of his race to be upgraded to a supervisor in the mammoth aircraft plant in Marietta." Hudson's promotion to a management position also made national news within the African American community, as the November 12, 1953, *Jet* magazine carried a brief story on Hudson and a photo.[50]

The *Southern Star*, too, announced Hudson's promotion but did not do so until four days after the *Daily World* piece appeared. The *Star* generally acknowledged low-level supervisory promotions in groups, with little individual comment. Hudson's promotion, however, merited a headline—"Harry Hudson Is Named Supervisor"—and a brief story. Most significantly, the story noted that with his promotion, "Hudson thus becomes the first colored employee to be assigned a supervisory position at the Georgia plant," though the next sentence assured readers that Hudson would not be supervising white workers: "Twenty colored employees, including lead men, are working under his direction."[51]

By 1958, two or three other African Americans had followed Hudson into supervisory positions, though all had authority only over black crews. These men included Charles Ferguson, who joined Lockheed in 1951, before Hudson, as one of the few hundred blacks hired into jobs considered traditional for African Americans. Although Ferguson had a year of college under his belt, he was employed as a groundskeeper, but he and some of these other early hires eventually were offered the chance to take tests and receive training for production work. Ferguson took advantage of these opportunities and moved into production work in 1953 before becoming a crew supervisor on the new C-130 transport aircraft that secured Lockheed's presence in Marietta for at least another decade.[52]

Like Ferguson, Reginald Kemp, who was hired as a janitor in 1951, received testing and consideration for movement to production work. Kemp, the fourth of nine children born to a man with no formal education and a woman who was a "self-taught teacher," had received no education prior to about age nine because the area where his family lived had no school for blacks. The family subsequently "began moving about for available black schooling, and he ultimately got his high school diploma." Kemp "constantly sought to improve himself" while at Lockheed, taking every training opportunity available, "and progressively held higher skilled jobs," retiring in 1996 as "a Manufacturing Experimental Technician, the highest paid skilled job in the aircraft industry." Ferguson and Kemp climbed the Lockheed ladder on their own initiative, but they would not have been able to do so if Lockheed had not offered advancement opportunities. Moreover, their progress was slow, and they constituted the exception rather than the rule.[53]

On Hudson's first day as a supervisor, a department manager introduced him to the quality inspector, whose name was Fisher, and informed him "that I was 'the first of my race' to become a supervisor at the Bomber Plant." Hudson suspected that a subtle managerial game was being played. By positioning Fisher, who was "white and a good southerner," as "the most knowledgeable and qualified cat in the area," Hudson believed that the manager was encouraging the inspector to offer "his help in getting me over my [supposed] ignorance and stupidity." As Hudson noted, "psychology is potent as hell." Hudson and Fisher went on to develop a good working relationship that conformed to the strictures of the segregated social order:

> Not only was he an inspector, he was also a teacher of quality workmanship. He proved, as most southerners, that us "southerners" could do as well as anyone in these United States when it came to doing a quality job.... [I]t is no effort to say that directly and indirectly, whites and blacks have worked together, unknowingly, for the benefit of us all, as long as we were under the impression that he was in his place and I was in mine. In other words, I did not expect him to invite me to his house for dinner and vice versa.[54]

Hudson recalled the sixteen men he supervised as "a good crew" who "were learning fast." But "there were some rough times" as well. One issue arose because the union contract prohibited supervisors and inspectors from laboring directly on aircraft. Hudson and Fisher nevertheless occasionally "drilled holes and shot rivets" to maintain "quality and schedule"; luckily, he recalled, "we . . . were not caught by the union or management."[55]

These "rough times" brought Hudson into contact—and conflict—with Harold Mintz, who took over as department manager after his predecessor died in January 1954. Mintz, according to Hudson, "considered himself God's chosen best"; Hudson, however, saw him as "ignorant about aircraft" and "a politician" who sought to "prove to some of those halfass characters from California . . . that he could handle 'Negras' even though the government required that all would be treated equal." Hudson associated Mintz's arrival with "the first big crisis I experienced" at Lockheed.[56]

Hudson recalled that Mintz "rode my ass"—and those of the white supervisors—"without a saddle for about five weeks." Hudson began to experience stomach pain as a consequence of the stress, and one day, when Mintz "told me I would either produce or get fired," Hudson exploded. He "snatched that . . . badge off my shirt and hit [Mintz] in the chest with it and told him to ram it up his ass." Hudson believed that he was insulated from retaliation because "after all the money spent on me to show the government that they could produce a supervisor (black, stupid or otherwise), they were not going to let me bust my own ass." He was right: Mintz "stooped and picked up my badge, told me to take it and cool off." With his crew watching and most of them "ready to go down with me," Hudson felt "pretty good." A few days later, however, Hudson had to be hospitalized for treatment of stomach ulcers.[57]

Mintz, a North Carolina native, came from a middle-class family: his father worked at a power plant and owned a farm, and Mintz graduated from high school and opened a service station with his brother. After Pearl Harbor, the Mintz brothers sold their business and paid $500 each to attend an aircraft training school in Nashville, Tennessee. Three months later, Vultee Aircraft hired Mintz to work at its Nashville plant, and he worked his way up to become a lead man at Vultee before moving to Marietta in the summer of 1943 to work for Bell Aircraft. By the end of the war, he had become a department manager, but he returned to the service station business and developed several other sidelines until Lockheed reopened the Georgia plant.[58]

Not surprisingly, Mintz's characterization of his time managing the segregated department with virtually all of Lockheed's African American production workers differed substantially from Hudson's. According to Mintz's recollection, he was brought in not because the previous supervisor had died but because the section—"Nine hundred black employees who had never worked on an airplane" before—was having significant problems: "It was way behind, and the "learning curve was outstanding," and he quickly righted the ship by instituting a series of "games" to encourage better housekeeping and more efficient production. For example, the supervisor who received the lowest cleanliness score each week had to place a dirty model duck on his desk. Mintz also "fired a bunch to get started, to get their attention."[59] Hudson clearly had little respect for Mintz's methods, yet Mintz clearly respected Hudson's ability. In June 1954, after the white supervisor of a larger crew accepted a voluntary downgrade to hourly production work, Mintz placed Hudson in charge of those thirty-five men. By the fall of that year, Mintz had assigned Hudson additional crews to supervise as other white supervisors quit. Less than a year after becoming a supervisor, Hudson found himself responsible for eighty-seven men. His salary, however, had not increased.[60]

But Mintz and Hudson clashed again over the issue of defects on the panels drilled by members of Hudson's crew. Close supervision by engineers and inspectors failed to locate the source of the problem, so, according to Hudson, Mintz blamed "bad workmanship" and gave a series of poor performance notices to all of the drill operators in Hudson's crew as well as to Hudson himself. Shop steward J. B. Mabry then filed grievances on behalf of the workers while Hudson continued to investigate the source of the problem. He discovered that the tooling department was saving money by resharpening and reusing drills and that "whoever had resharpened those drills had done so at an angle that was several degrees off the specified angle required." The drills then jumped out of the pilot holes and caused the defects. When the tool shop supervisor corrected the angle, the problem disappeared. Hudson observed, "Funny all those drills showed up in my work area."[61]

But Mintz refused to retract the poor performance reviews. Even though Hudson's status as a member of management prohibited him from helping workers craft grievances, he later declared with "great pleasure" that he had disregarded that stricture and "got together" with Mabry to come "up with one of the best grievances ever written against a company." Mintz consequently "had to eat every one of those performance notices and we went back to quality workmanship." For Hudson, race and fairness trumped job status and motivated him to risk disciplinary action, particularly since he believed that "upper management would have understood anyway." This belief reflected Hudson's overarching view that Lockheed's top management was committed to equal employment opportunity and that problems arose from resistance to that idea at the middle and lower levels. According to Gordon, upper management put up with Mintz and other white supervisors with less-than-enlightened racial attitudes because they got results.⁶²

Though Mintz later shied away from discussing racial incidents at Lockheed, another southern-born manager, Jack McLendon, was more revealing about white attitudes toward African Americans at the Marietta plant. McLendon grew up in the small town of Ashburn in south-central Georgia, where his father managed large tracts of farmland worked by African American laborers. After high school McLendon attended Georgia Tech until World War II cut short his studies. He later earned a degree in chemical engineering from the Southern Technical Institute (now part of Kennesaw State University) and went to work as a field service engineer for the truck division of International Harvester in 1950. In May 1951, McLendon accepted the position of tool planning trainee at Lockheed-Georgia, quickly moving into an engineering management position.⁶³

In a 2002 interview, McLendon observed that "a lot of the whites had the idea that [black workers] were being rammed down their throats, and they didn't like it." McLendon, however, had learned from his father that some African Americans were smarter and worked harder than others and that a good manager needed to find "the right man for the job": race should not be a factor in employment decisions. According to McLendon, from the time the plant opened, management had sought to identify and promote blacks, a goal that led officials to elevate one black worker who held a doctor of divinity degree to the position of tool planner. However, in McLendon's view, the man "never should have been" promoted to that position, which was beyond his capabilities. McLendon attributed the promotion to management's calculation that the man's race meant that he could not be left in his current position or transferred, so he had to be promoted. McLendon related several similar cases where he believed African American workers were either in over their heads or had poor attitudes, but he also singled out a few African Americans whose work he admired: Ferguson, for example, was "one of the most efficient blacks I came across."⁶⁴

McLendon's words reinforce Hudson's views about resentment of African Americans among lower and middle managers and production workers. However, McLendon also seemed to believe that involvement by upper management was unnecessary beyond making it clear that discrimination had to end, and he seemed reluctant to admit that discrimination existed. And his comments about black workers could easily be taken as a version of the good Negro/bad Negro" dichotomy or as a conservative reading of Carmichael's statement that blacks should be hired for jobs for which they were qualified and/or suited. McLendon's characterization supports the idea that outside of a few exceptional individuals, African Americans encountered difficulties when they moved more than a few rungs up the job ladder. Moreover, McLendon expressed sympathy for the position of recalcitrant white workers: "If [management] try to ram [integration] down my throat, I get my back up, too."[65]

The man who placed Mintz at the head of Hudson's division was H. Lee Poore, who became production manager for the entire Marietta plant in 1954. A native of Delmar, Delaware, located right on the Maryland border, Poore attended Nebraska's Lincoln Airplane and Flying School, the same place where Charles Lindbergh had learned to fly. After receiving training as a flight mechanic, Poore returned east by 1937 to work for Taylor Aircraft. From there, he made his way to California and joined Lockheed in 1939 as an assembler. During the wartime production boom, he was promoted to supervisor and then to department manager, and he was part of management there when Randall Irwin pioneered desegregation. After briefly returning to hourly work as an assembler during the brief postwar demobilization, he moved back into management with the outbreak of the Korean War. Poore transferred to the new Georgia division in 1951 and served as superintendent of assembly. Thus, although he was one of the California transplants, he had grown up in a locale that had much in common with the Upper South.[66]

Hudson met Poore soon after joining Lockheed when he came to welcome Hudson and his colleagues to the workforce. Poore was blunt and direct and could be very tough, but he appreciated ability and drive. Hudson and Poore had a mostly positive relationship: Poore and other management higher-ups often walked through the areas where segregated crews worked and offered compliments such as "You boys are doing a good job," and Hudson respected Poore's capabilities. On one occasion, Hudson improvised a solution to fix a door that would not fit correctly, resulting in a complaint from the tooling department. Poore surveyed the situation and essentially told Hudson to keep altering the doors to make them fit until tooling could correct the problem. Poore eventually began to call Hudson "Lad," which Hudson interpreted as a term of affection from the older man.[67]

By the fall of 1954, Hudson had completed two years of employment at Lockheed and a year as a supervisor. He had developed some good relationships with white managers and had the confidence of the Georgia facility's production manager. The plant now had a small but significant number of

African American employees in skilled positions, including a handful of supervisors. But Lockheed's black production workers remained separated from the remainder of the plant's workforce and were becoming increasingly dissatisfied with the slow pace of change. They turned to some bold actions to try to speed up the process.

CHAPTER 3

"Progress to Be Permanent Had to Be Gradual"

GRADUALISM AND ITS DISCONTENTS, 1954-1960

On February 2, 1954, just four months after highlighting Harry Hudson's promotion, the *Atlanta Daily World* congratulated Lockheed-Georgia on its third birthday, noting in the brief article's first sentence that the plant was "the state's largest integrated industrial enterprise at a single location." The article contained no other references to race, offering an overview of total employment, geographic reach (employees from thirty-three Georgia counties), and production statistics. But that lead, though it papered over several layers of complexity, spoke volumes in the heart of the deeply segregated South in the mid-1950s.[1]

Some of those layers of complexity had been exposed in Duke University economist Donald Dewey's 1952 analysis of the racial division of labor in the South. Dewey observed that although there were a "vast number of different racial employment patterns found throughout the South," one could, "without much difficulty . . . discern at least two uniformities—virtual 'laws' of labor use in the southern economy." First, "Negro workers seldom hold jobs which require them to give orders to white workers." Dewey found "virtually no exceptions" to this first proposition. One might rarely find "a Negro worker in a mixed crew serving as a lead man or assistant supervisor," but Dewey had "never heard of a case in southern industry where a Negro worker was placed over a white worker in a formal chain of command." Second, "Negro and white workers do not ordinarily work side by side at the same jobs." Both of those "laws" remained in effect at Lockheed through much of the 1950s.[2]

About a year after Hudson's breakthrough, Harry Alston, southern field director for the National Urban League, summarized the status of African

American workers at Lockheed-Georgia for the civilian staff at the Department of Defense. The eventual audience for the report was, however, President Dwight D. Eisenhower's President's Committee on Government Contracts (PCGC), which was inaugurated in August 1953.

The PCGC, like its predecessors under Franklin Delano Roosevelt and Harry S. Truman, had no real enforcement powers and had no objective standards or criteria by which to gauge compliance. Hugh Gordon recalled that no one in Lockheed management really gave much thought to appeasing or satisfying the PCGC: until 1961, the federal government made no direct attempts to compel firms to comply with fair employment. And Georgia, like other southern states but unlike New York and some other northern jurisdictions, had no state fair employment agency or regulations. Nonetheless, Gordon recalled, Lockheed made efforts toward desegregating the shop floor, in part to follow broader company policy.[3]

As Jennifer Delton argues, however, that though the PCGC did not act forcefully to promote contractors' compliance with antidiscriminatory practices, that does not mean that the commission had no impact. By maintaining fair employment as a goal of government policy, it kept the issue alive and promoted the idea that racial discrimination was un-American. "The PCGC normalized the existence of both non-discrimination policies and a government committee committed to such policies," Delton observes, both recognizing and nudging popular opinion. Eisenhower was the third consecutive president—and the first Republican—to create such a committee and reaffirm a commitment to nondiscrimination among government contractors. The symbolic commitment to fair employment practices became a pillar of the postwar liberal consensus.[4]

Alston's Urban League report reflected the complexities and difficulties of Lockheed's position as an ostensibly integrated employer in Herman Talmadge's segregated Georgia. Alston noted that while several job categories at the Lockheed plant included women, "there are no female Negro workers in these positions" and that Lockheed's James Lydon had said that he "did not see the possibility" of using African American women in any of these job categories. Alston also reported that black male workers remained concentrated in Hudson's section. In addition to Hudson, the sole "Negro supervisor," there were "a few lead men and several sub-assembly workers." There were no African American workers on the flight assembly line, where the various aircraft sections were put together. Moreover, the plant had "no Negroes in administrative or professional positions." When pressed about the potential for expansion of opportunities for African Americans, Lydon offered "a rather doubtful point of view" that he attributed to two factors: "the repercussions to the Supreme Court's decision relative to segregation in the public schools; and the limited budget with which Lockheed has to work."[5]

In May 1954, just five months before Alston submitted his report, the U.S. Supreme Court had announced its decision in *Brown v. Board of Education*, outlawing "separate but equal" schools and provoking outrage among white southerners. Lydon probably judged that with white workers on edge, obtaining cooperation within the workforce might become more difficult, and he may well have been correct. According to Hudson, the decision "upset a helluva lot of people in the south and other parts of the country," and the assistant foreman came "down to the floor with the request that [black workers] not put on a demonstration of glee." Although, Hudson remembered, "about half the guys did not know about any attempt to get a decision from the Supreme Court on anything, . . . the bosses were under the impression that there would be an outbreak of demonstrations as a result of that news."[6] Management appeared to be treading very lightly indeed when it neared the boundaries of Georgia's traditional social order.

Alston's report on the too-slow progress at Lockheed received a sympathetic response from James Evans, civilian assistant to the assistant secretary of defense. Evans saw "great significance" in Alston's findings: although the official believed that "great progress" had been made since the first efforts to promote desegregation in the aircraft industry around Dallas, Texas, he conceded that "a definite racial ceiling has been established . . . at the levels indicated." He encouraged Alston to remain vigilant regarding Lockheed-Georgia, adopting the language of rational personnel usage: "Anything less than full utilization contravenes current directives regarding economies in procurement and operations." Under this theory, including previously excluded groups such as African Americans would eventually yield lower average wage rates. However, the idea could hardly be seen as a short-term justification for action by any single firm, particularly one, like Lockheed, that was unionized and thus would not realize any cost savings in labor (except possibly in the longer term).[7]

The PCGC was, however, considerably less enthusiastic about Alston's report of a de facto cap on black employment at Lockheed. The report, according to the committee's director of information, Charles Livermore, did "not seem to provide a sufficient basis for investigation, or material necessary for a complaint." Alston lacked "a specific complaint in the form of some individual or group of individuals who have sought to be upgraded or transferred and have been unsuccessful in doing so."[8] In other words, statistics alone could not yet serve as evidence of discrimination; individual stories were needed.

Production at Lockheed-Georgia shifted in the aftermath of the Korean War. The company's production of B-47 bombers topped out in 1954 at 143, but the research and development team had a replacement in mind: the C-130 transport aircraft, nicknamed the Hercules for its lifting capacity. The plant's selection as the production site for the new plane secured a more stable long-term future for the facility, and Governor Marvin Griffin, a strong supporter of segregation, christened the first completed aircraft on March 10, 1955. The C-130 quickly became the staple transport aircraft for the U.S. military and proved popular with a number of foreign governments, and by 1957, Lockheed-Georgia delivered 143 of the planes. The U.S. Air Force's decision to purchase the C-130 was fortunate for the Georgia division, because the Boeing B-52 was replacing the B-47 as the primary U.S. strategic bomber, and Lockheed ceased its contract production of the latter in 1957.[9]

About two thousand African American men followed Harry Hudson and his small group of pioneers through the gates at Lockheed-Georgia during the 1950s, with black employment averaging about nine hundred (including six hundred or so in production jobs) until 1958. Among those workers was Ernest "Pappy" Ross, who joined Lockheed in July 1953. Born and raised in Donora, Pennsylvania, just south of Pittsburgh, where he played high school football, he acquired some industrial experience working for the American Steel and Wire Company during the summers. In 1949, Ross enrolled at Atlanta's Morris Brown College on a football scholarship, excelling at both sports and academics. Robert Kennon and other black Lockheed recruiters, among them Napoleon Johnson, visited Morris Brown, though Ross recalled that he made his way to the company after learning of job openings via word of mouth and newspaper advertisements. Ross applied for a position in the late spring or early summer of 1953 and was hired in July.[10]

African Americans at the time typically entered production work as "assembly helpers," but Ross's experience enabled him to start at a higher grade as a "structural assembler," where the starting pay was $1.60 per hour, which Ross believed made it the "best-paying job in the whole state of Georgia." Ross worked in several departments, starting out with the segregated crews on the B-47. As integration slowly proceeded, Ross was often chosen as the first man to move to mixed-race crews, since he had experience working with whites in Pennsylvania. Most black workers from the Atlanta area did not know whites, and Lockheed managers appeared to see Ross's experience as a resource that would help white workers adjust.[11]

In practice, Ross's role seemed to be to reassure whites that workplace integration did not mean integrated social relations. He told his first white partner, "We don't have to like each other to work together. We won't be socializing, won't be calling each other, but we can work together." When another work partner needed to read blueprints, an area where Ross had significant previous work experience but the coworker did not, Ross offered some pointers, prompting the coworker to announce, "There's two things that don't live long in Georgia. That's a smart nigger and a frisky dog." Ross responded, "I don't call myself a smart nigra, but I know a lot of things. But there's one difference, the dog can't fight back. I'm not like that, but we can get along."[12]

One white supervisor, Paul Casey, played an instrumental role in desegregating the shop floor. According to Ross, "Everywhere [Casey] went, he took those black workers into white areas. He would take these black workers to help get [cost] centers back on schedule, even into white work areas." By using black workers as troubleshooters, Ross believed, Casey helped impress on white workers the idea that competence could be color-blind.[13]

Nevertheless, tensions rose when departments integrated. Toolboxes were moved and occasionally broken into. African American employees found notes calling them "niggers." A man named Coleman found a piece of coal taped to his locker with a note that said, "You don't run this," and a sign reading "Niggers beware" appeared on a bulletin board.[14]

Another African American who joined Lockheed during this period was Gordon Kemp, an Atlanta native whose mother worked as a domestic, earning about seven dollars working "sunup to sundown, six days a week" and whose father worked as a chauffeur, making a "decent salary for the time." Kemp dropped out of school in seventh grade because he "felt that I didn't have the proper clothing" and went to work washing dishes in the Georgia Tech cafeteria at around age thirteen. A couple of years later, the manager asked Kemp to fill in baking bread, and the temporary assignment turned into a long-term position. When he turned eighteen in 1943, Kemp joined the U.S. Navy, which assigned him to galley duty. He soon found himself managing the all-black cooking crew.[15]

"In the evening," Kemp recalled, "the other men would come into my office and sit around diagramming sentences and doing math problems, and I realized, 'Here I am in charge of all these people'—many of whom were college-educated—'who are more educated than I am.'" He decided to go back to school when the war ended and focused on "read[ing] everything" he could get his hands on aboard ship. Discharged in 1946, Kemp earned a high school diploma via night school and then enrolled at Morehouse College. Upon graduation in 1951, he applied for a job at Lockheed, where "all the blacks they were hiring were college graduates." Lockheed offered him a position, but Kemp had already signed a contract to teach school in Thomaston, Georgia, so he declined.[16]

Married and with a baby on the way, Kemp applied again at Lockheed two years later and was hired as a structural assembly helper on the aft section of the B-47. Kemp, like Hudson, recalled the extensive training, which he believed to be excessive: general manager James V. Carmichael "said blacks had no knowledge of how to build an airplane," so the first African American hires "had to have one year of training to drill a hole and apply some fasteners, but this was not a requirement for whites." Over time, the amount of training for black employees was reduced first to six months and then to three months, where it stood when Kemp joined the company. Nevertheless, he claimed, "Every department I was in, I was the most trained person in that department." Kemp also observed "a funny thing": "All the projects we worked on were very complex. If they had any problems with any area, they would bring the blacks into that area." Management may have been looking for easy scapegoats: if these assemblies showed problems, they could be attributed to the workers' race.[17]

Gordon had a different take on what Kemp perceived as excessive training: though the personnel manager admitted that whites received some "preferential treatment," he claimed that Lockheed had "hired a lot of [white] former Bell workers who didn't need much training because they had experience" building airplanes, whereas blacks "got a disproportionate amount of training" because of their "lack of industrial experience." Kemp, however, recalled "three or four [white] people" who came to Lockheed "directly from the farm" but were not required to attend the intensive training. It is hardly surprising that white managers and black workers had varying definitions of equal employment opportunity.[18]

Kemp believed that one accommodation to racial resentment in particular impeded production efficiency. The main B-47 flight assembly line remained staffed by all-white crews, and when they found a problem with a subassembly (as frequently occurs in all aircraft manufacturing), workers from the subassembly department would move to the final assembly line to fix the problem. When those workers were African American, even though it "might be just one or two" in the white area, supervisors "allowed whites to vacate the area while blacks were working to fix the problem. It might take a day or two." During that period, all other work in the section would cease: the white workers "could go anywhere they wanted," killing time away from their assigned work area and in Kemp's view needlessly delaying production. Once again, however, Gordon saw the practice differently, defending it on the grounds that bringing blacks and whites together on the shop floor, especially under conditions where black workers were perceived to have made mistakes, could have led to tension and conflict. Gordon acknowledged the practice as less than ideal but viewed it as a practical accommodation to the everyday realities of life in the segregated South, an example of caution rather than a concession to white prejudice.[19]

After years of such policies, thirty-six African American workers filed complaints against Lockheed in 1961, challenging John F. Kennedy's new administration to live up to its promises about tougher action on equal employment. The vast majority of the complainants in 1961 had been hired in 1952–53 and had spent most of the remainder of the decade at the Marietta facility. The affidavits filed in conjunction with these complaints provide insight into life on the Lockheed shop floor during this era.

Expressing a common complaint, J. O. Wyatt, a Morehouse graduate who applied for work at Lockheed in 1955, noted that "after completing my training, I was assigned to . . . an all Negro manned department"—"all Negro," that is, with the exception of the white supervisor, who had a seventh-grade education and "no prior aircraft experience." Moreover, Wyatt did not receive an upgrade from assembly helper to assembly installer until he filed a grievance based on work performed: in essence, the company accepted his assessment that he had been doing the installer's job without the classification or pay increase. Further, Wyatt noted, in his six years at Lockheed, "there has never been a Negro apprentice in any trade."[20]

Another affidavit was filed by Willie T. Elkins, who had spent eight years in the U.S. Army and had attended Morehouse College before becoming one of the first African Americans hired by the Atlanta Police Department in 1948. After resigning from the department briefly to finish his Morehouse degree, Elkins rejoined the force and spent two years as a policeman and an additional seven months as a probation officer before seeking employment at Lockheed.[21]

Elkins, like Hudson, had been recruited by Robert Kennon. In early March 1953, Kennon told Elkins that Lockheed had an opening in the personnel department; however, managers at Lockheed's Atlanta employment office told Elkins that the personnel job "was not open at this time."

Instead, they invited him to apply for a temporary position in production and wait for the personnel job to become available. Elkins quit his job as an Atlanta probation officer and was hired as a production worker at Lockheed on April 3, 1953.[22]

Meeting with Kennon and John H. Patterson, president of the segregated black lodge of the International Association of Machinists (IAM), Elkins "was told, in essence, that Lockheed was a division of a California corporation and that discrimination was not company policy." Kennon and Patterson insisted that "every man had an equal right to advance according to his abilities." Further, according to Patterson, "There would be no 'Uncle Toms' on the job": supervisors were to be addressed by their last names, with no special racial etiquette. But Elkins had already noticed that the plant maintained the customs of everyday segregated life in the South— *White* and *Colored* signs on restrooms, drinking fountains, cafeterias, and even time clocks. Kennon assured Elkins that these symbols of segregation were "a result of local law and custom" and did not reflect the company's underlying attitude.[23]

After a month of training, Elkins, again like Hudson, was assigned to one of the crews working on the B-47 nose section. Hudson had not yet been promoted to supervisor, and the "department had all Negro laborers and all white supervisors." The time clocks designated for use by African American workers were located further from their work stations than those for white employees.[24]

According to Elkins's affidavit, after Kennon left Lockheed in the mid-1950s, Elkins renewed his request for a transfer to the personnel department and was interviewed for the position by Win LeSueur. LeSueur opened by asking about Elkins's background, but "the general discussion drifted to company policy." LeSueur declared that Lockheed had "no discriminatory policy" and observed that the California division had "a well-known Negro athlete on its personnel staff." LeSueur was referring to Woody Strode, who in 1946 had become one of the first two African Americans to play in the National Football League before taking a high-profile position recruiting black workers for Lockheed. LeSueur also pressed Elkins on his relationship with Kennon, leaving Elkins with the impression that the personnel official was interested primarily in fishing for information on Kennon and assuring Elkins that Lockheed did not discriminate, not in hiring Elkins. Nothing came of the interview.[25]

The personnel department hired another African American man, T. W. Hinds, who subsequently confided his disappointment in the position to Elkins. Hinds reported that he "had no job as such because he had no specific duties." According to Elkins, Hinds had no access to personnel files and had simply "been told to circulate among the Negroes and to report the general attitudes and feelings of the men in regard to any incident or occurrence that might warrant company interest." When personnel officials discovered that a black worker named Patterson had lost an eye in an off-the-job accident but had continued his employment—a violation of company policy for his particular position—Hinds was "sent down to talk Mr. Patterson into resigning." On another occasion, Hinds was directed to investigate the "attitudes of the Negroes" toward the "in-plant arrest" of a black worker. Hinds "considered this type of duty degrading," Elkins recalled, and "resented the fact that he had no opportunity to apply his administrative skills." When a frustrated Hinds finally left Lockheed and accepted a lower-paying job elsewhere, he was asked to "sign a statement to the effect that he would not divulge the nature of his position with Lockheed."[26]

John B. Mabry, another military veteran and college graduate, also joined Lockheed in April 1953. After training, Mabry became a structures assembler and received a promotion to inspector of structures in May 1957, only to be downgraded back to structures assembler five months later. Like most of the others who filed complaints in 1961, Mabry singled out segregated restroom and cafeteria facilities, time clocks, and discrimination in upgrades and promotions as the most important grievances, though he noted that the *White* and *Colored* signs had been removed from the time clocks in the past two years and replaced by a less overt system in which employee numbers—coded by race—were used to assign workers to time clocks. And like Elkins, Mabry accused the company and the union of colluding to keep black employees from advancing.[27]

Mabry's complaint alleged that the company had failed to take into account his education and experience when considering his applications for upgrades. Given that he held a college degree and had worked as a medical technician while in the navy, he believed that he should have had "an opportunity to hold a classification in areas other than 'shooting rivets.'" Mabry asserted that "the records will verify that members of the Caucasian race" with as little as sixth-, seventh-, or eighth-grade educations had held a half dozen or more job classifications and that whites who had "less than a high school education" had been promoted to production supervisor posts and given responsibility "over Negroes with college degrees."[28]

Moreover, during his service on the IAM's labor relations committee, Mabry had "observed evidence of many 'side agreements' made by [business] agents and other members of the official family of the union . . .

for the primary purpose of perpetuating segregation and racial discrimination." Mabry thus believed that the union did not truly represent its members' interests and was instead colluding with management to their detriment. According to Mabry, black workers believed that grievances regarding upgrades, transfers, and promotions were often mysteriously settled or dropped after going through the first couple of stages of the process.[29]

Elkins echoed Mabry's charges, contending that there had been "indications of collusion" and that "there exists a general feeling of dissatisfaction among the Negroes at Lockheed in regards to the union and its relations with the Negro membership."[30] The segregated IAM local had been a source of frustration for Lockheed's African American employees at least since the mid-1950s. Beginning in 1954, the IAM constitution prohibited the chartering of new segregated locals but allowed existing segregated locals to continue to operate as long as they did so on a "voluntary" basis. On October 13, 1957, the *Atlanta Daily World* published an open letter from Alfred "Tup" Holmes, an African American union representative and activist who had previously sued the city of Atlanta to force the desegregation of its golf courses. Holmes explained that fifteen months earlier, seven black Lockheed employees had filed a complaint with the PCGC alleging discrimination at the Marietta plant. The committee sent a team to investigate. "Sensing a whitewash," Holmes wrote, he and his colleagues had asked the NAACP to monitor the investigation to "insure a complete and accurate appraisal of conditions at Lockheed." After NAACP labor secretary Herbert Hill conferred with investigators and conducted his own inquiry, he met with black union members, probably in November 1956, and recommended that "to obtain complete equality," the segregated local should disband and its members should join the existing all-white Lockheed IAM lodges. The members present voted unanimously to accept the recommendation. The vote must have been considered unofficial or advisory, however, and according to Holmes, several subsequent "efforts to secure an official vote have been unsuccessful because a few persons have apparently taken a stand 'that we will not have representation if we merge, because our people will not go to union meetings.'" In Holmes's view, "the real reason" for opposition to the merger was that it would "cause some members of the [black] local to lose positions, [along] with the doubtful prestige that goes with such jobs."[31]

Although Holmes believed that the decision to create a separate local had been "well meaning ... in the beginning," the time for union integration had long since arrived. Only if all workers were truly united could the union effectively represent their interests. "The reactionary forces of the State of Georgia could ask for no better support of segregation than to have a vote from us to continue" to operate segregated locals.[32]

On the same day that Holmes's letter appeared, the members of the African American local again voted to disband. Nevertheless, the union's District 33 executive committee, which included the presidents of the four white lodges and the black lodge, recommended against the merger. In addition, the executive committee recommended that the district fight "any force[d] merger" by appealing first to the union's International Council and if need be to the National Convention, which would not meet again until 1960. In addition, delegates from one of the white lodges called for the attorney general of Georgia to be notified of the proposed "forced merger" and asked to rule on its legality vis-à-vis the state's Jim Crow laws. Finally, according to Elkins, G. H. Andrews, the president of the black local, had met with district and company officials and "challenged the validity of the meeting" at which the black employees had voted in favor of the merger, causing "the majority of the membership to become discouraged. There was a growing feeling that the president of the local was working to perpetuate himself in office and was indifferent to the attitudes of the membership." Attendance at meetings of the black local declined precipitously, making it impossible to achieve a quorum to take any further action, and the merger idea went no further. When Elkins, Mabry, and their compatriots filed their complaints in 1961, Lockheed's IAM locals remained segregated.[33]

As labor economist Herbert Northrup demonstrates, these black workers' experiences with IAM at Lockheed-Georgia in the 1950s were typical. As the IAM expanded into the aircraft industry in the 1930s, the union maintained its long-standing racially discriminatory policies, including limiting membership to "competent white" candidates, a provision that remained in place until the late 1940s. "IAM union policies" sometimes "proved a bar to Negro employment in the industry during World War II, but in most cases the IAM did not have a compulsory union membership contract and therefore could not adversely affect Negro employment," as was the case under Georgia's right-to-work legislation. But as also was the case in Georgia, union locals could hamper desegregation efforts without fear of national union intervention: as Northrup wrote in 1969, "The IAM attitude on race has been basically a passive one. Locals of the IAM are very independent, with the international exercising only limited interference. As a result, there is little or no affirmative action [by the union] in support of Negro employment and no national union interference when local unions either drag their feet or oppose affirmative action programs."³⁴ In this atmosphere, it was unsurprising that African American workers developed an ambiguous relationship with their union.

Black workers' discontent with both the union and the company percolated just beneath the surface, erupting in a little-known but nevertheless significant incident related to the C-130 contract. Probably in early 1955, Lockheed officials met privately with Donald Lee Hollowell, an African American who was Georgia's preeminent civil rights attorney and later the first director of the Atlanta office of the Equal Employment Opportunity Commission, in an effort to address black workers' grievances. Preliminary discussions to set up the meeting appear to have involved Lorimer Milton and Clayton Yates, owners of a drugstore at the corner of Auburn Avenue and Butler Street, in the heart of Atlanta's Sweet Auburn district, home to an array of black-owned enterprises. Milton and Yates were also activists involved with both the Atlanta Urban League and the local NAACP. Although many black Lockheed workers were reluctant to attend the meeting, fearing retaliation and loss of their jobs, Elkins, Mabry, and a few others joined Ross, who described himself as "either too young or too foolish" to restrain himself from going. On the way to Hollowell's southwest Atlanta office for the meeting, the group decided to call itself the Observatory Council on Race Relations at Lockheed, and the men brought with them a manifesto asking for black supervisors, nurses, and more African American workers overall. On the Lockheed side, attendees included Carmichael and, according to Hugh Gordon, who heard about the meeting from Hollowell, W. A. "Dick" Pulver, a future president of Lockheed-Georgia, and E. G. Mattison from industrial relations. Pulver did not move permanently to the Marietta plant until 1956 but was a key project engineer and coordinator of the C-130 project who succeeded Dan Haughton as general manager of the Georgia plant. The meeting took place outside the boundaries of any of the IAM locals, reflecting black workers' difficulties with the union.³⁵

The meeting apparently produced some tangible results: Mattison promised that company officials would take a look at the "bad attitudes" among white managers and employees that Ross and the others had observed. In addition, "there were some black supervisors appointed after that meeting." However, Hollowell also told the African Americans in attendance that they were not to discuss anything that had happened at the meeting.³⁶

The PCGC and the threat of outside pressure appear to have played no role in the meeting, though it seems to have been connected, directly or indirectly, to the C-130 contract. The company may have been seeking to avoid bad publicity resulting from an open airing of black grievances or to avoid losing productivity as a consequence of poor labor relations. Whatever their motivations, the participation of company board member Carmichael and other officials indicates that management took the matter seriously.

As Lockheed began scaling back work on the B-47 in late 1955 and 1956, supervisors and workers scrambled to secure new positions on the C-130 line lest they be bumped back down to hourly production work or laid off. White supervisors in the B-47 assembly area began trying to flatter and cajole department managers into recommending them for transfers, taking advantage of social opportunities outside of work to which Hudson and the other three black supervisors did not have access: Hudson recalled that the white supervisors would supply "the clay pigeons when the boss was taken on trap shoots. The boss did all the shooting. There were the fishing trips and the boss did not pay anything. The guys would tell me what great times they had with the boss on weekends. I never participated because I was never invited. I would not have gone because he had never invited me to dinner either."[37]

Social segregation made it more difficult for African Americans to develop social capital within the workplace, where advancement has never been determined purely by merit, however defined; personal relationships and simple good fortune always matter. Blacks not only lacked external networks to help in locating and navigating the job training and application process but also were generally excluded from the internal networks that offered "pull" within the firm.[38]

In 1955, Haughton assigned Harold Mintz to the C-130 line to get it ready to go. Mintz would get "to pick the people that I wanted out of that department to bring over there.... I knew who was good." On the C-130, however, subassemblies would not be made in different areas and then moved to a final assembly line, meaning that even if crews remained segregated, workers of different races would be working near one another. To maintain "the southern tradition," according to Mintz "a section of [the C-130] department ... was blocked off. This was planned by upper management where the blacks would work. They put a row of big parts racks in between." Black and white workers would be stationed side by side but with their views of one another blocked by containers. Desegregation had taken another baby step forward, and another one followed when the racks gradually receded to the edges of the department, ultimately removing the barriers between black and white crews. When Mintz told Haughton, "I'm working my whites and blacks together ... and I haven't had one complaint," the general manager just "scratched his head, and... said, 'My Lord.'"³⁹

Nevertheless, in March 1957, the NAACP's Hill reported on the results of an investigation into the racial division of labor at Lockheed and painted a relatively bleak picture of African American employment opportunities at the Marietta plant. The facility employed roughly 17,350 workers, about 1,350 (7.8 percent) of them African Americans. Given the plant's proximity to the city of Atlanta, where blacks accounted for nearly half the total population, employment fell far short of any sort of representation of the community. Moreover, more than a thousand of Lockheed's African American workers were employed in just two departments as "structural assembly helpers," a job category near the entry-level rank for production workers. A significant but smaller number had worked on the aft section of the B-47 assembly, which had recently been closed down. Some of those workers had been transferred to the C-130 line, but others had lost their jobs. Hill contended that of the 450 job classifications in the plant, African Americans could be found in no more than 20, and some of them were janitorial and other unskilled positions. According to the report, the concentration of black production workers in the two "colored departments," as they were "universally referred to throughout the plant," drastically limited the advancement of African Americans, and "whatever job diversification there is among Negro employees is within segregated Negro departments." Hill also reported that "Negroes are not employed in any clerical department or in the Personnel department," meaning that the company had apparently abandoned its pledge to the Urban League to employ African Americans in personnel. Though a very small number of blacks occupied a few "white collar jobs," Hill found that a "pattern of racial segregation and job limitation... exists at the Lockheed plant."⁴⁰

Hill also found, just as Elkins and Mabry later alleged, that blacks were being excluded from the apprenticeship program, which was jointly administered by the company and the IAM: though numerous African Americans had applied, the program had not admitted "a single Negro" in five years. Further, when black workers accumulated enough seniority to bid for jobs in higher classifications, "the company often reclassifies those jobs, or moves the job operation completely out of the Negro work group," placing it effectively beyond their reach. Hill noted that the union locals at the plant were effectively segregated, though IAM claimed that the existence of an all-black local was "accidental." In addition, the NAACP report criticized the company's practice of gathering racial employment data via a numerical classification system. And it indicated that as of March 1957, white and black workers remained separated on the shop floor, so Mintz's removal of the barriers must have occurred at some later point.[41]

For whatever reason, Hudson initially was not among those whom Mintz handpicked to move to the C-130 line, although, according to Hudson, Mintz "told me he had tried everywhere to find me a position in the new area." In Hudson's view, "This was the same bull that he gave most of the other supervisors." Instead, Hudson "found my own position" supervising a segregated crew on the C-130 line "based on my record and actually needed help from no one."[42]

Hudson assumed supervision of a night-shift crew working on the side panel assembly. His day-shift counterpart was a white man, Atlanta native Jack "Roc" Rochester, whom Hudson recalled as "a regular fellow" who "had had to hustle practically all of his life in growing up to make ends meet." Rochester and Hudson clashed over sloppy housekeeping and mistakes by the day shift that were passed along to the night shift, though Hudson attributed no racial overtones to the conflicts. They were ultimately resolved when production manager Lee Poore followed Hudson's suggestion and established a policy that all of the members of the day-shift crew had to vacate the work area before anyone from the night shift could enter.[43]

After close to a year on the night shift, Hudson took over the C-130's cargo ramp assembly during the day shift. Hudson continued to take advantage of training opportunities, taking "classes in time study, the foundations of human behavior as related to the industrial complex, tooling methods, and improving work attitudes." He also "learned quite a bit about the different chemical and physical reactions one might experience from the working with metal and other components in the manufacture of aircraft."[44]

Hudson's cargo ramp crew included Ted Ramsey, who had a master's degree and had completed work toward a doctorate in clinical psychology. Hudson believed it was a terrible waste of Ramsey's potential for Lockheed to have him "drilling holes and shooting rivets" when he might have been "one of the best human factor scientists at the plant." In Hudson's view, "a lot of talent was lost to both Negroes and poor whites because they were keeping Negroes in their place by sitting on them," and "a lot of things in general could have been accomplished for the people and the plant if middle management wasn't so continually telling upper management that everything was going fine."[45]

Although his situation at Lockheed was far from perfect, Hudson became a symbol of black economic progress. In October 1957, the Pet Milk Company featured Harry and Edith Hudson and their children in a quarter-page advertisement in the *Washington Afro-American*. The ad was part of Pet Milk's groundbreaking decade-long "happy family" campaign, which "used black spokespeople and unique ad copy to reach" the African American market. As early as the late 1920s, market researchers had identified the small but growing black urban middle class as a prime target, and Pepsi had pioneered the use of black salesmen and ad campaigns focused on the African American market. Mainstream advertising agencies, however, feared that such campaigns might lead to labeling as a "Negro product," thus hurting sales to the larger white market. Pet Milk had developed a remarkably successful campaign focused on the Fultzes, the first recorded set of African American quadruplets, in the late 1940s, and. African American advertising pioneer Leonard Evans helped convince the company to go further. Evans traveled around the country identifying successful middle-class black families to counter the stereotype of African Americans as poor and outside the mainstream. Pet Milk's campaign reflected the growing significance of the African American market, though most companies continued to shy away from marketing that explicitly targeted black audiences.[46]

"Pretty Edith Hudson," the ad copy began, "is the center of an active, happy family—her successful husband, a graduate of Morehouse College, and four husky boys." Edith Hudson's "favorite part of the day" was when her family came "hurrying home," with Harry Hudson from his "job as an assembly supervisor at Lockheed Aircraft Corporation." Edith loved "cooking for them and she always uses PET Evaporated Milk to make her meals extra rich, extra nourishing, and extra delicious." The Hudsons also enjoyed entertaining in their "large backyard," with Harry playing a steel guitar to accompany group singing at parties. Among the images featured in the ad were the Hudson family seated at the dinner table and Harry roughhousing with his boys on the living room floor—in every respect a typical middle-class American family. Pet Milk ran more than a hundred such ads in African American newspapers during the 1950s, never specifically mentioning race and positioning African Americans as members of the middle class, with the same goals as white America. The reality, of course, was much more nuanced, as blacks both made gains and chafed against persistent segregation and discrimination.[47]

In 1959, Hudson recorded another first, perhaps the most significant of his career and the most important for Lockheed in the 1950s. Production manager H. Lee Poore announced to Hudson that they were going to attempt an experiment: Poore "did not think that a Negro could supervise a mixed crew in the south without friction," but Lockheed was going to try.

Hudson was suspicious of the offer and thought he was being set up to fail. But he accepted the challenge.[48]

As Hudson assembled the integrated crew he would supervise, he specifically asked for older workers, those who were "dissatisfied with their present area," and any who "might seem to be misfits." He believed that any worker who "had a job where he felt needed and had full responsibility ... and also had respect ... would be happy not only in his work but at home." Hudson seemed to be putting into practice the human relations management style that Lockheed had long favored. "A few whites told me, 'I ain't never worked for a colored fellow before,'" Hudson recalled, but "my answer was standard—'me neither, both of us work for Lockheed.'"[49]

Hudson's new integrated crew received quite a few "rough looks and derogatory remarks" from whites in adjoining work areas, and he suspected that some asked for transfers to avoid having to observe this violation of the traditional social order. Nevertheless, Hudson did not record any overt racial difficulties, and he described his integrated crew as "building top quality aircraft on schedule and at a reasonable cost."[50]

In early 1961, with "things ... running well," Hudson asked for a significant raise. Hudson made his case to Poore, who said that "he thought that was a reasonable request and would give it positive consideration." Encouraged by that response, Hudson decided to go further, suggesting that the department could use an assistant manager and that he would be a qualified candidate for the position because of all the "training on my own time and company time" he had completed. Hudson was taken aback by Poore's reply:

> That sapsucker dropped an atom bomb on me. He told me in no uncertain terms that as long as he was production manager that no Negro (pronounced Nigra) would ever be a foreman in his production crews. Being stupid and not giving a damn, I demanded [to know] why! He said he could not see a Negro being boss over 600 people including at least 400 white people. There was no point in me giving in to the urgent desire to kick his butt as I needed the job. I reminded him that he was the person that requested me to take the first integrated crew in 1959. After that had been successful he must have ... also [been one] that lost his bet that it could not be done.

Hudson received a larger raise than he had requested, and a few other supervisors "got [a] little raise," but the cordial working relationship between Poore and Hudson "kind of cooled after that and actually was never regained."[51]

Lockheed-Georgia's contracts and total employment had changed substantially over the 1950s. When Robert Kennon was hired to recruit African American employees in 1952, Lockheed was in the midst of an effort to boost its workforce. But by the end of the 1950s, the market for Lockheed-Georgia's prime product, the C-130, had, in business parlance, matured. The aircraft would continue in production in one form or another for decades and continue to provide jobs, but the very high production numbers of the mid-1950s fell as the market became saturated. The long life of aircraft often created boom-and-bust cycles for aircraft workers, and by 1960, another bust was on the horizon: unless additional C-130 orders came in, layoffs loomed. Aircraft deliveries from the Marietta plant had fallen from 149 in 1957 to just 55 in 1960. Employment, which had grown from 10,695 in early 1952 to about 17,000 by May 1955, fell to 10,484 in March 1961, when the African American employees filed their complaints. In 1952, Lockheed had 457 black employees (mostly in custodial and other unskilled jobs); in March 1961, that number was 474.[52]

In February 1961, shortly after President Kennedy's inauguration, the Defense Department awarded Lockheed a contract for an additional sixteen C-130Bs. Lockheed vice president and Georgia division general manager Dick Pulver said the new orders "will keep our C-130B line intact, and will halt the layoff of aircraft workers on that line." He also indicated that some workers would probably be added but declined to speculate about how many.[53] Still, the new order would keep the production line running for less than another two years. Many in the Atlanta area feared that employment at the plant would shrink even further or that the plant would close entirely, short-circuiting regional growth plans. Lockheed-Georgia's record of progress in African American employment had been largely erased by the time Kennedy assumed office in January 1961. Reviewing his company's equal employment opportunity progress in 1961, Mattison insisted that Lockheed-Georgia management had realized early on that "progress to be permanent had to be gradual."[54] But the experience of the 1950s indicated that the difficulty of maintaining even modest gains in the face of fluctuating labor demand matched or exceeded the challenge of short-term equal employment progress.

CHAPTER 4

"A Problem That Was Already Here"

THE EARLY PLANS FOR PROGRESS ERA, 1961–1964

In early 1961, Lockheed-Georgia and its workers, white and black, faced an uncertain future. So, for that matter, did the metropolitan Atlanta area and the entire state. Lockheed's future was threatened first by maturing demand for its bread-and-butter product, the C-130 as well as by the discontent of African American workers, which meshed with the new Kennedy administration's civil rights initiatives to threaten a new contract that promised the firm long-term salvation, while the larger crisis involved school desegregation. By early summer, however, both storms had passed. Atlanta had added to its reputation both as the city "too busy to hate" and as an engine of economic growth. Lockheed agreed to far-reaching internal changes to meet new government expectations in the arena of equal employment, and company personnel took leading roles in evangelizing the gospel of affirmative action to the private sector.

In 1959, a federal judge had ordered Atlanta's schools to desegregate. But the state legislature, implementing policies that reflected the segregationists' "massive resistance" strategy, had passed measures earlier in the decade that effectively required the state to cut off funding for any school system that desegregated. An order to integrate a small rural district might not have triggered a crisis, but Atlanta had cultivated a reputation for having not only decent race relations but also—and not coincidentally—a climate friendly toward economic development: all of that work might well go down in flames if the public schools were closed.

Georgia governor Ernest Vandiver, though a staunch segregationist, had to choose between following through with the closure of Atlanta's schools (which might cause severe economic harm) or accepting some measure of desegregation (which would be politically unpopular). Vandiver and associates devised a scheme to create a commission, headed by prominent businessman and attorney John Sibley, to conduct hearings around the state and make a recommendation: that is, they tried to deflect at least some of the negative backlash by an apparent appeal to democracy.[1]

James Peters, a close associate of Herman Talmadge who chaired the state Board of Education, advised Vandiver to find a compromise solution rather than follow through with closing the schools, even though the Talmadge machine had made that threat part of its stock-in-trade. Peters warned that public sentiment, especially in the state's urban and suburban areas, was turning against a die-hard defense of segregation and maintained that "by compromising, the 'friends of segregation' could dominate the coming of desegregation, thereby ensuring that social change would be as limited and difficult as possible."[2]

Though also an ardent segregationist, Sibley, too, believed that any attempt at further massive resistance would be futile and would harm the state's business interests. Though a majority of witnesses before the commission favored a hard line on segregation, many residents of the northern third of the state—including Fulton County (Atlanta) and Cobb County (Marietta)—supported a "local option" alternative that would permit school districts to adopt limited desegregation. The Sibley Commission recommended this approach, though the legislature remained reluctant to go along until the courts issued a desegregation order for the University of Georgia in January 1961. With the state's flagship university—the alma mater of perhaps half the legislature—under threat, Vandiver pushed through the commission's recommendations on January 31, and Atlanta's schools remained open with limited desegregation. While this action averted a crisis, "it also provided tactics that local school boards could use to slow down the desegregation process."[3]

Perhaps not coincidentally, just a week after the legislature backed away from the precipice of school closures, the Department of Defense issued a $32 million contract for sixteen new C-130 planes. And in mid-March, the U.S. government offered Lockheed-Georgia an even larger prize: a $1 billion contract to produce a new transport plane with greater capacity, range, and speed than the C-130. Lockheed outbid Boeing, Douglas, and Convair to produce the new plane, which became known as the C-141 Starlifter. Lockheed pledged to subcontract 62 percent of the new aircraft and "place the subcontracts in economically distressed areas of the South and East." In other words, Lockheed promised to help the government manage the contract as an economic development program. The contract, which was slated to last between ten and fifteen years, would add five thousand jobs at Lockheed's main Georgia plant. In a front-page article announcing the contract, the *Atlanta Constitution* characterized it as "one of the biggest pieces of economic news in Georgia for a long time, with far reaching effects."[4]

"The recession-etched frown on Georgia's economic face gave way to a broad smile Monday night," wrote the *Constitution*'s Marion Gaines, summarizing the reaction of Georgia's business and political elite to the news. Ivan Allen Jr. lauded the anticipated spillover effects of related business activity," while the president of the state Chamber of Commerce called it "a terrific breakthrough for Georgia's economy." Commissioner Herbert McCollum called it "one of the happiest days we've had in Cobb County in a long time," adding that he believed that the contract would spark a resurgence of construction. Senator Herman Talmadge observed that the deal would "make possible the retention of Lockheed as Georgia's single largest manufacturing employer." General manager Dick Pulver echoed that view, saying, "This contract will mean much over the next 10 years to the stability of Lockheed's Georgia division and the economy of the entire area." The *Southern Star* observed that "the 'long face' disappeared from the Georgia Division" with the contract announcement, which "pick[ed] up morale among employees, the people of Cobb County, and the entire Atlanta area." The announcement "jammed" the plant's phone lines as people called to ask, "When will you start recalling workers? When will you start hiring?"[5]

The Atlanta area received more economic good news the same week when Delta Airlines added nonstop routes from Atlanta to both Los Angeles and San Francisco and the Southern Cement Company, headquartered in Birmingham, Alabama, announced plans for a new multimillion-dollar cement plant near Atlanta in anticipation of new construction boom. The president of the state Chamber of Commerce referred to the trio of announcements as "the beginning of a new era of expansion for the state." These "good tidings" should "serve as documentation . . . that the South is the last economic frontier in the country."[6]

Lockheed board member and former gubernatorial candidate James Carmichael linked the contract award to the defusing of the school crisis. "Had it not been for the legislature and the Governor clarifying the school situation," he said during a press conference on Georgia exports, "I don't think Lockheed would have gotten the contract." An editorial in the *Atlanta Daily World* expressed a similar view at about the same time. State leaders' commitment to maintaining basic public services such as education and avoiding protracted political conflict with Washington and the courts made Georgia a more attractive place to do business.[7]

A March 24 letter to the editor of the *Atlanta Constitution* chided Carmichael and others for seeming to claim credit for Lockheed's success. A reader wrote sarcastically that "it is heartening to those at Lockheed who worked on the newly proposed cargo transport that the contract was won not by the superiority of their design, but by the influence of our politicians, unemployment, and the clarification of the school situation." An editor's note clarified, "Carmichael's opinion was not that Lockheed got the contract because of these influences—only that it would not have gotten the contract without them." But influential senators such as Talmadge and Richard Russell and powerful House committee chairs such as Representative Carl Vinson, who helmed the Armed Services Committee, certainly did not damage Lockheed's chances. The potential to use the contract as a kind of economic stimulus, particularly with the company appearing eager to play along, also made the deal attractive. And Georgia's avoidance of a messy and prolonged school desegregation crisis may have tipped the balance.[8]

Longtime Atlanta mayor William B. Hartsfield, who as much as any individual embodied Atlanta's growth strategy, expressed much the same view. In a speech to an African American audience at the Butler Street YMCA, Hartsfield reflected that an agreement among merchants, student activists, and community leaders that had resolved a wave of sit-ins and boycotts of downtown businesses had enabled the city to accomplish "a good deal of things without explosions." Maintaining not just social and political stability but also "a climate of decency and fairness" marked by gradual change was the key to the city's success and that of the surrounding region. The Lockheed contract and other announcements offered evidence that the strategy was working, though Hartsfield cautioned that the battle between "the leadership of the progressive and retrogressive forces of the area" had not yet been settled conclusively and that progress remained contingent.[9]

Indeed, much remained undone. The African American students who had staged the sit-ins and boycotts were not satisfied with the agreement to end the protests, which had been negotiated by black lawyers and community elders. And Atlanta continued to lag behind other southern cities in desegregating public accommodations. Behind the facade of racial harmony, Atlanta's business leaders doggedly resisted full integration of public spaces and private restaurants and other commercial establishments.[10]

Nevertheless, Marietta, metropolitan Atlanta, and Georgia generally seemed poised for an era of economic growth supported and subsidized by what Noam Chomsky has called the "dynamic state sector," focused on aircraft, electronics, computers, transportation, and weapons technology. Observers who might have opposed massive spending on a variety of alternative public services and projects loudly cheered federal appropriations for programs in these areas. Indeed, many business and community leaders considered such expenditures "an essential part of our economy," as a 1958 Rockefeller Brothers Fund report put it. Within the broad liberal consensus sketched by analysts from Godfrey Hodgson to Jennifer Delton, what the Rockefeller report called "public expenditures in support of growth" were crucial. While there was room for debate within the consensus about just what kinds of public expenditures supported growth and which might be wasteful, defense-related spending generated little disagreement during the Cold War era.[11]

At this point, Lockheed-Georgia's path to long-term stability encountered a potential roadblock. During the 1960 presidential campaign, John F. Kennedy had promised action on equal employment, and on March 6, 1961, just a week before the Lockheed contract announcement, he issued Executive Order 10925. The order replaced the President's Committee on Government Contracts with the President's Committee on Equal Employment Opportunity (PCEEO). Much longer than previous orders on equal employment, Executive Order 10925 required contractors "to take affirmative action to ensure that applicants are employed, and that employees are treated during employment, without regard to their race, creed, color, or national origin." This requirement extended to "employment, upgrading, demotion or transfer; recruitment or recruitment advertising; layoff or termination; rates of pay or other forms of compensation; and selection for training, including apprenticeship." Moreover, the order contained a "but not limited to" clause that opened the door to unspecified aspects of the employer-employee relationship and recognized the role of organized labor in racial discrimination, instructing the PCEEO to "use its best efforts," directly and through contractors and contracting agencies, to secure union compliance with the order. Finally, the order took the unprecedented step of outlining penalties, up to and including cancellation of contracts, for failure to comply.[12]

In contrast to his predecessors, Kennedy issued the equal opportunity employment order with great fanfare, accompanied by a press conference, touting the "vastly strengthened machinery" that would enable "vigorous enforcement" and thus demonstrating a "concerted effort to place the full prestige of the presidency behind the moral imperative of nondiscrimination." As much as any substantive difference in language, the Kennedy administration's projection of activism and intent marked a break with the past. The PCEEO, to be chaired by Vice President Lyndon Baines Johnson, scheduled its first meeting for April 11, amid rising expectations among African Americans and civil rights organizations.[13]

Many African American workers at Lockheed-Georgia and in the surrounding area, however, believed that, absent dramatic changes in management policies and behavior, black gains would be as limited as they had been in the previous decade—a few more jobs but not much else. On March 20, a group of black workers unsuccessfully sought to be served in one of Lockheed's white-designated cafeterias, provoking "considerable unrest" among black workers. On March 27, 1961, Lockheed-Georgia's director of industrial relations, E. G. Mattison, reprised his 1955 meeting with African American employees at the office of civil rights attorney Donald Lee Hollowell, with Carmichael again called in to help mediate as a consequence of company officials' fears that "any incident of sufficient magnitude could cause the Government to switch the contract to ... one of our competitors." African American employees attending the meeting presented Mattison and Carmichael with a list of demands that reiterated their complaints from six years earlier—too few black hires, lack of opportunity for advancement, and segregated facilities, which had assumed an increased importance. Mattison assured the workers that the "company would continue to give consideration to the problems of the Negroes."[14]

The following day, current and former black Lockheed employees formed the Observatory Council on Discrimination, again echoing the Observatory Committee on Race Relations from 1955. Members of the original group joined with new and former black Lockheed employees to launch "an all-out campaign to eliminate ... unfair, discriminatory, and segregated practices" at the Marietta location. According to the *Atlanta Daily World*, the Observatory Council immediately "set up active contact and communications with certain federal agencies whose interest lies in discrimination at government contracted companies" and had already initiated a complaint with the PCEEO. The group was determined that "Negroes must have a fair share of the" job opportunities created by the new contract. In addition, the group aimed to root out segregationist practices in all areas of the plant, including cafeterias, restrooms, and other facilities, and claimed "100 percent backing of its program by the entire Negro force at Lockheed." And, the Observatory Council warned, "alleged unfair or discriminatory practices at the plant could hamper final decision of the contract."[15]

At the same time, NAACP president Roy Wilkins wrote to Johnson and the PCEEO to protest continued segregation and discrimination at Lockheed-

Georgia, suggesting a "reexamination and possible cancellation" of the contract. The letter included a litany of by-now familiar charges drawn from the complaints, among them discriminatory hiring and promotion practices, segregated time clocks and race coding of time cards, and segregated facilities. The Marietta facility was "operated on a rigidly racially segregated basis . . . in direct contravention to the letter and spirit of the President's executive Order." The Reverend Samuel Williams, president of the Atlanta branch of the NAACP, declared that "we have been concerned about Lockheed for a long time" and suggested that it was "time for Lockheed to get in step with the rest of the nation." In the days following Wilkins's letter, thirty-six African American Lockheed employees signed affidavits making specific allegations of discrimination to buttress the NAACP's case.[16]

Lockheed officials defended the Georgia division's record over the previous decade and shifted blame toward prevailing social mores. According to a Georgia company official who was not named in either the *Atlanta Constitution* or the *Atlanta Daily World*,

> The problem that is being faced today is not one that we brought to Georgia. It was a problem that was already here. Lockheed has very conscientiously and vigorously done everything humanly possible to comply in all regulations in the operation of this facility. We are quite proud of our record in dealing with our employees over the past 10 years. . . . We recognize that there is more progress yet to be made, but . . . we believe we have made more progress than any individual employer in the South in providing for all its employees. We think that any objective look at the record will show how well we have done.[17]

By alluding to the "problem that was already here," Lockheed came close to stating publicly that although it had found local customs distasteful, it had been forced to engage in a delicate balancing act, following custom as far as possible while trying to provide opportunity for all its employees, implicitly including black workers. However complex the Lockheed problem was, this statement expressed the views of many in management, including personnel executives Gene Mattison, Howard Lockwood, and Hugh Gordon, who played leading roles in shaping Lockheed's response to the 1961 complaints and who evangelized for affirmative action and private-sector equal employment policies throughout the 1960s.

The PCEEO took up the Lockheed controversy at its initial meeting on April 11. Vice President Johnson subsequently declared that the federal government would take whatever action was needed to bring Lockheed into compliance with Executive Order 10925, prompting the company to release a statement declaring simply, "We are willing as always to work with the President's Committee."[18]

PCEEO executive director John G. Feild did not associate the threat to Lockheed's contract with the NAACP complaints. In 1967, Feild recalled that after reading a routine U.S. Air Force compliance report on the Marietta plant, he decided, "I'm not going to accept this report. The Lockheed Company in Marietta, Georgia, is not in compliance." Regardless of the trigger for the PCEEO's involvement, Feild became the agency's principal negotiator with Lockheed on the matter.[19]

As the negotiations got under way, Mattison responded to the complaints filed by black workers. Born in Pasadena, California, Mattison had earned a political science degree from UCLA before becoming a Lockheed career man. He began work in the industrial relations department of the home office in Burbank in 1944 and moved up to labor relations manager at Lockheed Aircraft Service, one of the firm's numerous subsidiaries, in 1951. Three years later, he moved to Lockheed's Georgia division as industrial labor relations manager and was groomed to succeed Jim Lydon as industrial relations director for the Marietta site. In 1956, Lydon was transferred to Burbank to serve as the company's vice president for industrial relations and Mattison took over in Georgia.[20]

Mattison signed affidavits responding to each complaint individually as well as a separate statement on the Georgia division's general nondiscrimination policies and procedures in which he insisted that for reasons of "policy, cost, convenience, and efficiency," the company "would have preferred to start with a completely integrated work force" when it reopened Air Force Plant 6 in 1951. Management "recognized, however, that this preference had to be tempered" for several reasons. First, Mattison deployed a version of the educational feedback loop. At the time of the factory's reopening, the top priority had been getting it back into operation and refurbishing B-29s as soon as possible. During that initial year, "there was no time for extensive training," so Lockheed tapped into the area's "reserve of skilled aircraft mechanics" left over from the Bell Aircraft operation. Consequently, "the vast majority of these workers were white since very few Negroes in this locality had been trained in aircraft skills during World War II."[21]

Moreover, according to Mattison, "we were informed that those Negroes employed by [Bell] on production work were assigned to a separate facility in Marietta, several miles from the main plant at which its white employees worked." Only blacks employed in what were considered traditional jobs were visible to white workers. The small amount of desegregation of work attempted by Bell was essentially invisible; the work*place* remained totally segregated. "This background," according to Mattison, "could not be ignored."²²

Bell's extreme reticence regarding any hint of desegregation in the workplace highlighted a broader concern. Lockheed had to consider "community laws, attitudes, and customs." "To have attempted complete integration of the work force at that time," Mattison argued, "could have resulted in serious friction between the races and probable failure of the re-activation effort"—"a risk which the Company felt, under the circumstances, it could not take." Mattison did not offer any details on precisely what difficulties the company envisioned, but "for the company to disregard completely local attitudes and customs would have precluded community acceptance and seriously impaired the war effort."²³

Lockheed management had settled on a long-range "plan for progress" toward the eventual integration of the Marietta plant. "If an integrated work force with an integrated facility was to become a reality," he wrote, "it was judged that progress to be permanent had to be gradual, and if the plan were to succeed, we could not move too far ahead of prevailing community attitudes and community judgments." Mattison explained that the segregated work areas for the B-47 had enabled the promotion of six African Americans to supervisory positions by October 1955. According to this line of reasoning, segregation in the form of all-black work crews and departments had opened a path for upward mobility without threatening that local custom. By 1957, Mattison claimed, "substantial progress had been made in eliminating segregated departments," and as of May 1961, "segregated departments at Lockheed-Georgia no longer exist." Further, the company had promoted "Negroes to professional positions within its Engineering branch."²⁴

According to Mattison's affidavit, at Lockheed's production peak in the 1950s, total employment had briefly exceeded 19,000, including 1,287 African Americans in 52 of the plant's 290 occupations. By the end of the decade, when production slumped and layoffs occurred, the company employed about 450 black workers in 39 classifications. For comparison purposes, Mattison referred to a "Record of Progress" for 1953–58 compiled by the Eisenhower-era President's Committee on Government Contracts. This report showed that as of 1958, McDonnell Aircraft's St. Louis plant had employed 379 blacks in 25 job categories, while Chance-Vaught, located in Dallas, had a total workforce of 18,000, with 134 black employees, among them 1 supervisor and 2 skilled and 25 semiskilled workers.

Boeing's Wichita, Kansas, plant had 749 blacks in a workforce of more than 30,000. Those numbers compared favorably with Lockheed's.[25]

The complainants had also alleged discrimination in Lockheed's training programs, which included classroom and on-the-job training in basic aircraft manufacturing—the type of training that had been provided to African American workers in 1952–53 and for which trainees were paid. In addition, advanced courses were available to enhance existing skills or prepare workers for higher-skilled and/or management positions; such courses generally took place outside of working hours but sometimes were offered on company time. In addition, Lockheed had a joint agreement with the Cobb County Board of Education to provide vocational training and made courses available for personal enrichment, strictly on employees' own time. J. B. Mabry and other complainants had charged that the company ran segregated courses, offered more training opportunities for advancement to whites, and colluded with the union to restrict the apprenticeship program. Moreover, Harry Hudson, Ernest Ross, Reginald Kemp, and others believed that black workers, even those with college degrees, were required to undergo needlessly extensive basic training that was not required of white workers who lacked even high school diplomas. To African American workers, the issue of basic skills training seemed to represent a way for management to act on old prejudices about appropriate jobs for blacks without explicitly acknowledging them.

Mattison briefly responded to these allegations but deferred to training department manager Robert H. Hudson for a more detailed response. A Georgia native, Hudson had graduated from Georgia Tech with a degree in chemical engineering just in time for World War II, when he served on the staff of General Elwood Quesada. Hudson remained in the military until 1953, when he retired as a lieutenant colonel and became training department manager at Lockheed-Georgia.[26]

According to Hudson's affidavit, Lockheed had provided 2.25 million man-hours of classroom training on company time since the Marietta plant opened in 1951. Although Lockheed did not keep records on the "racial composition of training classes," a "special report" compiled in 1958 had found that African American workers received about 6.7 percent of the total classroom training hours to that point while comprising 6.1 percent of the plant's workforce. However, Hudson confirmed that "to ensure that newly hired unskilled Negro employees possessed basic job skills, the majority of Negro employees hired in 1953 were given a 120 hour basic shop skills course," while "the majority of newly hired white unskilled workers were given an 80 hour course." He presented this information in such a way that it implied a racial standard to which some exceptions were made, with a few blacks getting less than 120 hours basic training and some whites getting more than 80 hours. Hudson's statement also implied that after 1953, the initial extra basic training for black unskilled workers ceased, aligning with the impressions of African American employees.[27]

Hudson distinguished between training courses offered by the company and those sponsored by the Cobb Board of Education. While both programs offered classes in which employees had demonstrated an interest or that had been specifically requested, the Board of Education generally was responsible for "trade and vocational" courses that enhanced skills to help hourly workers qualify for upgrades and transfers within the production ranks. The company, in contrast, generally took responsibility for job-related courses in "scientific, engineering, and management development subjects" with the goal of helping workers cross the threshold into lower-level management and other salaried positions and move up the salaried ranks. The company's "professional" courses were "usually taught at a comparable college level on an integrated basis." But such courses required previous college classes: for example, to enter a company course in aircraft structures design, Hudson noted, "an employee would be expected to have completed a math course equivalent to college algebra and trigonometry." Once again, because segregated labor markets provided black schools with no incentives to offer courses in scientific, technical, and professional subjects, lack of preparatory opportunities may have hindered black advancement.[28]

Further, Hudson explained, "largely through the efforts of the company," Georgia's Department of Vocational Education had "agreed to support non-segregated vocational classes," although Cobb County had not yet "agreed to integrating these classes." Hudson pledged to "make continuing efforts" to convince Cobb County to change its policy but acknowledged that the only way to avoid segregated classes in the interim would be to discontinue Board of Education–sponsored classes for all employees. Hudson did not explain why the company would not or could not pursuing that idea.[29]

Further, because the Cobb Board of Education required a minimum enrollment of twenty students, a standard that was much easier for courses aimed at whites to meet given the much larger pool of white employees, classes for blacks were routinely canceled as a consequence of low enrollment numbers. "Since 1956," Hudson reported, "223 specific classes have been scheduled for Negro employees, and of these 14 were started and

13 were completed." The company had sought "to make training opportunities more available to" African American employees who lived in Atlanta by arranging to have the city's African American Carver and Washington High Schools offer training classes. In the fall of 1953, Hudson declared, 250 black employees had submitted requests for a blueprint-reading course. The company then scheduled classes both at the plant and at Carver and notified employees that they could sign up for either location. Eighteen black workers enrolled at Carver, and just five completed it. At the plant, twenty-seven African Americans started the course, but it was canceled when attendance slipped to two. A 1956 electronics course had suffered a similar fate, leading Hudson to claim "that only minor interest is shown in these classes by Negro employees."[30]

Nevertheless, according to Hudson, Lockheed was still trying: he had recently convinced the state and local boards of education to reduce the minimum enrollment for vocational classes to twelve. In addition, to "encourage Negro employees to continue their education," the company had intensified the publicity surrounding such classes and "regularly" brought "counselors from our local Negro colleges . . . into the plant to offer advice and assistance to interested employees." The company had also begun offering home study courses with "encouraging results": as of April 1961, blacks accounted for about 38 percent of the 205 employees enrolled.[31]

Though Hudson offered no explanation for African American employees' seeming lack of interest in training, it might well have resulted from their perception that the lines of advancement for blacks within the corporate system appeared to be blocked at low levels. Why should they invest time and effort in improving their skills when upward mobility was not available? In addition, Mattison and others in Lockheed management contended that systemic educational disparities played a role: blacks educated in segregated schools lacked the background and preparation needed to successfully complete the classes. And as Harry Hudson observed, those who had completed previous training but found it excessively elementary may have believed that further courses would not be useful.[32]

In response to the employees' charges about segregated recreational opportunities at Lockheed-Georgia, personnel department manager Win LeSueur explained that the company itself did not run the Lockheed Employees Recreation Club; rather, it was a nonprofit corporation formed by employees to various sports teams and to sponsor group activities such as family days at local parks and Christmas parties. LeSueur served as liaison between the club and the company, which contributed $6,000 per month to subsidize club activities. LeSueur acknowledged that no black candidates had won election to the general council that managed the club's activities but contended that the balloting process for the council was secret and that ballots "have not indicated race, creed, color, or place of birth of any employee." However, because production areas were segregated, simply knowing an employee's department would have indicated his race, and the *Southern Star* consistently printed candidates' photographs. Moreover, given that the number of white employees was far higher than the number of blacks, black candidates were highly unlikely to win election. LeSueur also insisted that virtually all family day and Christmas party activities were nonsegregated, though photographs in the *Southern Star* implied otherwise. The one exception, according to LeSueur, was the distribution of Christmas gifts to employees' children, which occurred "in separate, but adjoining, lines for white employees and their families and Negro employees and their families," although "toys and gifts of the same type and cost have been distributed . . . without regard to race creed, color, or place of birth."[33]

Despite what he portrayed as the lack of formal segregation at recreational events, LeSueur reported that he had recently "advised the [club's] General Council that the Company feels very strongly that, in light of the President's Executive Order 10925, progress should be made immediately" in desegregating sports and hobby activities. The council had informed him that the upcoming annual golf tournament would be open to blacks and whites; the softball leagues would be integrated; and the separate gift lines at the Christmas party would be abolished in 1961.[34]

In sum, Lockheed responded to employee complaints regarding real and apparent discrimination by citing the company's good intentions, its unwillingness to upset the delicate balance of local customs and practices, and the gradual progress that had nevertheless occurred. Except for International Harvester's Memphis, Tennessee, plant, Lockheed-Georgia had probably gone further than any other southern employer during the 1950s. Yet critical decisions at the outset had limited the impact of the company's efforts without testing the limits of white racial attitudes. The decision to create segregated production sections created another feedback loop, reducing incentives for black workers by limiting both perceived and real opportunities for advancement. The racial segregation of International Association of Machinists local lodges and the discrimination within the apprenticeship program to which the union's officers acquiesced, dovetailed with the company's walking-on-eggshells approach to depress expectations.

Moreover, the up-and-down nature of the company's workforce, from rapid buildup to layoffs, made a slow and gradual pace of progress difficult to maintain and hard to notice. As Mattison admitted, many assembly "helpers, white or Negro, remain helpers, particularly when reductions in force are as frequent and progressively severe" as they had been since the division's peak employment. Though promotion decisions had always been made on the basis of training and performance, "promotions... [had been] seriously curtailed or even stopped in certain periods."[35] And although the situation affected both African Americans and whites, black workers' small numbers and low levels of seniority made them particularly vulnerable to layoffs and more likely to feel the sting of delayed advancement.

Lockheed's Georgia-based management—Mattison, Gordon, and others—believed that the NAACP had unfairly targeted the company even though many other firms were far more deserving of the bad publicity and stockholder heartburn that resulted from the controversy. Yet the frustrations of African Americans at Lockheed were real and of long standing, as Mattison and some of his colleagues increasingly realized.

Later in 1961, Lockheed management, in consultation with John Feild and the PCEEO, drafted an affirmative action plan to increase minority hiring, promotion, and retention. Feild recalled that he and Jim Lydon, Lockheed's corporate vice president for industrial relations, "finalized the plan" after extensive meetings in Georgia and California with industrial relations directors from all Lockheed subsidiaries. Because the Georgia division was the primary target, Mattison played a major role, and he remained deeply involved for the remainder of the decade.[36]

Lockheed president Courtlandt Gross joined Lyndon Johnson in the Oval Office for a ceremonial signing of Lockheed's plan on May 25, 1961. President Kennedy labeled the agreement a "voluntary action" that would establish a new "pattern which can open new doors and new opportunities for members of minority groups throughout this country." Kennedy further claimed that "few actions of my administration have been more significant than the signing of this agreement." The high-profile signing ceremony raised the political stakes for equal employment opportunity, investing a much larger share of the president's political capital in the effort than previous administrations.[37]

Lockheed announced the signing of the plan for progress in the June 2 issue of the *Southern Star*, the first time that Lockheed-Georgia's house organ had even acknowledged the existence of any controversy over equal employment opportunity. The front-page story in some ways paralleled Lockheed-California's 1941 announcement that blacks would be entering the Burbank workforce but evidenced a great deal more caution. The story's headline avoided any reference to equal opportunity, instead proclaiming "Kennedy Praises Lockheed: Gross Signs U.S. Progress Plan." Lockheed workers would already have known about the plan from the area's major daily newspapers, which had reported the event with the employment of African Americans as the central focus. The *Southern Star* avoided the words *Negro* and *colored*, instead announcing that the company had "pledged to broaden opportunities for employment and advancement of members of minority groups." The *Star* noted that the recent executive order had required all government contractors to take "'affirmative action' to assure equal treatment for all employees and applicants without regard to race, creed, color, or national origin" and insisted that Lockheed had "historically followed a policy of giving fair and equal treatment to members of minority races." Management was confirming its "long-established policy" of equal opportunity employment and announcing "additional steps" that would "place the company in a position of leadership in the elimination of discrimination." Lockheed would "initiate and actively participate in appropriate programs to extend equal opportunity," pledging to widen minority recruiting, review current African American employees for potential advancement, work toward greater representation of minorities, and report annually on the progress of such efforts but offering no further substantive details.[38]

Shortly thereafter, Robert Battey Troutman Jr., a white Atlanta attorney and member of the PCEEO, suggested that Lockheed's affirmative action plan might serve as a model for a new approach to equal employment opportunity. Rather than threatening to cancel contracts as a means of forcing companies to comply with the executive order, the federal government could work with the companies, a collaborative, voluntary approach that Troutman believed would prove more efficacious. The new initiative would be known as Plans for Progress (PfP) and would be run by volunteers from the private sector. They would lobby businesses to develop similar plans, which would then be presented to the public at White House signing ceremonies with great fanfare. The PCEEO would gather statistics and evaluate the performance of the various plans, offering certificates of merit to companies that achieved significant progress in equal employment opportunity. From 1961 until 1965, when the equal employment provisions of the Civil Rights Act of 1964 became effective, the quasi-voluntary, public-private PfP program represented the chief national response to African American demands for action on jobs.[39]

With the crafting of the PfP approach, personnel executives began taking a leading role in what Frank Dobbin calls "a new social movement" that differed dramatically from the civil rights movement, which was based on popular mobilization and which had spurred executive orders and legislation. The new movement "emerged within the personnel profession to carry the civil rights project forward." The weak U.S. federal system, characterized by multiple centers of authority and points of both action and blockage, left corporations with ample room to maneuver. According to Dobbin, the U.S. state prohibited discrimination but did not codify or specifically define what constituted discrimination. Similarly, Jennifer Delton points out that although the National Association of Manufacturers was quite sympathetic not only to the idea of nondiscrimination but also to the concept of affirmative action by businesses to promote a more inclusive workplace, the organization balked at Executive Order 10925's vague language and at its potentially expansive interpretation.[40]

Mattison, Lockwood, and Gordon played major roles in this "new social movement." Mattison and Lockwood, high-level executives whom Lockheed loaned to Plans for Progress, helped define national programs. Gordon, increasingly Lockheed's designated equal employment specialist, became perhaps the most important figure in promoting equal employment practices and policies to other businesses and community organizations.

Participants always characterized PfP as voluntary, even though the program was initiated in response to Executive Order 10925 and the threat of canceled contracts. From the beginning, advocates of this quasi-voluntary approach struggled against advocates of a compulsory approach based on tough enforcement, registering success until the Civil Rights Act of 1964 created a path for the compulsory approach.

Troutman was a longtime friend of both President Kennedy and Georgia senator Herman Talmadge. Troutman and JFK's older brother, Joseph P. Kennedy Jr., had known each other at Harvard Law School, and Troutman met the future president in the summer of 1940 at the Kennedy family's Hyannis Port compound. Troutman worked for Kennedy's 1960 presidential campaign, leading the *Atlanta Daily World* to characterize him as Kennedy's "closest political adviser in Georgia." During the campaign, Troutman had become involved in a minor controversy that arose when JFK scheduled an early October speech at Franklin Roosevelt's Little White House in Warm Springs, Georgia. After rumors circulated that the Kennedy campaign had requested integrated seating, at least in the front rows, a move that might have antagonized the state's white voters, Troutman had been forced to deny that he or anyone with the campaign had made such a request. With the help of Troutman and the state's Democratic establishment, Kennedy won Georgia by a wide margin, though his 62.4 percent of the vote trailed the margins of Adlai Stevenson, who polled more than 66 percent in 1952 and 1956. Just four years later, after Kennedy's assassination and the passage of the Civil Rights Act, the Democratic presidential candidate lost the state for the first time since the Civil War.[41]

When Governor Ernest Vandiver and other Georgians met with Robert Kennedy at the 1960 Democratic National Convention, Troutman had convinced Vandiver to support JFK in spite of his seemingly liberal civil rights platform. Because the candidate supported only lawful protests and the sit-ins were illegal under Georgia law, Bobby Kennedy saw no problems arising with Georgia authorities. Vandiver traveled to Washington during the August congressional session and "exchanged his support for the Kennedy campaign . . . for the promise that, if elected, Kennedy would not send federal troops to Georgia in the event of an integration crisis."[42]

Troutman's influence in these events is unclear. These negotiations occurred after the Sibley Commission had made its recommendations regarding school integration in Atlanta but before the governor and the legislature had decided to keep the schools open. The Sibley Commission, Vandiver, and the legislature began to implement limited desegregation in early 1961. While there is no direct evidence that Troutman devised PfP as a scheme to control and limit desegregation of employment, it is easy to see how observers including NAACP labor director Herbert Hill and New York senator Jacob Javits could have concluded that such was the program's real goal.

John Kennedy appointed Troutman to the PCEEO in March 1961 and asked him to head up PfP in June. Troutman spent the next year promoting the PfP idea and jousting with PCEEO chair John Feild over the voluntary versus compulsory approach. Troutman brought in a young protégé, Joseph Kruse, to do much of the PfP fieldwork. Troutman advanced $44,000 of his own money and instructed Kruse to travel the country working to convince companies to develop affirmative action programs modeled on the Lockheed agreement. Over the next year, eighty-five firms, mostly large companies, pledged to create such plans, with Troutman then lining up White House signing ceremonies for most of those companies. CEOs traveled to Washington and posed for pictures with Vice President Johnson.[43]

The PfP approach, however, represented a schism within the PCEEO. Troutman ran the initiative with Kruse and a small staff but clashed with other committee members as well as with Feild. According to Feild, Troutman sought to make the voluntary approach "the whole of the Committee's basis of operations" and was "horrified" at the PCEEO's million-dollar budget"—he "didn't want to spend the taxpayers' money." Moreover, the Atlanta attorney "didn't like all this business of regulation, and he didn't think anybody else in business liked it either." Indeed, Troutman expressed deep skepticism about an approach that relied on forcing compliance with regulations. Feild insisted that PCEEO staffers and members believed that both approaches were important and that no companies escaped scrutiny and possible enforcement action against contracts merely by signing a plan. Such assurances from the committee staff and Vice President Johnson had little effect on civil rights leaders. Herbert Hill became a particular thorn in the PCEEO's side.[44]

Troutman's initiative had drawn criticism from civil rights leaders from the outset, but the complaints mounted after he hosted a November 1961 banquet for two of Georgia's most powerful congressional leaders, Representative Carl Vinson and Senator Richard Russell. Defense secretary Robert McNamara, who had been assured that the dinner would be integrated, ran a gauntlet of "contending Negro and Ku Klux Klan pickets" only to find that the event was all-white, leaving "Troutman saddened, the administration embarrassed, and the NAACP furious."[45]

Through the spring of 1962, Troutman advocated the formation of a business advisory council and a more structured PfP organization, but civil rights leaders and some within the PCEEO feared that doing so would cause the voluntary approach to overwhelm any effort to develop tougher regulations for contractors. In June, Javits echoed the concerns of Hill and other civil rights leaders and suggested that Congress should create a legislative basis for the PCEEO's operations, removing it from the exclusive domain of executive orders and presidential control. Javits and NAACP officials were particularly concerned that Troutman had such close personal relationships with avowed segregationists such as Talmadge and Russell. The November banquet and Troutman's recent comment that "segregated plant restrooms and cafeterias are not worth the 'fuss' of integration" contributed to the impression that he might have other motives for pushing the voluntary approach. Troutman insisted that he was interested principally in jobs, not in changing social attitudes, a characterization of segregation that Javits found "disturbing." The New York Republican pressed the point to the Oval Office, rhetorically asking if the PfP were "yet another effort on the part of the President to appease the southern wing of his party?"[46]

On August 19, veteran labor attorney, mediator, and PCEEO member Theodore Kheel completed an extensive investigation of the voluntary and compulsory options, concluding that "purely voluntary approaches are not likely to produce lasting results." Businesses must be convinced, he argued, that the committee would use the "leverage" created by the possibility that contracts would be canceled, creating "the proper blend of persuasion and enforcement." Troutman had suggested severing the relationship between PfP and the PCEEO, allowing the initiative to function as a private organization with privately raised funds, but Kheel firmly rejected this idea, instead proposing the creation of a new executive vice chair of the committee who would oversee both the PCEEO staff and PfP. The committee approved Kheel's recommendations. A few days later, Troutman, having lost the battle to make persuasion the primary implement of EEO policy, resigned from the PCEEO.[47]

Lyndon Johnson named Hobart Taylor, an African American, to fill the newly created post of executive vice chair. Taylor's father, a prominent Houston businessman, was a Johnson political ally; the younger Taylor, a University of Michigan law school graduate, had accompanied Johnson to Washington as an adviser after the 1960 election. Immediately after Taylor joined the PCEEO, the Kennedy administration demanded that he shut down the PfP program. Taylor "got an extension," and when administration officials "saw it was working, and after the Negro leadership became convinced it was working, then everybody said, 'Well, forget about closing it up. Let's go ahead.'"[48]

Taylor implemented a Troutman idea that had never flown because of the distrust of the Atlanta lawyer's motives—an advisory council drawn from the business community. Although, as Jennifer Delton notes, some companies no doubt joined PfP in part as a "self-serving" effort to deflect attention from government regulators, "for some companies, it was more significantly a genuine attempt . . . to prove their commitment to a positive program for minority employment. It collected and analyzed statistics on minority employment patterns. It sponsored hundreds of conferences and workshops to help companies begin integration. It developed scholarship and training programs. It sponsored vocational guidance seminars at high schools with predominantly black populations." The advisory council led the way in these initiatives, and Lockheed executives played a significant role.[49]

Lockheed allowed Lockwood and Mattison to devote a full year of their time to PfP's advisory council while continuing to pay their salaries. Taylor had "asked the companies to give us men as an earnest of their good faith, because if they're paying the salary . . . they have to follow up their investment, you might say, in it, and fellows take pride in what they're doing."[50]

The advisory council's first chair was G. William Miller, appointed to a two-year term in August 1963. Textron had hired the thirty-one-year-old Miller away from a Wall Street law firm in 1956; four years later, he became president of the company. Miller kept Kruse on the PfP staff to continue to recruit firms to sign agreements.[51]

Scholars have not generally had favorable views of PfP. "Enforcing JFK's affirmative action order, obviously, was a problem that was not going to be resolved by voluntary plans," observes historian Terry Anderson. The PCEEO "put pressure on companies" but "never canceled a contract," and many companies signed plans but continued their discriminatory hiring, training, and promotion policies. Aside from a few high-profile exceptions such as Lockheed, Chrysler, and Westinghouse, the private sector's "record was mediocre."[52]

Delton and Dobbin offer somewhat more positive assessments of PfP. Delton argues that a narrow focus on "'results' . . . obscures the real achievement of Plans for Progress": "it presented a business model for how employers might begin the process of integration." PfP drew on the experience of firms such as Lockheed to legitimize the idea of corporate action and expand business executives' horizons regarding equal opportunity employment. And the results were somewhat more impressive than critics had claimed. By 1963, Dobbin notes, participating firms "were hiring 10 times the number of blacks they had hired just three years earlier." Whitney Young of the Urban League was initially a vocal critic of the program but in late 1963 "announced that 115 companies in Plans for Progress had hired nearly 15,000 new blacks in the third quarter of that year—25 percent of new workers in these companies were black. Before Plans for Progress, blacks had never made up more than 3 percent of new workers in any quarter."[53]

The Southern Regional Council, probably the most significant interracial reform organization that promoted civil rights in the South, conducted a study of twenty-four PfP companies with branches in the Atlanta area. Only three had effectively implemented their affirmative action plans and made significant progress—Goodyear Tire and Rubber, Western Electric, and Lockheed-Georgia. Nationally, the first one hundred companies to sign PfP agreements increased nonwhite salaried employment from just over twenty-eight thousand to about forty-seven thousand, or from 1.5 to 2.5 percent of their combined workforces. Delton, echoing Steven Gelber, points out that the deficiencies of most southern PfP firms made the progress of the few that took serious actions even more impressive; the gains of Lockheed, Goodyear, and Western Electric padded the much less impressive gains of the remaining companies. Given that most southern companies seemed not to take their voluntary affirmative action plans seriously, "the actual gains made in those PFP companies that fulfilled their commitments were even higher than the national [aggregate] statistics indicate." PfP made some headway, but as William Collins and Robert Weaver note, opening real opportunity for minority employment gains was a greater challenge in the South.[54]

African American workers made some significant gains during the PfP period but continued to bump into familiar limits. An April 1963 *New York Times* article reported on the "quiet side" of integration in Atlanta. Gilbert L. Kelly had been hired at Lockheed in 1953 and had "worked up to that rarity among Southern Negroes, a supervisor," and according to Kelly, "For the past year, I've been working with an integrated" crew. Prior to the initiation of Lockheed's plan for progress, Harry Hudson had been the only black supervisor of an integrated crew, so Kelly's crew almost certainly resulted from the plan. For Kelly, it was "a personal challenge to keep both races on an even keel." To minimize friction, "when we get a new white man on the job, I never put him to work at first with a Negro. I know he'd be resentful. Instead, I ask one of the white persons to keep him under his wing. After a few weeks, he finds out that we all do our work, and that different folks get along OK with each other." Kelly projected optimism, but it was tempered by a clear-eyed assessment of the racial sensibilities of white workers in the Deep South.[55]

The *Times* story included a statement from Harold Arnold, director of vocational services for the Atlanta Urban League, that many African Americans had recently gained jobs in businesses that had previously hired only whites, but he did not wish to name the firms. A longer version of the same story, published in Missouri's *St. Joseph News-Press*, offered an explanation that did not appear in the *Times* version: Arnold "would not name the firms involved" because they had requested anonymity, fearing that the news that they were equal-opportunity employers "would be harmful in handling other employees." The message was none too subtle: keeping quiet created space for progress; agitation might wreck the entire integration enterprise. The echoes of "good Negroes" and "bad Negroes" continued to reverberate.[56]

During this era, the Lockheed-Georgia chapter of the National Management Association finally invited black supervisors to join, eight years after telling Harry Hudson "that I would not be expected to apply for membership." Less positively, the Lockheed Management Club ceased sponsoring an annual Christmas dance after some supervisors expressed concern about black men asking white women to dance.[57]

In addition, Hudson was invited to interview for a position in the materiel department, though he had never sought such a position. When he arrived for the meeting, department staffer Owen Malcolm explained that "the department had an opening for a buyer" and that the work "was similar to what I had done when purchasing materiel for my service station business but more complicated."[58]

The next day, Lockheed-Georgia vice president Bill Rieke sought out Hudson and asked about the interview. The two men had met in 1959, when Rieke stopped by Hudson's desk during a management walk-through. As Hudson recalled that meeting, Rieke had seemingly thought that Hudson's crew was not working fast enough but had changed his opinion after reviewing Hudson's production records. Rieke's interest in the purchasing interview surprised Hudson and gave him the impression that top management had taken an interest in moving him to a new position. Moreover, Rieke explained that he had begun his journey through the Lockheed ranks in purchasing, which offered the best overview of the entire company operation. Rieke elaborated on the virtues of the buyer's position, detailing "all the different people and companies" with which Hudson would come into contact and how he "would have to deal with every organization within the company," thereby developing extensive networks of contacts. Hudson inferred that the Lockheed-Georgia vice president was suggesting that Hudson might be upper-management material.[59]

Swayed by Rieke's words, Hudson accepted the position of buyer—a nonsupervisory salaried job—in August 1961. This move was lateral rather than vertical, though Hudson retained his supervisor's salary, which exceeded that of any of his colleagues in purchasing. Lockheed employed dozens of buyers, or purchasing agents, whose job was to locate and negotiate with suppliers of a wide array of items, including toilet paper, fasteners and screws, machine parts, and tools. Moreover, the C-141 contract had required Lockheed to source a large percentage of such purchases locally and regionally to increase the economic boost for the area. Buyers were thus some of the most public faces of the company to the business community. In accepting the post, Hudson recorded yet another breakthrough, as no African American had previously worked as a purchasing agent at Lockheed-Georgia. When Hudson reported for work in his new position in early September 1961, he found that "the only other Negroes in that two-story old barracks type building were one janitor and one maid."[60]

Three weeks after Hudson transferred to purchasing, Jack Rochester was made assistant foreman in Hudson's old department. This news prompted Hudson to consider other motives for his transfer offer, and he concluded that management had decided to move him aside so that Rochester could move up. Rochester's promotion called into question Poore's assertion that the department did not need an assistant foreman, particularly since Poore had stated that he did not think that white employees would accept an African American department manager or assistant manager. Rieke's knowledge that Hudson had interviewed for the purchasing job means that it is highly likely that Hudson was considered for the assistant foreman position, which management certainly knew was coming. Such a position would also have constituted a breakthrough—arguably a more significant one. There is no way to determine the reasons for upper management's decision. Mattison and others in employment and industrial relations may have thought that the time was not right or that despite his success at the crew level, Hudson was not suited to manage the larger departmental unit. Rieke and others may really have believed that purchasing might prepare Hudson to move higher up the corporate food chain. Whatever motivations lay behind the transfer, it had significant negative ramifications for Hudson's subsequent career path.

When Hudson was introduced to the other purchasing department employees, who included a number of white women who did clerical work, he received "curious stares": "Everyone was pleasant, but I only got about two 'welcome to the group' expressions." He considered such a response "normal" and started unpacking. After all, he observed, "breaking up red Georgia clay for planting ain't no easy job." As Hudson demonstrated his competence and politeness, "the ladies began to get a little more friendly." "Their gazes turned to 'good morning,' then to 'hello,' and finally to 'hi'" in a progression of familiarity that would have been unthinkable in an interracial workplace just a few years earlier. He knew that personal relations on the job had turned a corner about three months later, when one woman confided to him that "her father was a drunkard who beat her mother, her husband wasn't much of a provider, and her son was one of those new juvenile delinquents. I knew my presence was finally acceptable."[61]

Under the informal tutelage of Paul Hale, who was now occupied with purchasing larger and more expensive parts for the C-141, Hudson received responsibility for procuring small shaped-metal parts called forgings valued between five and several hundred dollars. The two men developed a solid relationship that endured until Hudson's retirement twenty-seven years later. Hale was "a very good teacher," helping introduce Hudson to suppliers, office staff, and the rules of the purchasing game.[62]

Hudson encountered few problems with salesmen and vendors. He had spent most of his life dealing with people and had learned to let passing remarks slide. On one occasion, however, a sales representative from New Jersey made a presentation in which he stated that "the plant was in a 'nigger' neighborhood and therefore housekeeping could not be as well under the conditions." Hudson immediately stopped the man, told him that "we did not use that terminology in this office," and terminated the meeting with the comment that "if that was the best excuse he could use for the housekeeping and cleanliness of the plant, what the hell would his excuse be in case his quality was not what it was proclaimed to be?" The salesman went to Hale's office but was rebuffed there as well. Hudson, who was light-skinned, surmised that the salesman did not realize he was talking to an African American and saw the man as an example of "people from other areas of the United States [who come] into the South . . . expecting better acceptance by being derogatory, in other words prejudiced."63

In the summer of 1964, nearly three years after his move into purchasing, Hudson met with a delegation from a presidential committee (probably the PCEEO). Though committee members visited Lockheed each year, this was the first time he had been invited to speak with them, and he was reluctant: "From all I heard, they were given the same BS each year and they went back and probably told the powers that be what they wanted to hear[, which was that] everything is going fine, minorities are progressing and advancing as fast as experience and ability will allow." But despite his reservations, he met with the committee.64

When asked if he had recently been promoted to buyer, he bluntly replied that in his view, "I had been demoted from manager to buyer . . . not as a disciplinary measure but to make way for an individual whom I respect but who" was less qualified to serve as an assistant foreman. Hudson was happy that his pay had not been cut, but he noted that he had not yet traveled for the new job, though buyers normally did so: after "almost three years," his supervisors apparently considered him "still gaining experience," though he was increasingly unsure what the relevant experience might be. He strongly suspected that the real reason he had been restricted to dealing with local sellers and hosting salesmen who called at Lockheed's Georgia offices was that "the powers that be" did not believe that African Americans could be trusted with the expense accounts involved in traveling. After telling the committee that he had no confidence in its efforts, Hudson declared that he had to get back to work and terminated the interview.65

Hudson was becoming increasingly frustrated. He took pride in his work, particularly in the fact that he saved the company tens of thousands of dollars, efforts that earned him numerous commendations and company awards. But he saw himself languishing in purchasing, with diminishing hopes for further advancement, and he believed that his race and his outspokenness on racial matters were factors in his career stagnation. Despite Rieke's explanation of the benefits of a move to purchasing, Hudson later reflected that Rieke had neglected to mention "that he was a Vice President and my chances of ever reaching that position were about as possible as two grains of sand raising the ocean levels one foot."[66]

Harry Hudson (*on the far right*) receives a safety award along with members of his integrated crew. Lockheed Executive Assistant to the Executive Vice President Charles Wagner (*on the far left*) would become president of Lockheed-California in 1965. Hudson family photograph.

Carl Smith (*on the right*) joined Lockheed-Georgia as a structures assembler in 1963; Roslyn Smith (*on the left*) was employed as a sealer the same year. The story "Up through the Ranks at Lockheed" highlighted the Smiths' advancement to manpower analyst (Carl) and the logistics department (Roslyn). *Lockheed Southern Star*, November 21, 1968, 6. Courtesy Lockheed Martin Aeronautics Company.

J. B. Mabry (*standing, behind banner*) receives a safety award on behalf of his crew from Lockheed-Georgia president Dan Haughton (*holding banner, left*). *Lockheed Southern Star*, March 17, 1955. Courtesy Lockheed Martin Aeronautics Company.

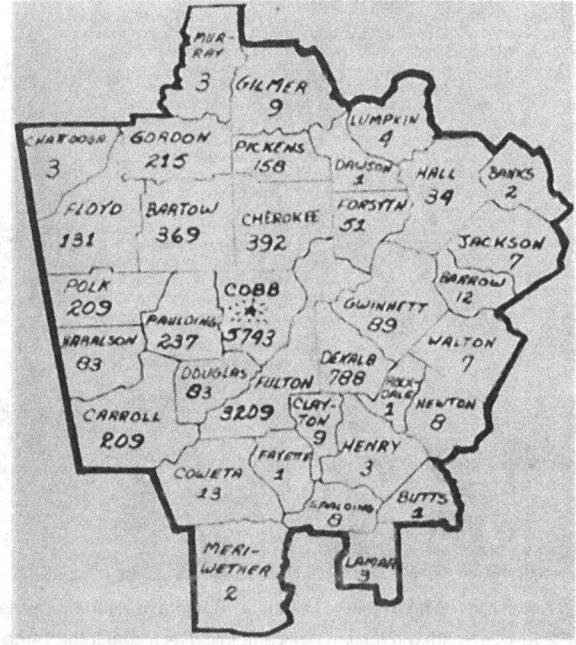

Georgia counties from which Lockheed's Marietta plant drew employees, 1953. Many of Lockheed's African American workers resided in Atlanta, in Fulton County. *Lockheed Southern Star*, June 25, 1953. Courtesy Lockheed Martin Aeronautics Company.

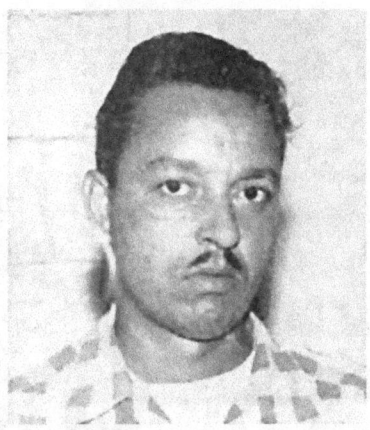

Harry Hudson. *Lockheed Southern Star*, August 18, 1960. Courtesy Lockheed Martin Aeronautics Company.

Representatives of the Plans for Progress Business Advisory Council at the Lockheed-Georgia plant, April 28, 1964. The African American man in the center of the front row is Hobart Taylor. Taylor is flanked on the left by E. G. Mattison and on the right by G. William Miller. From "Plans for Progress First Year Report," August 1964, folder 10, box 12, Kruse Papers. Used by permission of Kennesaw State University, Department of Museums, Archives, and Rare Books.

Whitney Young addresses Plans for Progress Third Annual Conference, January 26, 1965. *Seated, left to right*: Marvin Oberg, vice president, Northwestern Bell Telephone; F. D. Fennagen, director of public relations, National Brewing; Roy Wilkins, executive director, NAACP; Dwight Zook, personnel director, North American Aviation; G. William Miller, president, Textron, and chair, Plans for Progress Business Advisory Council; E. G. Mattison, director of industrial relations, Lockheed-Georgia. Folder 10, box 12, Gordon Papers. Used by permission of Kennesaw State University, Department of Museums, Archives, and Rare Books.

Panel including Hugh Gordon (*fourth from left*) and *Time* columnist Hugh Sidey (*fifth from left*) at a National Alliance of Business conference, 1976. *Working* (NAB publication), Fall 1976, folder 4, box 6, Gordon Papers. Used by permission of Kennesaw State University, Department of Museums, Archives, and Rare Books.

Members of the NAB-dominated Private Industry Council of Atlanta, 1979. *Clockwise from bottom*: Leo Benatar (back of head); Hugh Gordon; Tom Hamall; Bob Sparrow; John Gillman. *Atlanta Business Matters*, April 18, 1979, folder 24, box 6, Gordon Papers. Used by permission of Kennesaw State University, Department of Museums, Archives, and Rare Books.

Hugh Gordon at a Merit Employers Association meeting, ca. 1984. Folder 29, box 6, Gordon Papers. Used by permission of Kennesaw State University, Department of Museums, Archives, and Rare Books.

CHAPTER 5

"Build the People"

THE ERA OF UNCERTAINTY, 1965-1970

In 1967, Lockheed-Georgia employed a team of psychologists from Georgia Tech to survey employees on a range of workplace issues from wages and benefits to job satisfaction and management responsiveness to employee needs. The survey does not appear to have included any questions about racial integration. Production workers generally expressed a high level (60 percent or more in most categories) of satisfaction with the insurance benefits, rates of pay, and savings plan and other benefits. These workers also overwhelmingly rated the company's reputation as positive. Clarence Sinkfield, an African American hired in 1965, attested to the significance of being a Lockheed employee. Born and raised in the predominantly black Pittsburgh neighborhood of southwest Atlanta, Sinkfield recalled that employment at Lockheed brought with it a definite sense of improved status: "Especially in the neighborhood I was from, when you had that Lockheed badge on and you walked in a store, you got a certain amount of respect. If you needed credit, they didn't run an extensive credit check on you. They would just about give you credit immediately because you were a Lockheed employee. I can remember, you might get off from work at 3:30 or 3:45, and it might be 7:00 and you're still walking around with that badge on."[1] Even the psychological benefits of the job could have material consequences.

Supervisory personnel expressed the highest levels of satisfaction overall, though managers at all levels—like Harry Hudson—were less than fully happy with what they saw as their chances of promotion and of changing jobs. Hourly employees, too, expressed doubt about their chances for promotion and management's responsiveness to their needs. One hourly worker observed that "the main disadvantage of working for Lockheed is that job security is almost non-existent," while another noted a prevailing sense of expendability: "I believe when [layoff] time comes, more concern should be given to those in the [lower] labor grades.... It costs the Company to train a new group every time a new program comes along!" Lockheed-Georgia—and, indeed, the entire aircraft industry—had long followed a buildup-layoff-rebuild pattern that workers had to balance against the advantages of employment.[2]

In the fall of 1969, Lockheed-Georgia's total employment peaked at 32,945; by August 1970, less than a year later, that number had fallen to 24,400, and the cuts were just beginning.[3]

In the late 1960s, Lockheed management seemed eager to participate in public-private partnerships in the equal employment opportunity arena. In early 1967, a full year before the National Alliance of Businessmen (NAB) was formed to address this particular problem, Lockheed collaborated with the Georgia State Employment Service to develop a training program aimed at the "hard-core" unemployed. Funded primarily by a grant from the federal government through the 1962 Manpower Development and Training Act (MDTA), the program initially offered training with the promise of employment at Lockheed. In 1969, training department manager Robert Hudson prepared a slide show that was intended to recruit other Atlanta-area industrial employers for the MDTA initiative and was shown at meetings of the Georgia Chamber of Commerce, the Atlanta Merit Employers Association, and the local chapter of the NAB. In a memorandum accompanying the slide show, Hudson expressed his full concurrence with Daniel Patrick Moynihan's "disintegration of the black family" thesis as an analysis of the root causes of African American unemployment and poverty. "As you know," he confidently announced to his readers, "one of the biggest problems in our urban society is the abdication by negro males of their family responsibilities," resulting in the development of "a matriarchal society . . . which creates a major problem in the big city ghettoes." Hudson claimed that Lockheed's program had met with great success and expressed confidence that it "offer[s] real promise as a solution of one of the basic problems of urban society." He also insisted that it made for an "interesting contrast" to other programs around the country that focused on "hard-core females." Such programs, he contended, "tend to perpetuate rather than solve urban problems."[4]

Lockheed's program reflected the tensions among policymakers in Washington. Members of the Johnson administration had two main views of the problem of disadvantaged workers. According to economist Harry Holzer, the Council of Economic Advisers (CEA) argued that the best way "to increase overall employment, including among the poor, was through macroeconomic policy, particularly tax cuts to spur aggregate demand." The CEA also recognized a structural component in the persistence of high rates of unemployment among groups subject to racial discrimination and poor educational backgrounds. For such groups, the CEA advocated "human capital investments" including both enhanced education (Head Start, for example) and job training programs such as Job Corps and an expansion of MDTA initiatives. The CEA also strongly advocated enforcement of the employment provisions of the Civil Rights Act. These advisers viewed unemployment as a structural problem, as had many in Congress in the 1950s, but defined that problem in different terms—racial discrimination and its attendant impact on education (especially though not only in the South), motivation, and labor market connections.[5]

Other Johnson advisers, most notably Labor Secretary Willard Wirtz and Assistant Labor Secretary Daniel Patrick Moynihan, "argued for a broader effort focused not only on job training but also on job creation for the poor." Moynihan became notorious for his views of the weakness of black families, and both he and Wirtz focused on men, similar to Hudson's justification for the hard-core training program. But Wirtz and Moynihan also seriously advocated job creation on a scale not seen since the New Deal era, in part to provide an economic stimulus but also as a tool to attack structural unemployment among the poor and minorities. "Even in a relatively healthy economy, the low skills and weak job market contacts of the poor (plus discrimination) might prevent them from finding enough private-sector jobs to fill on their own. [Moynihan and Wirtz] thus perceived problems for the poor on both the supply (workers) and demand (employers-jobs) sides of the labor market."[6]

Members of both camps within the administration agreed on the need to focus on job training, leading to the MDTA-funded contracts at Lockheed and other companies as well as to other Great Society programs, including the Job Corps, an updated version of the New Deal–era Civilian Conservation Corps. But such programs could serve only a tiny fraction of the disadvantaged population at the funding levels approved by the Johnson administration. In October 1966, a massive coalition of civil rights organizations endorsed the Freedom Budget, a plan that called for moving beyond the simple removal of barriers to employment, voting, and economic progress by spending $185 billion on a vision that could best be described as positive liberty. What would it take to give meaning to the ideal of freedom? The sponsors of the Freedom Budget insisted that poor education, poverty, and persistent unemployment made freedom meaningless to a great many Americans. This view implicitly criticized what A. Philip Randolph had called the "haphazard, piecemeal approach" of the Great Society initiatives. The price tag for the Freedom Budget was steep, and the civil rights leaders who endorsed it worked hard, though unsuccessfully, to justify the expense in terms of future social savings.[7]

In early 1967, Lockheed prepared an off-site training facility near the main Marietta campus to "provide a realistic industrial environment" with enough "shop space and equipment to" provide trainees with instruction in a variety of basic skills and types of equipment operation. Rather than teaching job-specific skills for employment at Lockheed, the program provided training in the operation of general-use machines found in many manufacturing environments. In short, it offered general-purpose industrial-readiness training. The twelve-week program could be extended to allow some workers who were deemed to be making progress to take up to twenty-four weeks, and the average cost per worker in 1968 was just under $1,000, the bulk of which was paid by the U.S. Department of Labor under Lockheed's $306,000 MDTA training contract.[8]

During orientation, trainees were "indoctrinated on work policies and standards," including "rules on appearance, personal safety, and attendance," and "quickly develop[ed] acceptable work habits." After orientation, trainees received classroom training in "basic arithmetic or shop math" and "an introduction to blueprint reading." The facility's staff used booklets that allowed trainees to progress at their own pace and "enabled instructors to devote maximum time to individual learning problems." Program participants then moved to the shop to learn "elementary metal working" techniques, including filing, layout, drilling, and riveting. The program also featured a "specially adapted, easy to use projector" and "a series of film cartridges" that allowed employees to screen instructional films as often as needed, with the capacity to stop film to look closely at single frames. After becoming acquainted with basic skills, trainees moved on to common machines used in metal fabrication, such as belt sanders and band saws. Class assembly projects required trainees to bring together all these skills. After mastering assembly, trainees were exposed to specialized skills "common to metal-working industries"—welding, pipe fitting, and spray painting. Trainees who demonstrated an aptitude or who were designated for particular jobs at Lockheed received additional instruction in specialized areas.[9]

Program participants also received individualized counseling in which "unrehearsed role-playing" simulated "hypothetical situations which relate to the industrial world." These activities helped trainees "channel their own personality traits into acceptable behavior patterns." Finally, potential employers interviewed trainees. Lockheed initially hired most of the trainees, but after employment reductions in late 1967, the company invited other area employers to interview and hire trainees.[10]

To convince prospective corporate participants of the value of and need for more employers, Hudson argued that the fluctuation in individual firms' personnel needs meant that "a single employer cannot perpetuate such a program"; rather, the program needed "a pool of employers to generate a continuing job market for graduates." Hudson invited other employers to "join Lockheed in its efforts to combat one of the community's most serious social and economic problems."[11]

In January 1969, Lockheed's industrial relations director, C. A. Jenkins, reported that between the program's inception in March 1967 and the end of that year, ninety-nine people had enrolled, fifty-four had completed training, and all were employed—forty-three with Lockheed, the rest with other firms. However, thirty-one enrollees had dropped out or been dismissed. The report attributed this high washout rate to "absenteeism and lack of interest" or to problems with "motivation." In the first few months of 1968, when Lockheed's internal job openings disappeared, Hudson pitched the program to other companies. Beginning in March, Lockheed's employment needs skyrocketed as the company ramped up to produce the C-5A, and over the final ten months of that year 120 people completed training and were employed by Lockheed-Georgia, while 14 others found work with other firms. Throughout the initial twenty-two months of the training program, managers engaged in "a constant effort to improve methods of motivation and training," and these improvements helped to raise the completion/employment rate from less than two-thirds in 1967 to nearly three-quarters the following year. Though the absolute number of people trained remained relatively small, Lockheed managers believed that the program's real potential lay in developing models that could be replicated elsewhere and on a much larger scale.[12]

The program emphasized "close monitoring" of trainees, which alerted officials "to many individual problems that led to trainee failure." Most dropouts left within the first two weeks, some because of hardships caused by forgoing income during the pretraining assessment, for which they were not paid. For those with no economic security, even two weeks without pay could be an unbridgeable gap. Once in training, some trainees "developed a feeling of failure because they were 'dropping behind' the others in their group." Lockheed responded to both these concerns. The company negotiated with the U.S. Department of Labor, which administered the MDTA funds, to permit payment of an allowance during the assessment period. In addition, instructors and training department managers closely examined the first phase of the training program and decided "it could be broken down into smaller increments and rearranged," thereby helping to "ensure the trainee a certain amount of success and create[ing] a feeling of accomplishment." Counselors also visited dropouts in their homes to explain these changes and encourage them to return to the program. Moreover, counselors helped trainees with personal problems that contributed to absenteeism, identifying community resources to aid trainees with medical and dental issues, arranging part-time employment in off-training hours, and "advis[ing] trainees with unacceptable work habits and attitudes."[13]

Because "many trainees enter the program with belligerent and distrustful attitudes that inhibit successful entrance into the industrial society," counselors organized "special psychodrama sessions" in which trainees participated in role-playing sessions regarding hypothetical workplace issues and met with their peers "to discuss their problems, express opinions without fear of being reprimanded, and in general 'get things off their chest.'" Having trainees play the roles of boss, job interviewer, and employee with a complaint forced them to think about problems from different perspectives. Trainees could "see themselves as others see them" and, organizers hoped, "gain insight into the necessity of discipline and basic ground rules." The psychodrama sessions "contributed greatly to the trainee's adjustment to the everyday problems of the industrial world."[14]

As of December 1968, Lockheed's program had trained 320 people. Eighty-four percent were members of minority groups, while 77 percent were aged between eighteen and twenty-two. Among those who enrolled, 46 percent had police records for offenses ranging from public drunkenness to robbery; members of that group averaged 2.33 arrests, with one individual alone accounting for 15 arrests. The average trainee read at the equivalent of the sixth-grade level, and 74 percent were high school dropouts, including one man who had left school in eighth grade and read at the second-grade level. Even those who had graduated from high school averaged only a seventh-grade reading ability.[15]

In January 1968, in the wake of the July 1967 unrest in Detroit and other urban areas, President Johnson convened a meeting of business leaders at the White House to form the NAB. Johnson then asked Congress to appropriate funds for the NAB to use to provide on-the-job training and temporary wage subsidies. This new public-private program would expand on the pilot hard-core training programs in which Lockheed had participated under the MDTA. Johnson called on NAB to move half a million hard-core unemployed into jobs within three years and to create two hundred thousand summer jobs for disadvantaged youths in 1968. Johnson emphasized the waste associated with "the man and the woman blocked from productive employment by barriers rooted in poverty: lack of health, lack of education, lack of training, lack of motivation"; "the citizen who is barred from a job because of other men's prejudices"; and "the boy or girl from the slums whose summers are empty because there is nothing to do." Such untapped human potential, Johnson argued, was something that "an enlightened nation should not tolerate" and that "a nation concerned by disorders in its city streets cannot tolerate." According to Johnson, the private sector should have substantial control of this new government-supported training effort because "industry knows how to train people for the jobs on which its profits depend." The NAB constituted the "first federally funded effort to subsidize employment of low-income people in the private sector, though ... at quite modest levels." Johnson "rejected the Moynihan-Wirth arguments in favor of a more fiscally conservative ... approach, consistent with the views of his economic advisers," Holzer argued.[16]

After Johnson declined to run for reelection and Richard Nixon moved into the Oval Office, the old Plans for Progress organization was merged into the NAB, whose supporters included Lockheed executives. The hardcore program continued under NAB auspices, and in June 1968 Hugh Gordon explained to Atlanta-area business colleagues what Lockheed had learned from its efforts. Participants responded well to "demands made clear to them," and "the higher the standards for workmanship and personal attire, the better the response." The "hard core veneer is thin," and underneath lay "a rather classic set of middle class values." Trainees understood that "reliability in attendance," workmanship, and other values were necessary, but such attitudes had not previously "been important to them" in their daily lives. Employers also had to provide "a sense of dignity," "the main source of" which was a job. Gordon acknowledged that the trainees often received jobs near the bottom of the market, even with firms such as Lockheed, but emphasized all employees nevertheless should be treated as worthy and dignified. "If you can't change the job" by moving trainees into higher-status categories, "change the environment." Lockheed had learned to be "hard-nosed in production standards" yet "permissive in personal relations," broadening the definition of acceptable conduct and comportment on the job. "You have a right to expect more of these people than you probably think," Gordon insisted, "but only if you structure the job to give the employee what he is looking for."[17]

Gordon also worked to counter misperceptions of affirmative action and the hard-core unemployed within Lockheed. In February 1969, Gordon wrote to Jenkins to "clear the air" about "the discipline of our Negro employees." According to Gordon, "There is a myth generating about the disinclination of supervis[ors] to discipline Negroes" and a "lack of management support" for such discipline. Gordon provided data to back up his contention that such charges were indeed myths: in 1968 African Americans had constituted 31 percent of all Lockheed dismissals, though blacks accounted for only 9.4 percent of the workforce. Further, the company had faced 184 equal employment opportunity (EEO) charges dating back to 1965, and "not one Negro dismissal has been reversed."[18]

Gordon bluntly asserted that the myth originated from poor supervision. "Too many of our supervisors shy away from rule enforcement of any kind"; though some supervisors could probably improve with proper training, others were "misplaced in supervision." Many of the "gun shy" supervisors were "inept or clumsy" in interpersonal relations, and Gordon had seen "hundreds of examples over the years of inadequate personnel handling" in the company's grievance procedure. Despite the "growing trend" toward blaming discipline problems on black employees, the issue was more accurately a general problem with supervision. Not only might that misplaced focus permit the lack of discipline to escalate, but "in defaming a large number of our employees racial prejudices are further polarized and the tinderbox becomes bigger, more explosive."[19]

"The myth" did not go away. In late June 1969, Gordon constructed a more in-depth analysis, pushing back harder and with more data. Over the preceding eighteen months, Lockheed-Georgia had hired 12,550 new employees, all but about 1,000 of them in manufacturing, as the company set up the production lines for the new C-5A transport planes. Beginning in late 1968, the focus had gradually shifted away from line workers to more highly skilled mechanics, technicians, and engineers, a significant proportion of whom were hired with the proviso they would undergo "pre-hire training," much as African American workers and some whites had in the 1950s. The company had also promoted 398 employees into supervisory positions, 103 of them in the new C-5A section. Many of these new supervisors were quite young—under the age of thirty. With a wave of baby boomers finding their first jobs, Gordon noted, the workforce of the future would not only feature growing proportions of young people but also "likely include more minorities and people with disadvantaged backgrounds" as a result of EEO policies. Already, Gordon pointed out, the company had used the C-5A employment boom to boost its minority hiring, with the African American percentage of the company's workforce rising from 5.7 percent in 1967 to 9.95 percent in mid-1969. Nevertheless, he stressed, "our work force is a normal one—there is a marked absence of hippie or weirdo types" and "few of the Negro employees" wore an "Afro haircut"—not that the company would "consider this indicative of performance potential any more than" a white employee's "long hair or heavy sideburns."[20]

Gordon explained that the more diverse workforce would "present a continuing challenge to a younger, relatively inexperienced" group of supervisors, a challenge "with no quick solutions through discipline or other singular techniques." Gordon suggested that a more sophisticated form of management would be required and that it would need to be characterized by what he termed "optimum objectivity." Management would need to set clear performance standards and hold all employees to those standards regardless of race, appearance, socioeconomic status, and any other non-performance-related characteristics: "When optimum objectivity prevails, Negroes and whites are supervised, helped, trained, and disciplined *by the same standards.*" All managers had to ask themselves "whether or not double standards are being applied," particularly in "race related matters, a fair question for fair-minded people." Though "human frailty" made it difficult for individuals to judge their own objectivity, "it's something we have got to work on."[21]

Gordon explained away employees' charges of discrimination at Lockheed as the work of "a few militants." Those complaints had started to arrive at the regional office of the new Equal Employment Opportunity Commission (EEOC) when the employment provisions of the Civil Rights Act of 1964 became effective on July 1, 1965. The agency had authority to investigate discrimination charges and issue advisory opinions on whether discrimination had occurred but as yet had no enforcement powers. Complainants could use EEOC findings as evidence in civil suits, but the agency itself could not file suit. In the ensuing four years, Lockheed had faced 153 EEOC complaints and eleven lawsuits, actively denying the allegations.[22]

At the same time, some supervisors "have expressed concern over 'favoritism' accorded Negroes by our policies." These charges, however, had proven "most difficult to pinpoint" with a "marked absence of specific complaints" that could be investigated. The only specific grievance Gordon could identify was a charge by a production manager that "he could not get his job done because of excessive time spent answering EEOC complaints" and that "he and his supervisors were being harassed by EEO investigators." And that inquiry revealed that this foreman "had spent less than 15 minutes answering EEOC charges," and "all supervisors contacted asserted they had not experienced any harassment." Moreover, before filing his complaint, this department manager had been the subject of "charges filed by three Negro employees who were dismissed on the same day" as well as of other complaints regarding discriminatory behavior.[23]

Gordon's memo also included a discussion of the hard-core program, no doubt because many within the company associated it, not incorrectly, with the affirmative action program. Over the preceding sixteen months, the company had hired 576 workers through the NAB program; 404 (70 percent) remained on the payroll. Most had completed their probationary employment periods, and their retention rate was "competitive with all other non-hardcore hires during a comparable period." In fact, when he compared random samples of one hundred workers from the hard-core program and from the regular "pre-hire" training program, the hard-core sample was overwhelmingly black (94 percent), while most of the regular hires were white (71 percent): both groups had retention rates of 71 percent.[24]

Gordon added sample data showing that the absentee rates for blacks (0.037 per employee) and whites (0.027) were similar; because the workforce included many more whites, on any given project, 2.9 man-days were lost to white absences while 0.8 days were lost to black. Thus, Gordon argued, black absences could not be viewed as the main contributor to lost time and schedule delays.[25]

Gordon's data also showed that during the first half of 1969, the dismissal rate for African Americans had risen to 42 percent, a significant jump from the 29 and 31 percent rates in 1967 and 1968, respectively. Gordon bluntly declared, "Negroes have been dismissed disproportionate to their numbers in the work force." Although some people "categorically feel that Negroes are lazy, poor workers, prone to absenteeism, unresponsive to direction, and non-conforming," "838 Negroes have been promoted this year," and only 7.7 percent of black workers had quit their jobs. He warned that the disproportionate dismissal rate "could become attributed ... to management's concern for discipline of Negroes in the work force and be another 'cause celebre,'" thereby setting the company up for serious EEOC charges in the future. Moreover, Gordon emphasized, the data demonstrated that Lockheed-Georgia management did not hesitate to dismiss "Negro employees notwithstanding persistent rumors that Industrial Relations will not permit management to 'get rid of' unsatisfactory Negro employees."[26]

Gordon concluded by weighing in against any sort of written or verbal reaffirmation of the virtues of imposing discipline: "We believe the dangers of the encouragement of further Negro discipline ... outweigh the advantages otherwise attainable." What was needed was "better understanding of the unique human relations aspects of racial differences" and better personnel-management skills in general. To this end, his department recommended that the company develop and implement "a 'Personnel Awareness' training program." A Lockheed Training Department task force had already begun work on such a program, "designed to provide supervisory awareness of human relations responsibilities inherent in providing equal employment opportunity."[27] Eventually labeled Build the People, the program made its debut around the end of 1969.

In February 1970, Lockheed competitor McDonnell-Douglas submitted an affirmative action plan to the Department of Defense as part of the negotiations for the new F-15 fighter contract. The McDonnell-Douglas plan was the first submitted and approved under the more stringent rules imposed by Office of Federal Contract Compliance Order 4, which required contractors to develop affirmative action plans. Hugh Gordon visited McDonnell-Douglas vice president Robert C. Krone in early March 1970 to discuss the details of the plan and reported back to Jenkins, who would share the information with top management.[28]

McDonnell-Douglas's plan had emerged from a "crisis-type negotiation." The Defense Department had awarded the company a $1 billion F-15 contract in December 1969, but U.S. Civil Rights Commission hearings in St. Louis the following month determined that McDonnell-Douglas had not received clearance from the department's regional contract compliance office. On January 30, 1970, the department announced that McDonnell-Douglas would be required to submit an acceptable affirmative action plan or the contract might be canceled. During a series of tense bargaining sessions, negotiators hammered out a plan that the department approved on February 10. Lockheed and other contractors were keenly aware of the requirement's significance of affirmative action plans and sought as much information as possible about what might be acceptable to government contract offices.[29]

In Gordon's view, "in many respects, McDonnell-Douglas has just reached a point of sophistication" that Lockheed-Georgia had reached a year earlier. Krone admitted that his firm's prior EEO policies had been of the "'Motherhood' type," evoking empty praise of motherhood and apple pie, "based on such time-worn expressions as 'will aggressively seek out qualified minorities'" but including no specific targets or goals, no substantive management procedures to ensure execution, and no meaningful metrics for success. In contrast, the company's new program was "quite comprehensive," leading Krone to express "some concern as to whether or not they had gone too far." Nevertheless, Krone indicated that top management was generally satisfied with the program, and Defense Department contract administrators had already asked to have elements of the McDonnell-Douglas plan incorporated into Lockheed's next EEO plan. Gordon focused the remainder of his report on "major distinctive items" that Lockheed-Georgia needed to address."[30]

Lockheed had previously used numerical targets, but they generally applied broadly—that is, to entire departments or to such categories as "non-managerial salaried" employees. McDonnell-Douglas, in contrast, had made much more specific commitments, accepting "more detailed numerical and/or percentage goals by organizational unit and job category." To illustrate his point, Gordon reported that McDonnell-Douglas had no minorities employed as assistant project planners as of February 1970 but anticipated three openings in that category over the coming year and set a goal of filling one of those jobs with a minority candidate. Further, McDonnell-Douglas pledged to strengthen its EEO staff presence and appoint a corporate director of equal opportunity programs as well as an EEO manager for each factory with more than five thousand employees. The company also agreed to develop "a potpourri of training programs," including affirmative action workshops for all supervisors and employment personnel, special skills training for lower-skilled workers, a clerk-typist program, and "remedial education for all service workers, laborers, and low skilled operators." Finally, the company would develop charts to track EEO progress to be displayed in the Management Chart Room, which tracked important production and sales numbers. Lockheed's previous agreement had called for the development and tracking of such charts by a special EEO task force led by Gordon, but the McDonnell-Douglas plan had agreed to give these charts coequal status with other critical management tracking charts.[31]

Gordon again reported on the status of Lockheed's equal employment opportunity policies to the Lockheed-Georgia president's staff in March or April 1970.[32]

Lockheed-Georgia's history was "full of contradictions," he began. Since the company's arrival in Georgia, it had been "the acknowledged leader in the South in changing racial practices and policies," but "despite this leadership role," and despite receiving praise from "national publications as a model or example of harmonious integration of southern industry," the company had also "been singled out for attack." The company's racial difficulties had not been "enough to make headlines, but [were] enough to be painful for a few employees and their families." Gordon detailed a number of similar contradictions, including the fact that though Lockheed had successfully resolved more than a hundred EEO complaints since 1965, the backlog continued to grow, and a number of employees had refused conciliation agreements and filed suit. Thus, although Lockheed was "the only company to my knowledge ever cited in a major press release by the EEOC for having such a progressive program," it also might well face more complaints than any other firm in a single location. In addition to facing a class-action lawsuit by blacks alleging discrimination, Lockheed had "had to defend a lawsuit from a Caucasian alleging that we are giving preferential treatment to blacks." Lockheed seemed damned if we do, damned if we don't. But, Gordon emphasized, "there is no doubt in our minds as to the correct course of action." If discrimination were "defined as the pervasive nonuse of minorities in employment," he argued, "it follows that we must take specific affirmative steps to change the patterns of employment" that impeded full usage of minorities.[33]

In the current EEO climate, "business is expected to find solutions to social problems," and in the case of McDonnell-Douglas, Gordon understood that the Department of Defense had taken "the position that they were not just buying airplanes but management know how in hiring and training which was essential in solving national urban problems." EEO considerations were rapidly becoming a part of the government-contracting landscape, and Gordon believed that "vigorous enforcement efforts will continue or increase": the Nixon administration's Department of Labor had recently required specific quotas of minority employees on government construction projects.[34]

The Office of Contract Compliance's Order 4, which Gordon characterized as "the toughest EEO regulation ever issued to federal contractors," required contracting firms to analyze and identify their affirmative action deficiencies, set goals and timetables, and demonstrate a good-faith effort to achieve those results. There was "certainly no indication that this administration is letting up on EEO," Gordon warned.[35]

On a recent visit to Lockheed-Georgia, the EEOC commissioner had impressed on Gordon and his associates that upgrading and promotion of minority employees "in *all* categories of employment, especially in decision-making jobs of management and key staff assignments," would be an area of increasing attention. Large numbers of low-level production workers would no longer be sufficient. Gordon also expected a continued "push for 'hard core' hiring." Attention would also go to new categories of EEO focus, including women, Mexican Americans, and older workers.[36]

Gordon then turned to the current EEO situation at Lockheed-Georgia, highlighting the February 1969 conciliation agreement with the EEOC that had been "cited by the commission as an industry standard." Having learned from its experiences of the previous decade, Lockheed had formed a special unit that tracked equal employment opportunity progress. Gordon himself led the unit, which included five full-time staff members dedicated solely to EEO matters. Gordon presented employment data showing that Lockheed was neither a leader nor a laggard compared to five other aerospace companies. Black employment at Lockheed had mushroomed during the 1960s, with overall employment rising 214 percent and the number of African Americans in salaried positions increasing by 328 percent. But those percentages reflected the small starting numbers, and "government agencies will not be satisfied until our Negro employment figures are more comparable with the Negro population in the community."[37]

African Americans constituted nearly 32 percent of the 5,400 entry-level workers hired for the C-5 project in 1968 and 1969. But among the 602 salaried employees hired during that period, only 13 were black. Those numbers reflected "market conditions for Negro engineers," Gordon observed, but "this is a 'do better' area for us."[38]

The company was likely to face a challenging environment going forward. The company had exceeded its "goal of 54 Negro production supervisors" in the fall of 1969, "but as layoffs started, some of the last Negroes promoted got caught in the downturn." According to Gordon, "The massive layoffs we've experienced . . . have put pressure on us in several ways," one of which was that they "threatened to wipe out our EEO [progress] during the past several years." In addition, it had presented line managers with "some tough decisions on other potential surplus people." In an effort to contain the damage, Lockheed had created a "special presidential review board" comprising the Lockheed-Georgia president, vice presidents, industrial relations director, and relevant branch heads. The board would "review surplus action of lower level committees on any salaried employees in one of four categories"—minorities, the physically disabled, those near retirement, and older workers. Gordon reported that the committee had already overruled a number of lower-level layoff decisions: "Of 50 Negro supervisors designated for surplus, the committee overruled and retained 18." Lockheed had also formed a survey team comprising "key management people from all branches" that would review the effectiveness of the company's EEO programs. The team had added "2 Negro managers," who had "brought a freshness to our program."[39]

Gordon next noted that the hard-core training program had been "temporarily discontinued ... in view of our layoff situation" but then turned to Build the People, which he described as "a natural sequel." Build the People provided "training for all supervisors to help them understand their role, not only in supervising hard core types." Gordon presented the program as an attempt to address the needs of a changing workforce. Build the People would promote "good human relations practices" for a workforce that would include "more blacks, more females, more young people." The program's title came from Robert Gross, who had said, "If we build the people, the people will build the airplanes."[40]

In the early spring of 1970, "every supervisory employee" was going over the Build the People course content with "his immediate supervisor." The program had started at the top with branch heads and percolated down through the organizational chart, with all supervisors working through the material with those just below them. The program's two booklets contained everything necessary for "each manager to conduct his own training in staff-type meetings." "Unlike sensitivity training so prevalent in industry today," Gordon explained, Build the People stressed the importance of setting reasonable, "tightly defined performance standards" and managing all employees according to those standards. The program should assist managers in "defin[ing] success in down-to-earth terms for all employees" and providing them with individualized help "to reach or surpass the minimum standard for each part of the job." Helping managers develop a "better understanding is embodied in the course material," Gordon observed, but the Lockheed approach was "rather subtle." The program sought to attach racial sensitivity as a low-profile rider on a vehicle that appeared to be principally about performance standards, and, Gordon reported, "early evaluations have been favorable."[41]

With Build the People, Lockheed addressed what Gordon had already identified as an ongoing problem with supervisors' racial attitudes. The program was implemented in 1970, a year before the Department of Defense institutionalized racial sensitivity training, which corporations and the government developed in part as a response to continuing public protests demanding racial and social justice, including those associated with the Black Power movement. As the opening paragraphs of the Build the People training manual asserted, "Lockheed believes that the solution of our country's social problems [is] part of industry's responsibility." According to the manual, "Lockheed believes that the right to work is meaningless without the opportunity to work and advance in that work."[42]

Each supervisor received a copy of the *Supervisory Awareness Manual*, which presented detailed instructions for creating performance standards.

Department managers also received *Build the People: A Manager's Guide*, which offered step-by-step instructions for instituting Lockheed's "rather subtle" approach to implementing affirmative action and improving sensitivity regarding workplace diversity.

The guide acknowledged that Lockheed managers probably believed that they now faced "two demands that conflict with one another": "the Government's demand that industry help solve the country's social problems" and the company's demand that managers "do the same or more work with fewer people." Despite couching the need for equal employment policies in terms of government requirements, the manual reiterated the company's commitment to such policies and cautioned managers against taking the view that social goals such as reducing discrimination were impractical in an atmosphere of declining employment and greater attention to efficiency: "Such an attitude guarantees that further demands will NOT be met!"[43]

Implicit in this formulation was the idea that although Lockheed—or any firm—might be able to operate efficiently without fully utilizing the productive potential of people of all races, society as a whole could not. The *Manager's Guide* asserted both that the government required action on equal employment opportunity and, perhaps more significantly, that Lockheed management accepted the need to create a nondiscriminatory workplace.

The key to Lockheed's approach was an old device in the personnel manager's toolkit, the performance standard. U.S. personnel managers, including those at Lockheed, had long used formalized performance reviews and other bureaucratic measures to standardize employment practices. In the 1970s, personnel managers realized that such reviews offered a way to respond to the federal government's equal employment imperative and insulate firms from lawsuits, as the use of standardized evaluations could provide proof that decisions had not been made for discriminatory reasons.[44] The *Manager's Guide* spread this idea through the Lockheed hierarchy, touting the idea that properly crafted, enforced, and detailed performance standards for each activity within the plant could solve both of the company's problems, both increasing productivity and promoting equal employment goals.

A separate *Supervisory Awareness Manual* for line supervisors then provided instructions for properly evaluating tasks and scientifically setting time and quality standards. In addition, supervisors were instructed to discuss and revise performance standards based on worker input. "*We meet the EEOC and top management demands,*" the manual declared, "*by giving* all our people the equal right to get out production according to the standard we apply equally to all in the same job."⁴⁵

According to the *Manager's Guide*, when managers established "one single minimum performance standard," they were "insuring equal opportunity" in their respective departments. When managers evaluated worker performance against the same standards, they guaranteed equal treatment. Managers could "eliminat[e] bias and prejudice" by "communicat[ing] what must be done for a person (any person) to enter the ranks of superior, high potential employees." And, the manual advised, when managers "communicate your agreement to give extra help to all those employees who are not performing up to standard or as high as they could, you are practicing affirmative action." The purpose of setting performance standards was not to speed up the weeding out of inefficient employees; rather, it was to offer guidance for managers in providing on-the-job extra training and advice for poorer-performing employees. Although disadvantaged (and potentially lesser qualified) workers might require more training and supervision, the company was committed to helping them meet the standards, and that help was offered based on workers' need rather than their race. Build the People shifted the emphasis away from mere EEOC compliance—that is, advising managers on what or what not to say or do in regard to race, gender, or ethnicity—and toward identifying positive, production-related goals.⁴⁶

Department managers bore primary responsibility for the program, and the *Manager's Guide* essentially provided a detailed but flexible syllabus for a course they would implement within their departments. "The program could have been designed so that each person would merely read his book, then sign a pledge saying he had read it and promised to do what it said," the guide's authors observed. But "all of us with experience in management know that would never work." The program's "two major concerns" were "much too crucial for us to give them lip service." Therefore, department managers essentially were required to conduct the training course, a strategy that the program's developers no doubt hoped would encourage those managers to take ownership of and buy into the program. It also meant that training department personnel crafted the program but would not conduct the training.⁴⁷

The guide optimistically stated that the program had "two features that almost guarantee that your supervisors become involved and take action": a series of staff meetings that would function as training sessions, and "homework assignments." The guide sought to "reduce the amount of planning necessary" to launch the program, but it would "not stand without" the managers. In addition, they were encouraged to adapt the program to the needs of their departments and tailor the presentation to fit their personalities and management styles. "The worst thing that could happen," the guide warned, "would be for a manager to read aloud or parrot the material in this book to his supervisors." Managers who liked "the thoughts in the manager's manual" should "put them into your own words and add your own thinking." The guide was "not a substitute for thinking—it is an aid, a spark, a generator for your own thoughts."[48]

The *Manager's Guide* also addressed why Build the People was necessary. Acknowledging that "there are some whites who do not like blacks," the manual declared that "management wants to change this situation, but realizes too that change must come from within the people involved." Though management could "create rules" and enforce compliance, "this does not create the kind of change it wants." However, the program's pragmatic, performance-based approach could provide "the basis for creating that change from within the people."[49]

Lockheed's strategy may well have been based on assessments by the training department (and upper management) that racial attitudes were deeply embedded within the psyches of white supervisors and workers and might not be amenable to alteration through sensitivity training. By focusing on productivity and urging managers to avoid trying to reshape supervisors' attitudes, officials sought to create an atmosphere where people managed by standards, not feelings. The manual encouraged an emphasis on the idea that "with performance standards, you can work people to the same standards, no matter what your feelings towards them may be." Even aside from factors such as race or gender, managing by emotion could lead supervisors to "have a different standard for each person and no one would know what their performance is measured by." In addition, a supervisor might inadvertently discriminate by "demanding too much of a guy I didn't like so I could fire him, and too little from the friend I admire so he'd go on liking me." And such discrimination took on a more ominous cast when race and other characteristics were added to the mix.[50]

Build the People instructed each branch head and department manager to lay out for supervisors "my performance standard for you all." It consisted of three elements, which managers were supposed to write on the board and discuss. First, supervisors would use rationally crafted performance standards "as the basis for managing." Second, they would apply those standards "equally to all people." Third, supervisors must "use no derogatory names, concepts, or phrases on any of our people at any time." By *derogatory*, the manual meant "any name or word by which the other man feels discriminated against": "HE determines what is discriminatory, YOU DON'T." Supervisors were to communicate with each employee "in words that *do not offend* him."⁵¹

The manual then offered suggestions for a general discussion with supervisors: "By now, Mr. Manager, some of your people may feel emotionally charged about 'Niggers are having the last word,' or some equivalent feeling. Here is where you both live and demonstrate your performance standard by respecting *any feeling they may express, but you define again that they can NOT use that feeling as a basis for managing or to belittle any worker*. You manage the situation, not the person's feelings."⁵²

The *Manager's Guide* then turned to how supervisors should develop performance standards. The productivity of lowest-performing workers should serve as a baseline for the creation of attainable goals, and those expectations had to be clearly communicated to all workers. The booklet included a page featuring a single sentence in all capital letters, intended to be posted prominently on a bulletin board near the work area: "WE CAN'T BLAME A MAN FOR NOT KNOWING WHAT WE HAVEN'T TOLD HIM!" The emphasis on this statement targeted African American employees' longstanding complaint that white supervisors did not make explicit their performance expectations and applied different standards to whites and blacks.⁵³

Build the People also included a few exercises that resembled sensitivity training. Supervisors were presented with three hypothetical situations and instructed to come up with solutions. Two of the situations did not mention race and involved veteran workers—an hourly employee who was also a union shop steward, and a professional employee—who had received a string of stellar performance reviews but whose recent performance had declined. These scenarios were intended to drive home the importance of meaningful standards and reviews.⁵⁴

The third case dealt with layoffs and African American workers: "Your work force is being cut back one person, and of the thirty staff people you supervise, one is Black." Further, "You have already surplussed the only other Black you had in the previous cut along with ten whites." The remaining African American worker was not only performing below established standards but was "'semi-militant,' i.e., Afro hair, comb, and talks about Black Power at every opportunity." This worker also regularly and loudly threatened to complain to the EEOC if he were laid off "because he has been given satisfactory to outstanding [ratings] in his reviews to keep him off your back."⁵⁵

By invoking the conception of the "bad Negro," this hypothetical maintained the focus on the importance of standards and managing to those standards but also opened an opportunity to explore supervisors' attitudes toward black workers. Despite his long history of work on behalf of equal employment opportunity, Hugh Gordon had evoked the same stereotype a few months earlier with his characterization of Lockheed's workforce as "normal," testifying to the continued potency of such images. Writing in *Ebony* magazine in 1963, Sarah Patton Boyle, a white dissenter from the southern racial orthodoxy, explained that "even while looking squarely at real Negroes," segregationists "could see only stereotype twin images of the Negro, one good, one bad—both false." And in his study of the 1965 Los Angeles riots, Nathan Cohen concluded that public statements regarding the unrest were "centered around the effort to distinguish between the 'good' Negro and the 'bad' Negro. A correlate" to this effort was "the belief that the riots are the work of outside agitators, 'riffraff,' or the 'mad dog' element of Negroes. A guessing game follows: What is the percentage of 'bad' Negroes in the population?"[56]

Treated with care by a department manager with an interest in exploring and debunking stereotypes, the third scenario could have been a valuable example. But given the prevalence of such stereotyping even among sympathetic human resource professionals, it is not clear that the hypothetical was used in this way. And the manual offered no commentary on the stereotype or guidance about how managers should act in such a situation, simply presenting it for discussion.

A few pages later, however, the guide book went against such stereotypes, using Gordon's data on dismissals to emphasize the falsity of the widespread rumor that supervisors could not and did not discipline African American workers and noted that "discipline, consistently applied to those unwilling to meet defined standards DOES WORK." Handing out harsh disciplinary actions in the form of notices, suspensions, and firings could work even in the absence of clearly defined standards and extra training, with remaining workers adapting to their supervisor. But the manual advised that the method laid out in the Build the People program was superior to the discipline-heavy approach. Supervisors should work closely with lower-performing workers, offering constructive guidance and extra training to help them meet clearly defined expectations, a strategy that was preferable to dismissal and hiring of new workers. "If a person is meeting the standard," the manual urged, "fine. Let's encourage that person to 'overmeet' the standard." But if a worker were not meeting the defined expectations, "let's give him an opportunity to become at least satisfactory": "*Equal opportunity here means to teach him all that the average and outstanding producers know and do. This 'equals' his opportunity for success."* In short, a hard-nosed disciplinary approach could work, but "GIVING THE MAN THE INFORMATION AND SKILLS HE NEEDS TO SUCCEED, WORKS BETTER."⁵⁷

In early October 1970, Gordon wrote a memo in which he offered some insight into his deeper views of the affirmative action/EEO enterprise. He had observed a "tendency" at Lockheed "to lump all blacks into the hard core category." Moreover, officials' use of language that referred to groups of blacks or whites as monolithic could "easily be misunderstood and can appeal to race prejudice." In response to officials who had questioned the human-relations-oriented focus of much of the industrial relations department, Gordon declared that he saw nothing "wrong with human relations training that teaches 'the virtues of personal interest, respect, [and] human values.'" Although Gordon admitted that he did not "know the 'right' approach" and that "maybe industry cannot be proud of its state-of-the-art training in human values," he thought it "fair to say much integration (and consequently much acceptance of Negroes by whites) has come about by leadership which says it's the law, it's social responsibility, it's good personnel policy, it respects human dignity, it's fair, it's *right*. In my opinion, we have come a long way in 10 years *on that approach*. It's easy to forget just how segregated we were in this plant a few years ago."⁵⁸

Gordon also pushed back against the assertion by some in management that it seemed necessary for white supervisors to view black workers "in an emotional way": "My own view is that what whites lack is a factual view of blacks which does not require that they be looked at 'in an emotional way.'" In that regard, Build the People "is the first major effort to deal with that side of the coin." But the program "is compromised heavily . . . until there is a combination of skill and desire to do a better job on what other companies address simply as 'race relations.'" He hoped that "someday we will be as skillful in 'conditioning' the redneck in human relations as we have been in 'conditioning' the hard core black in industrial environment and values." Despite the success of the hard-core training program, Gordon believed that training had not yet "reached its full potential in supporting corporate EEO affirmative action policies." Until it did so, "we will have to continue to rely heavily on management leadership."⁵⁹

CHAPTER 6

"The Competitive Economic Advantages of Having an Excellent Minority Hiring Record"

THE BANKS CASE AND ITS AFTERMATH, 1966-1972

The employment provisions of the Civil Rights Act took effect on July 1, 1965. Approximately eight months later, African American Lockheed employees began filing discrimination charges with the newly created Equal Employment Opportunity Commission (EEOC). Among the complainants were longtime workers such as Ernest Ross and Willie Elkins. More than fifty complaints filtered into the Atlanta EEOC office, headed by civil rights attorney Donald Hollowell, between March and December 1966. The agency began serving notice of the charges to Lockheed in September and continued through January 1967. The EEOC office reported its findings in September 1967.[1] The charges and investigation led to an addendum to Lockheed's original plan for progress, ongoing efforts to reach conciliation agreements with the complainants, and eventually to a lawsuit, trial, and settlement in 1972. Lockheed's voluntary efforts collided with the new compulsory provisions of the Civil Rights Act, while changing business conditions complicated the implementation of affirmative action strategies.

According to the EEOC's September 1967 report, Lockheed was "the largest defense contractor in the United States." The Georgia division employed 23,365 workers, of whom 1,463 (about 6 percent) were black, a far lower ratio than that of metropolitan Atlanta's overall population, which was 22.8 percent African American. Some employees alleged that they had been denied specific positions for which they were at least as qualified as whites who received similar promotions, but in essence, the charges boiled down "to the fact that Negroes, as a class, are not treated equally with whites" in terms of promotions among both salaried and hourly workers. Blacks held salaried positions in only 44 of Lockheed-Georgia's 366 departments. Meanwhile, "several thousand other salaried employees," none of them African American, worked in the many remaining departments. Overall, African Americans could be found in only 27 of 925 salaried job classifications within the plant. Blacks were represented in just 183 of 652 hourly job classifications and as hourly workers in only 115 departments. Even when counting just the departments that had black salaried employees, African Americans occupied less than 3 percent of such jobs. The complaints against Lockheed also targeted the International Association of Machinists, which now operated on an integrated basis but had no African American "officers, business representatives, or clerical personnel."[2]

The report detailed the company's promotion procedures. A Management Development and Selection Department had developed a "complex screening process." When vacancies for salaried positions occurred, department managers forwarded requests to higher-level managers, who in turn forwarded requests to the Management Development and Selection Department. The department then sent a list of what it considered qualified candidates to a Placement Committee, which would make a final decision, subject to the veto or approval of the department manager. In keeping with the original 1961 plan for progress, Lockheed "employ[ed] a representative to 'identify' qualified Negro candidates." The EEOC determined that at a minimum, this procedure needed significant refinement and enhancement.[3]

The Management Development and Selection Department screened candidates on the basis of "minimum educational level," "basic experience," and "performance reviews," but the company lacked definitive standards for minimum educational levels for many jobs, basic experience was judged capriciously by supervisors and committee members, and performance reviews seemed to reflect mostly intangible factors that were subject to wide discretion in interpretation. The EEOC's random sampling of white supervisors revealed that 80 percent had no more than a high school diploma. Of the twenty-one black complainants who sought salaried positions, a dozen had college degrees, while eight others had at least two years of college; only one sought promotion with only a high school education. Lockheed's management selection committees and department managers appeared to implicitly assume—as Harry Hudson and others had long alleged—that a high school diploma for whites was equivalent to a college degree for African Americans.[4]

The EEOC found that black workers had more difficulty learning about job openings than did their white counterparts: "Negro employees are not informed of job vacancies, knowledge of which is communicated by white employees to each other by word of mouth." Further, many white managers remained recalcitrant about promoting employment opportunity for black workers: one department manager "admitted that he considers Negro employees with long seniority generally less qualified for salaried positions." Company officials claimed that they "look[ed] for 'specific experience' in making promotions," but the investigation seemed to indicate that such experience was not made available to black candidates. Not surprisingly, therefore, management's attempts to find black candidates for promotion had thus far yielded meager results.[5]

Moreover, the evaluation process called for the judging of candidates on "vague criteria such as 'stretch'"—candidates' ability to work beyond their current job classification and to see the larger picture and the interconnections among crews and departments. Such judgments were subjective and highly sensitive to bias. There was also no guarantee that a placement committee would consider all candidates put forth by the Management Development and Selection Department. And even if a black candidate survived such scrutiny, department managers "have the final word on whether a candidate, agreed upon by the Committee as best qualified, will be promoted, and no check or restraint against possible bias on their part is provided" by the company.[6]

Hugh Gordon often spoke of "culture change" as perhaps the most important goal of equal employment policies. Implicit and explicit in many of his assessments both contemporaneously and in retrospect was a recognition that such change came hard and grudgingly. When African American Joseph Jones ran for office in the IAM local at Lockheed in 1965, one white opponent circulated literature that described Jones as "a bad reflection on his race" and criticized "mixing of the races." Jones complained to the company and the union that such language violated the antidiscrimination pledges and policies of both the company and the union. Lockheed declined to take further action, declaring that it did not wish to be perceived as interfering in a union election and that it had already reminded union officials of the company policy on the distribution of literature. But that reminder consisted only of a housekeeping-related admonition about leaving literature scattered about work areas; it did not mention content. Union officials, too, did nothing. In addition, black workers charged that shop stewards and union grievance screening committees simply would not process grievances from blacks concerning racial discrimination. As of July 1966, ninety-three grievances awaited arbitration, but "only three were filed by Negroes and none of these related to discrimination." The union's president had stated that he "was not very interested in non-monetary matters" and apparently believed that he had no need for "knowledge of Title VII" (the section of the 1964 Civil Rights Act that dealt with employment discrimination). The union's attorney "refused to recognize that, in fact, shop stewards act as agents of the union" and thus denied that the union needed to inform shop stewards of the IAM's antidiscrimination policies, citing an old southernism: the stewards were "free, white, and 21." Lockheed's culture clearly had not changed enough, and the EEOC found sufficient evidence to indicate that Lockheed had discriminated on the basis of race.[7]

As Timothy Minchin points out, early complaints under the Civil Rights Act at Lockheed and elsewhere were aided and often organized by the NAACP, which "spearheaded the fight to ensure that federal legislation was forcefully implemented. As the group's strategists realized, equal rights laws were not self-enforcing." Indeed, the NAACP had played a large role in helping organize pressure from workers to make the federal government and contractors live up to the spirit of antidiscrimination regulations from the beginning of Lockheed's occupation of Air Force Plant 6 in 1951; many of the complainants in the 1960s were active members of the organization's Atlanta chapter. The NAACP "dispatched Herbert Hill to Georgia to help the workers prepare their charges." Hill was already well known among Lockheed personnel department officials, including Hugh Gordon, having investigated discrimination charges at the Marietta plant at least twice in the 1950s and helped to organize the 1961 complaints that led to the initial plan for progress.[8]

In November 1967, the EEOC issued a decision on complaints by Ralph Banks and Kendrick Chamberlain, who had been among the 1966 complainants and who charged that Lockheed had retaliated against them for filing discrimination charges. Banks not only held a college degree but had earned some graduate credit. Lockheed hired him as a "bonded assembly worker" in April 1965 and moved him up to the next classification, "bonded assembly fabricator," seven months later. Both Banks's crew supervisor, David Turner, and the manager of the larger department, Harold Westbrook, were white. Turner was a high school graduate who had joined the company in 1962 and had been promoted to supervisor in March 1965, taking over Banks's cost center eighteen months later. Westbrook, too, had only a high school education. He had been with Lockheed since 1952, was a longtime supervisor, and received a promotion to department manager in 1966.[9]

In the late fall of 1965, Banks asked to take the management selection test, and he did so in December. According to Lockheed officials, Banks performed poorly on the test and for that reason received no serious consideration for promotion to supervisor. But Lockheed representatives also told EEOC investigators that Banks had taken the test again in the fall of 1966, and in October of that year, Banks had received a positive performance review declaring his "work satisfactory and his attitude good. He was rated 'outstanding' in demonstrated job knowledge and was commended for his 'ability to aid and instruct new employees.'" Indeed, Turner acknowledged that Banks "did a good job in the casting operation . . . knew more about the assignment than I did and was helpful in training new employees." Yet Lockheed officials including Turner and Westbrook insisted that Banks's attitude and performance had deteriorated steadily in the six months or so after he did poorly on the management selection test—in the fall of 1966. But, as investigators noted, Banks "took the Management Selection Test nine (9) months prior to the time Turner became his supervisor, and six (6) months prior to the time Westbrook became department manager. Also, the six month period ending October 21, 1966, for which the outstanding performance review was issued, was subsequent to the [first] time Mr. Banks took the test." Shortly after the performance review, Banks took a leave for medical treatment, and when he returned in mid-December, he was transferred to another position that involved somewhat more complex tasks. Thereafter, Turner and Westbrook alleged, Banks's attitude and performance had deteriorated steadily.[10]

According to Turner and Westbrook, Banks had requested the transfer because, as the commission paraphrased their remarks, "he thought his assignments were beneath him," and Westbrook had referred to Banks as a "colored boy." Westbrook also alleged that Banks displayed a "bad attitude" and "seems to want something he can fall into without any instruction or supervision." Managers and union officials claimed that Banks had taken five months to learn the basics of his new position, compared to three to four weeks for other employees. This inability to adapt "naturally" led to more intense scrutiny from supervisors and eventually resulted in Banks's return to his former position as a fabricator.[11]

Banks disputed his managers' statements that he had initiated the transfer request and alleged that he had been "given an unfamiliar work assignment" and was "bird-dogged," or constantly watched, and harassed after the transfer. Banks also insisted that white employees had taken as long as five months to learn his new job. Further, when Banks, Turner, and Westbrook had met to discuss performance issues and Banks's charges of discrimination, the department manager had used the term *persecution complex*. Westbrook acknowledged having used the phrase but argued that he had simply been trying to convey the idea that if Banks continued to cry discrimination at every turn, he would develop such a complex. Banks, however, insisted that Westbrook had used the term in an insulting fashion as a way to dismiss Banks's charges of discrimination. The EEOC found probable cause to believe that Banks had suffered retaliation. The investigator noted the absence of any documentation showing that three to four weeks constituted a typical training time for Banks's new job and reported that supervisory personnel had also told him that "the amount of training time is highly variable and subject to the discretion of individual managers and supervisors."[12]

Lockheed-Georgia had hired Chamberlain as a "wash rack attendant" in 1957. He was eventually moved into production work and held a number of classifications that involved machine operation, progressing to "Drill Press Operator A" by late 1966. In December of that year, after he had filed discrimination charges with the EEOC, Chamberlain became the first African American accepted into the tool inspector training program.[13]

Chamberlain satisfactorily completed the program's classroom component in mid-January 1967 and began the on-the-job training segment. Eight days into this portion of the training, Chamberlain fell in the plant parking lot and separated his shoulder. Both the company's physician and another doctor consulted for a second opinion recommended surgery to insert pins. After having the surgery, Chamberlain returned to work in early February, when the company doctor restricted his duties, ordering him not to use his right arm until a second surgery to remove the pins. Although this limitation prevented Chamberlain from doing some aspects of the tool inspector's job, training department supervisors allowed him to continue performing other aspects of the work. However, supervisors claimed that Chamberlain made too many errors and worked too slowly, leading to his dismissal from the training program and demotion to his former classification.[14]

Lockheed's supervisor of technical training told the commission that Chamberlain had a "defeatist attitude" and that it was "obvious ... that Mr. Chamberlain would not be able to complete the training. ... [H]e was bound not to succeed." He compared Chamberlain's likelihood of success to "the probability of 'an elephant learn(ing) to run a four-minute mile.'" At worst, here and in Banks's case, such references to the "bad Negro" stereotype certainly could be construed as evidence of discrimination. At best, white line supervisors, managers, and training supervisors had apparently done nothing to help the two men succeed and arguably actively undermined their chances.[15]

Chamberlain was one of only two employees to fail the on-the-job portion of the tool inspector program: the other was a white worker who had been placed in the program after filing a grievance through the union. Other than these two men, no one else had entered the training program "subsequent to filing complaints against the Company." In addition, the company had attempted to fire Chamberlain after he missed a week of work to have the second surgery, though personnel records showed that he had properly notified Lockheed about his absence. Even after acknowledging the error, management forced Chamberlain to file a grievance to retain his job. In the only other case EEOC inspectors found in which an employee's training had been interrupted by sickness or injury, J. T. Lawman, who was white, had missed about a month after been injured in an auto accident and had been allowed to return and begin his training again. Moreover, Chamberlain's demotion meant that as of mid-1967, none of the ninety-nine tool inspectors were African American. The commission therefore concluded not only that "Respondent's Tool Inspection training program, Tool Inspection Department, and Tool Inspector classification have traditionally been reserved for white employees" but also that they still were.[16]

As the EEOC investigation was ongoing in late 1966, Lockheed negotiated an agreement to expand its original plan for progress, announcing the additions to its equal employment program in the January 5, 1967, issue of the *Lockheed Southern Star*. The company characterized the new agreement as "Another First for Lockheed: Equal Opportunity Expansion." Lockheed's chair, Courtlandt Gross, and U.S. vice president Hubert Humphrey met in Washington to sign an "amendment to our Plan for Progress," presenting the agreement as a purely voluntary expansion of the affirmative action program. Lockheed had helped "conceive the idea" of Plans for Progress in 1961, Humphrey said, and "Lockheed is now saying it will do even more," setting "a splendid example for other companies around the country." Humphrey encouraged other firms to "examine the avenues that Lockheed proposes to explore in its future programs."[17]

The announcement made no mention of the EEOC complaints, though Lockheed would have been aware of them by this time, and it seems likely that some connection existed between the two. The announcement itself might have been part of the agreement, or the company might have been hoping to influence the EEOC's findings—a way of demonstrating that the complaints had been heard and were being addressed. Whatever the motivations behind the agreement, neither the *Atlanta Constitution* nor the *Atlanta Daily World* carried the news, and later in his life, Gordon either did not recall the agreement or did not think it significant enough to mention.

Lockheed's new commitments included a pledge to expand its community outreach. In 1965, under the auspices of Plans for Progress, Lockheed had helped to organize a program that targeted vocational guidance counselors at Atlanta-area high schools with significant numbers of disadvantaged and minority students. Going forward, this program would also send minority employees to schools to offer motivational speeches and provide materials publicizing minority employees' achievements.[18]

Lockheed also made a commitment to more tangible goals, pledging to develop "pre-employment on the job training programs to help disadvantaged applicants attain higher levels of education and training"—what ultimately became known as the hard-core training program (see chapter 5). The personnel department agreed to step up its counseling to help minority workers identify and take advantage of advancement opportunities within the company. The company committed to establishing cooperative programs that offered employment to college students for a portion of the year and to including minorities in summer youth employment initiatives, recruiting applicants from newly created federal programs such as the Job Corps. The company further pledged to "monitor job requirements and applicant selection procedures to make certain they are consistent with qualifications needed for expected work performance" and to "include in management training programs discussions of responsibilities of supervisors in carrying out equal employment opportunity policies"—in all likelihood the origin of Build the People.[19]

A separate article in that issue of the *Southern Star* announced the appointment of John H. "Pat" Patterson to the post of equal employment opportunity coordinator, apparently a new position. Patterson had joined Lockheed in 1952 and had become "one of the first Negroes promoted to supervision in Manufacturing Operations." Patterson was promoted to the quality assurance branch as an inspector in 1960 before moving to the personnel department, where he became a labor relations representative. Patterson had long played a leadership/advisory role among black workers, and Willie Elkins had observed in his 1961 complaint that Patterson appeared to have been delegated to speak with new black employees and counsel those who voiced dissatisfaction.[20]

A 1943 graduate of Atlanta's Booker T. Washington High School, Patterson had served in the U.S. Army during World War II, helping to conduct "aptitude tests for new recruits." Patterson had been stationed at Georgia's Fort Benning, a base that reflected the complex history of race and the U.S. military. It was the home of the first African American paratroopers, the 555th Battalion, which served with the U.S. Forest Service as fire jumpers rather than in combat to avoid potential negative responses from white paratroopers. Fort Benning was also the site of the 1941 murder of Felix Hall, the only known lynching to take place on an American military base. Patterson and other black veterans who had trained or served at Fort Benning nonetheless took pride in the shared experience and milestones achieved. Patterson attended the University of Michigan, earning a bachelor's degree in business administration before returning to Atlanta, where he began real estate and accounting businesses.[21]

Like many other African American Lockheed employees, Patterson was firmly ensconced in Atlanta's black middle class as well as exceptionally active in civic affairs. He served on the boards of the Butler Street YMCA, the Atlanta chapter of the NAACP, and the Atlanta Merit Employment Association, which Gordon had formed as part of the Plans for Progress initiative.[22]

As EEO coordinator, Patterson initially reported to the director of personnel programs, Win LeSueur. About eighteen months after Patterson took over the new position, LeSueur was placed on special assignment and replaced by Gordon.[23] For the next two decades, Gordon and Patterson worked together on matters related to equal employment, developing a friendship along the way.

These new programs did not, however, amount to a conciliation agreement with the EEOC, as is evidenced by the fact that no complaints appear to have been settled or withdrawn. Indeed, after the EEOC informed Banks, Chamberlain, and six other complainants that it had been unable to reach an agreement with the company to end discriminatory practices, the men filed a discrimination lawsuit against Lockheed in March 1968, with a ninth plaintiff joining the case three months later. The NAACP agreed to represent the Lockheed plaintiffs as part of a strategy to press the issue of affirmative action.[24]

In February 1969, Lockheed eventually reached a conciliation agreement with the EEOC and some of the complainants. Lockheed agreed to maintain promotional profiles of both hourly and salaried employees containing frequent updates on performance and promotion potential, create career counseling units, develop career plans for individual employees, and offer advanced and specialized testing. Perhaps most important, the company formed an industrial relations EEO Action Committee, and one of its "key functions" was "to review tracking charts on minority representation in various sub-categories and take steps as necessary to implement upward minority representation." By mutual consent, the company and the EEOC agreed not to publicize the deal or the number of complainants involved, and it is not clear whether any individuals received money.[25]

In April 1970, fifty African American Lockheed employees met for two hours "to discuss what they say is blatant racial discrimination at the Marietta facility," the *Atlanta Constitution* reported. Among the attendees was James Woods, an African American personnel representative, whose presence led to "a minor hassle." Though Woods argued that he "was interested in what is going on in the community," other attendees objected to his presence, probably fearing that the company had sent him to report on the group's membership and strategy and/or to influence the discussion by offering Lockheed's perspective. After the other attendees voted overwhelmingly that Woods should not be allowed to remain and he departed, the group heard from J. O. Wyatt, a representative from the Atlanta office of the EEOC who had previously worked for Lockheed and had been among those who filed complaints in 1961. Responding to heated criticism of the EEOC's glacial pace in investigating complaints, he explained that the commission's resources were quite limited: the organization's 1969 budget was only $6.5 million—almost comically low in light of the volume of complaints, which topped twenty thousand in fiscal 1970. Consequently, Wyatt emphasized, "legal action was the best anti-discrimination weapon created by" the EEOC. Even though the agency had no power to issue cease-and-desist orders and could not yet file lawsuits on behalf of complainants, the Civil Rights Act of 1964 had granted private individuals the right to sue, and EEOC findings of discrimination could be offered as evidence in these proceedings. Only a federal court, Wyatt argued, had the power to "enforce a quota system to insure that blacks will be hired."[26]

The group met again a month later, seeking "to get our part of the action" at Lockheed. Representatives of the NAACP, the Metropolitan Atlanta Summit Leadership Conference, and the Atlanta Urban League addressed those in attendance and pledged support for their efforts to combat discrimination. Lyndon Wade, the Urban League's youthful new director, warned the group "that Lockheed management would attempt to pick out a few people and satisfy their demands 'in an effort to diminish your struggle.'" Wade drew applause from the crowd when he promised to ask Whitney Young, the Urban League's national director, for help in pressuring Lockheed. The workers drew up a "manifesto of grievances" and agreed to send copies to Lockheed management, all members of the U.S. Senate and House, federal administrative officials, and national magazines.[27]

No trace of the workers' demands seems to have appeared in the national press. In the Atlanta area, only the *Great Speckled Bird*, an underground alternative newspaper popular within the radical community, devoted any more significant attention to the group or its demands. The *Bird*'s June 1970 issue carried the only extensive published account of the group, which called itself Black Lockheed Employees, a name that reflected the emerging identity politics associated with African American empowerment. The manifesto traced "Lockheed's hiring and promotion practices since the early 1950s" before turning to a critique of the company's implementation of the 1966 agreement with the EEOC. Moreover, as layoffs snowballed, "black employees are saying, in effect, that they are tired of being the main victims of the economic ups-and-downs caused by an imperialistic foreign policy and a man-versus-man economy at home." Topping the Black Lockheed Employees' list of demands: "(1) that black women be hired immediately (within 90 days); (2) that no black employees be laid off until Lockheed's employment ratio is equal to the racial population rate of metro Atlanta; and (3) that all black salaried employees who have been downgraded or laid off be reinstated in their salaried job classifications." The second item dramatized the zero-sum game that had emerged at Lockheed: with massive employment cutbacks, black representation could be increased only by taking jobs away from whites. The organization called for Congress to investigate these grievances and withhold future contracts from Lockheed until the company reached equal employment goals.[28]

Improving productivity was a vital consideration for Lockheed's managers at this time, and the emphasis on performance standards seemed calculated to help as much with trimming the labor force as with developing sensitivity on issues of race and diversity. In February 1971, Lockheed's corporate management in Burbank went against Lockheed-Georgia's history by appointing new leaders from outside the division. Both new president Robert Fuhrman and new vice president Larry Kitchen were veterans of Lockheed Missiles and Space, the defense giant's most successful unit, and both were rising stars. According to Lockheed historian Walter Boyne, the two men were brought in to right a sinking ship.[29]

Since receiving the C-5 contract in 1965, Lockheed had faced growing cost overruns, redesigns of significant portions of the aircraft, and production problems, and Fuhrman assigned Kitchen to fix these issues. Kitchen found the C-5 production line in complete disarray: "I'd go down and go through the fuselage . . . and could not see through [it]—it was jam-packed with people." He continued, "Some [workers] would be making initial installations and some would be making changes; behind them would be another crew, ripping out what they had done and putting in another change." When Fuhrman and Kitchen arrived, "there were over 20,000 people and production chaos." "Hatchet man" Kitchen "set to work paring the work force," and by 1975, when Kitchen left Georgia for the corporate office, "ten thousand people were employed on a rational production line." In 1969, Lockheed's profit margin had been only 3 percent, and over the next few years, the company recorded losses. But by the time of Kitchen's departure, profits had risen back to a healthy 9 percent.[30]

In the summer of 1972, top management redoubled its efforts to impress on all management personnel the importance of making a good-faith effort to implement the strategies for promoting equal employment. The issue took on increased urgency in part because amendments to EEOC regulations would now allow the commission to file lawsuits on behalf of complainants under certain circumstances. That June, Lockheed chair Dan Haughton sent a memorandum to all management personnel that signaled a change in the way high-level officials sought the cooperation of middle and lower management:

> Lockheed has for many years emphasized the compelling moral, social, and economic reasons for providing equal employment opportunity to all persons.
>
> We have also been aware of our legal and contractual obligations.

Haughton briefly summarized the recent changes to EEOC policy before exhorting supervisors and department managers to recognize and act on the realization that "our performance under" the affirmative action plans "is just as much a part of doing business with the government as attaining schedule, cost, and performance goals." Haughton reminded managers that "results are what count," implicitly sending the message that consistently missing targets and goals would complicate the company's attempts to show that it was making good-faith efforts to comply.[31]

At Lockheed's midyear corporate meeting in July, E. G. Mattison, now vice president for industrial relations for the entire Lockheed family of companies, delivered a tough assessment of its recent equal employment opportunity record. He opened with a cautionary tale from Lockheed Electronics's Tucson, Arizona, facility. The small plant employed fewer than 250 people but had been found wanting in its first EEO evaluation by a government contract compliance officer. This finding led to delays in two payments to Lockheed-California and might have had more dire consequences if the compliance office had not agreed to give Lockheed more time to respond. As Mattison told the assembled executives, "Non-compliance with the government's EEO contracting provisions at the smallest, most remote Lockheed facility could jeopardize all Lockheed government contracts." Consequently, all Lockheed divisions and subsidiaries not only had to have affirmative action plans but also needed to demonstrate "good faith efforts to achieve our projected results."[32]

Mattison also noted that the status of women would now be included in EEO reviews and warned of the need for "a reorientation of our thinking." Gender-based discrimination was so widespread that it was essentially invisible, he observed. And Lockheed had done deceptively well overall in minority hiring by filling the lowest rungs of the work ladder—jobs classified as *laborer*, for example, and the semiskilled categories. Suits on behalf of individuals or particular groups had been relatively rare, he reminded his audience, because potential complainants generally lacked the resources to mount serious legal challenges: the Banks lawsuit, financed by the NAACP, had been an exception. But with the changes that allowed the EEOC to file suit on behalf of victims of discrimination, "the legal resources of the federal government" would now be brought to bear against companies, undoubtedly increasing the number of lawsuits.[33]

Though "many people within Lockheed, and possibly some of you, think Lockheed has done an outstanding job in hiring minorities," Mattison bluntly declared, "I wish it were true." A government official had recently told Mattison that Lockheed was "not doing as well as some of" its competitors, an assessment that Mattison had confirmed via data obtained from the Southern California divisions of three of Lockheed's competitors. Lockheed had fallen behind in percentage of minorities in supervisory, salaried nonsupervisory, and clerical positions and led only among laborers.[34]

Lockheed did fare better in a comparison against sixteen other major corporations in a variety of industries for which Mattison had acquired data, placing sixth in minority representation in supervisory positions, second in terms of laborer jobs, and fourth in both semiskilled and skilled jobs. The company fell in the middle with regard to salaried nonsupervisory and office/clerical jobs. Beyond the statistics, Mattison knew "from personal experience" that "many other companies have black executives." Even "little Northrup," with "only 18,000 employees overall," had "a black lawyer and black assistant director of public relations." McDonnell-Douglas had "a black vice-president of administration in one of its California divisions." Some of these competitors had "taken imaginative and bold steps," seeking out "highly qualified blacks and other minorities." Lockheed must "do the same," he insisted, or risk being "viewed as a laggard instead of a leader."[35]

Doing so, Mattison argued, would require Lockheed to internalize the logic of affirmative action. The way forward most definitely did not include "rush[ing] out and hir[ing] people just because they are minorities." Rather, the company must "aggressively recruit minorities—and women—for all available openings." When managers identified candidates, "we must carefully see that whites—who actually may be overqualified for the job opening—are not always chosen over the minorities." There were "many qualified minorities, and women, but we must aggressively compete for them." In the light of history, managers would "almost always find in a given selection situation a white male who has more experience," but Lockheed had to take the bold step of promoting "some minorities and women who are qualified—but not necessarily the most qualified in terms of experience"; otherwise, "we will make little progress." The company must also work to advance minority workers and lower-level management personnel, citing the case of "one black supervisor" who had held the same position for almost ten years. Although his performance was good, he had remained stuck on the corporate ladder because his department had few promotions. Such employees should be identified and moved into "a line of progression" so that the company would have "more minorities at the department manager level," even if doing so necessitated a transfer to another division. Mattison's message echoed Gordon's words to a frustrated department manager who had objected that the personnel department was sending him too many black candidates and who was convinced there must be more qualified whites: "What about the last time when I sent you [all] whites? It's time to be moving along."[36]

Also in July 1972, North American Rockwell defeated Lockheed, McDonnell-Douglas, and Grumman in the competition for the multibillion-dollar contract to develop and build the space shuttle. Four months later, *Washington Post* journalists Thomas O'Toole and Leon Dash published an article on the inner workings of the bidding and selection process in which they reported that "the most interesting edge that North American had over its three competitors was in its approach to minority hiring." This advantage "figured importantly in the award of the shuttle contract." North American's relatively high level of minority employment was, however, a quite recent development. Just three years earlier, black workers had confronted top management about the lack of promotions, absence of blacks in middle and upper management, and other grievances.

The workers also filed EEOC complaints. Shocked, according to the reporters, North American executives worked out an affirmative action plan with the Department of Labor and took it seriously. A NASA official privy to the decision process remarked, "We're not crusaders for civil rights, but the fact that North American moved forward on this front tells us something about how this company is thinking ahead," particularly in terms of "labor relations."[37]

Mattison subsequently sought out and circulated some more detailed information on North American Rockwell's EEO status. North American's space division employed 6,316 people, with about 14 percent minority representation—360 African Americans, 354 Mexican Americans, 163 Asian Americans, and 26 American Indians. But the firm's real advantage over any Lockheed division came in the managerial and professional ranks, where North American had increased minority representation from near zero to 7.1 percent in managerial positions, with African Americans now holding 2.7 percent of management positions. Mattison concluded, "We have all been well aware of the possible economic penalties for not meeting equal employment opportunity goals," and the shuttle contract story "should emphasize to us *the competitive economic advantages of having an excellent minority hiring record.*"[38]

Ironically, Lockheed may have been at least partially responsible for North American Rockwell's EEO progress. In July 1969, North American's Dwight Zook, a special assistant to a company vice president, had asked Gordon for information about Lockheed's affirmative action plan. With the blessing of industrial relations director C. A. Jenkins, Gordon had outlined the steps in Lockheed's recently negotiated conciliation agreement with the EEOC, even though "we have not publicized our Conciliation Agreement by understanding with the Commission." While there is no way to know what effect the information had at North American, Zook's inquiry demonstrates that competitors recognized that Lockheed managers had relatively long experience with affirmative action programs and sought guidance from the procedures that the company had developed in conjunction with the EEOC.[39]

The Office of Federal Contract Compliance also changed its rules in 1972, requiring contractors to demonstrate plans to disseminate EEO policies to all employees, particularly managers and supervisors. Gordon helped to develop Lockheed-Georgia's three-step dissemination plan, which opened with a videotape presentation of Mattison's July 1972 talk. Step 2 was a ten-minute video of Lockheed-Georgia president Larry Kitchen addressing EEO policy specific to the Marietta location. Finally, branch (major division) heads would discuss the videos and review branch and department goals.[40]

Gordon gathered data, drafted, and helped edit the script for Kitchen's message, suggesting relatively strong statements and backing them up with data. He also included information on the space shuttle case. Kitchen opened his seven-minute video with a stern warning: "Failure to be in compliance cannot be excused by our layoff situation." He declared it "a practical business fact" that "the key element in getting compliance certification so far has been our performance against EEO goals and timetables." For the immediate future, three goals had to be met: targets for African Americans and women in salaried professional and technical job classifications; a continuation of the individual placement and career advancement advising service; and "minimum utilization targets" for minorities and women if and when "we have an employment turnaround."[41]

Then Kitchen got down to the nuts and bolts: "On a current basis, we are talking about providing opportunities for 83 Negroes and 123 females out of 4,000 salaried people." To "maintain fair representation," management committees "may make decisions to retain qualified but less experienced persons." Most of the personnel considered for retention under these circumstances had "already proven [their] capability." Moreover, "we are in the business of developing and advancing people." Retaining qualified but less experienced women and minorities among professional and technical staff might require extra effort but was "a basic part of our managerial responsibility." If cuts in these fields proceeded on a traditional basis, with experience playing a major role in layoff decisions, the gains already made would be lost.[42]

Kitchen then laid out those gains and losses. The proportion of African Americans in the Lockheed-Georgia workforce had risen from 6 percent in 1965 to 9.5 percent at the end of 1969, but subsequent reductions had reduced that number to 6.8 percent. And if anyone had questions "about the role EEO plays in government contracting, you should have been given an idea" by the shuttle story. Whereas minorities made up about 7 percent of North American's management and 12 percent of its professional employees, Lockheed-Georgia had a "2.12 percent overall minority representation in salaried jobs, 3.07 percent in supervision, and 1.79 percent in professional jobs." Viewers of the video might be surprised to learn that Lockheed-California "today has more black supervisors and managers and more black professionals than we have in Georgia, despite the differences in black population from which the work forces are drawn." In this atmosphere, Kitchen declared, Lockheed's "future as a government contractor may depend largely upon *your personal responsibility for* EEO *results"*—and his: "I also *will* do what *must* be done to meet our contractual obligations."[43]

In the fall of 1971, as Lockheed struggled to adjust to competitive conditions and to the EEOC's new powers, the Banks case moved to trial. In the discovery process, NAACP attorneys learned that Lockheed had conducted an internal self-study of its affirmative action programs in 1970. Prompted by a suggestion from contract compliance officer Kenneth Eppert, the company had appointed five or six survey teams to gather data, interview managers and workers, and assess the successes and weaknesses of Lockheed's program. The NAACP requested all documents related to the self-study, including the final summary and recommendations. When the company balked at turning over the report, U.S. District Court judge William O'Kelly ruled that it did not have to: equal opportunity employment compliance was "an important issue of public policy," and making the report available to the plaintiffs would, in O'Kelly's view, "discourage frank self-criticism and evaluation in affirmative action programs." All "factual and statistical data" developed and used by the survey teams was fair game and had to be turned over, but the conclusions drawn from that data by Lockheed's internal study teams were protected. The decision drew on a precedent from a 1970 medical malpractice case involving minutes of hospital staff meetings, but the case constituted the first time that the "self-evaluative privilege" was recognized in an employment discrimination lawsuit.[44]

With the self-study issue resolved, the Banks case finally went to trial in December 1971. In *Griggs v. Duke Power Company*, a decision released nine months earlier, the U.S. Supreme Court had found that testing and job requirements not related to job performance or business necessity violated the intent of the Civil Rights Act, and the NAACP lawyers challenged not only Lockheed's promotion and advancement procedures but also its use of a variety of tests.[45]

Called as a witness, Gordon provided testimony, filled with requests for clarification and responses that sometimes appeared deliberately to miss the point of a question, that often confounded the plaintiffs' attorneys. When asked about the departments and divisions that reported to him as personnel manager, he did not mention the equal opportunity coordinator's office, and neither side made any reference to Plans for Progress or the National Alliance of Businessmen (known after January 1979 as the National Alliance of Business), omissions that were striking in light of Lockheed's long history with these quasi-voluntary programs.[46]

NAACP counsel pressed Gordon on the relationship between job qualifications and the Wonderlic test and the Management Test Battery, both of which Lockheed had used, as well as on the issue of disparate treatment of white and black candidates and the composition of and criteria used by management selection committees.

Trial testimony from black employees reprised the charges from the EEOC complaints of Banks, Chamberlain, and others. Black workers "had been channeled to low-paying posts regardless of their qualifications," denied opportunities for advancement, and harassed when they complained. The criteria used by management selection committees were shrouded in mystery. At times, tests were administered to blacks but not to whites in similar situations. African American employees had been bird-dogged. At one point, "whites used a doll to enact a fake lynching." College graduate Lincoln Woods testified that when he had asked about the possibility of promotion, managers "just told me that the only thing available was a wash rack attendant or a utility worker."[47]

After several weeks of testimony, the trial recessed, and it remained in limbo for most of 1972. Lockheed ultimately reached a settlement with the plaintiffs before the judge delivered his verdict. The delay and the decision to settle were probably influenced by the deteriorating employment situation in the Marietta plant: on November 1, Kitchen announced that Lockheed-Georgia's employment was expected "to decrease from its present 12,000 to around 7000 by mid-1973. *It is my hope to stabilize at that figure.*" The C-5 was being phased out, leaving only limited production of various models of the C-130 at the facility. Beyond that, most of Lockheed-Georgia's work would involve modifying and upgrading existing aircraft, engineering and testing research, and subcontracting work. The era of declining military budgets and Pentagon spending had led to a "lull in the aerospace business," though top management hoped and expected that the outlook would improve after 1975. In the interim, the main goal was to maintain a "work base" sufficient to allow Lockheed to "emerge as a strong competitor for future business when it develops." The company remained determined "to *stay in business*, not get out."[48]

The memo—and particularly the anticipated decline to seven thousand employees—played a significant role in the settlement that ended the Banks case. In the settlement agreement, Lockheed agreed to "maintain and retain a sufficient number of black salaried employees in order that blacks will comprise at least 2.3% of its salaried work force." Further, Lockheed pledged to inform plaintiffs' attorneys at the end of any sixty-day period in which black employment fell below 1.8 percent. Kitchen and Gordon's subsequent emphasis on the importance of retaining as many African American supervisory and management personnel as possible reflected not only EEOC and Office of Federal Contract Compliance guidelines but also this agreement. If black salaried employment fell below 1.8 percent, Lockheed would supply the NAACP attorneys with the personnel records of all employees who had been recently laid off. However, in recognition of the precariousness of the company's situation, the percentage goals would "lapse during any period in which Lockheed's total employment is less than 7000."[49]

Lockheed also agreed to use its "best efforts" to ensure that blacks received a proportionate share of promotions into the salaried ranks. This goal was contingent, however, on Lockheed having at least eleven thousand employees, excluding training or temporary hires. Lockheed was quite certain to fall short of that number for the foreseeable future, rendering this pledge at best aspirational. In addition, Lockheed agreed to drop the Wonderlic test as a prerequisite for entrance into the apprenticeship program, another empty concession given that the apprenticeship program, always quite small, had recently been discontinued. The company also stipulated that it would not reinstate the Wonderlic test "for any purposes related to selection, promotion, or retention of its employees." Other tests of reading or mathematical ability remained permissible as long as they were correlated with specific job requirements, in keeping with the *Griggs* decision.[50]

The agreement called for an affirmative action program that included a number of things that the company was already doing. The company would actively recruit at African American colleges and graduate schools, publicize job openings in African American media outlets, solicit referrals from black employees and area organizations, and conduct further reviews of black employees in search of candidates for promotion. Lockheed pledged its "participation in area high school career days and black-oriented youth motivation programs." The nine plaintiffs also received a total of $160,000 in damages, a relatively paltry sum.[51]

On December 14, 1972, one of the plaintiffs, C. W. Hill, wrote to NAACP attorney Isabelle Gates Webster to detail "inadequacies of the proposed settlement." The agreement did "not address itself to the basic problem of segregation" at Lockheed, and the NAACP's monitoring would lapse in three years, not long enough "to provide adequate long-term protection or the plaintiffs." Hill also questioned the efficacy of the measures included for "the upgrading of qualified black employees" and deemed the financial settlement inadequate, "taking into consideration the amount of money that has been taken from black salaried employees through low salaries." Moreover, the NAACP was "not being adequately provided for." Hill and presumably other plaintiffs did not see the settlement as an unambiguous victory.[52]

The Banks case typified the challenges that confronted the NAACP's legal strategy. A large firm with deep pockets even in the midst of its difficulties, Lockheed was a formidable opponent. Even if the judge found in favor of the plaintiffs, appeals were certain and would be expensive and time consuming. After forty volumes of testimony and exhibits and nearly a year of off-and-on trial time and negotiations, the NAACP's legal team and the plaintiffs finally decided that even an imperfect settlement was preferable to continuing the legal ordeal and risking a negative verdict. Moreover, Lockheed was hardly the behemoth it had seemed when the complaints were originally filed in 1966, and a bigger victory would have carried little weight, just as the textile industry's decline somewhat diminished the significance of victories at J. P. Stevens, for example.[53]

More broadly, however, the case shaped Lockheed's EEO policies. The complaints had intensified the ongoing dialogue between company officials and government representatives. Though the threat of enforcement actions by the EEOC was minimal and lawsuits by complainants were difficult and time consuming even with the aid of the NAACP, Lockheed had to go through regular EEO reviews and submit plans, forcing management to devote time and effort to the issue. And the space shuttle contract had taught officials that failing to improve the company's EEO record could have concrete negative impacts. Members of Lockheed's upper management continued to learn by doing in the arena of equal opportunity, even if they still had difficulty persuading line managers and the bureaucracy to go along.

For some time after the Banks settlement, Lockheed presented a much lower profile as a litigation target. As Lockheed's designated equal employment leader, Gordon's activities brought him into closer contact with Atlanta's emerging African American political power. Lockheed and Gordon had brought the equal employment message to the broader community since the mid-1960s, and those efforts acquired even more importance in the 1970s and early 1980s as white business leaders confronted an increasingly restive black community.

CHAPTER 7

"Atlanta Will Be a Problem"
LOCKHEED-GEORGIA AND THE MEA, THE NAB, THE CETA,
AND THE EQUAL EMPLOYMENT CONUNDRUM, 1973-1982

Lockheed and Hugh Gordon played leadership roles in a pair of public-private partnerships from the 1960s through the 1980s that helped shape policies and business attitudes toward equal employment opportunity. National-level efforts associated with Plans for Progress (PFP), which had grown out of Lockheed's encounter with Executive Order 10925 in 1961, have been the subject of some scholarly attention, although local programs have not. Nevertheless, they represent an important part of PFP's legacy, at least in the Atlanta area. The National Alliance of Businessmen (NAB), conceived as a response to the economic dimension of urban unrest in the late 1960s, also developed significant local programs. Gordon was probably the single most active individual in establishing, maintaining, and promoting the expansion of PFP's signature local programming effort, merit employers' associations (MEAs), in the Southeast and beyond. Under the Nixon administration, the PFP's programs were merged with those of the NAB, and Gordon went on to organize NAB metros—local councils whose membership was often nearly or entirely coterminous with those of the MEAs. The metros were the key agents charged with implementing NAB's government-subsidized job training and hard-core employment programs. The overwhelmingly white business executives who controlled these programs clashed with emerging African American political leaders over the management of new, more generously funded job programs in the mid- to late 1970s, when U.S. macroeconomic and social policies took a neoliberal turn. Gordon helped lead the business community's efforts to rein in political control over these new programs and reassert the primacy of the private sector in such partnerships.[1]

Gordon outlined the origins of Atlanta's MEA at the annual PFP conference in Washington in January 1967. Georgia had just been through a tumultuous gubernatorial election. In 1962, a year after the compromise on school desegregation, Georgia elected a moderate governor, Carl Sanders, who encapsulated the emerging official consensus in the state around issues of race when he stated, "I'm a segregationist, but I'm not a damn fool." Sanders had stressed promotion of economic growth and acceptance and accommodation, if not enthusiastic embrace, of federal mandates. But, as James Cobb observes, "the old era was not quite over in Georgia." Lester Maddox, who had become infamous for "waving ax handles in the face of pickets at his segregated Pickrick restaurant" and campaigned as a diehard defender of Georgia's "traditional" way of life, defeated liberal Ellis Arnall in the 1966 Democratic primary. With Arnall waging a write-in candidacy, neither Maddox nor Republican nominee Howard "Bo" Callaway won a majority of the vote, throwing the election into the overwhelmingly Democratic Georgia legislature, which elected Maddox. Many observers feared that Maddox would attempt to hold back or reverse the tide of change.[2]

Gordon opened his talk with a brief reference to the election, joking that "it might ... be hazardous for me to speak to you about how we solve our problems in Georgia." But, Gordon reassured his audience, "the programs offered by the new Governor were ... generally conceded to represent progressive views ... hopefully in keeping with the progress we are making in Atlanta." Gordon's boss, Lockheed industrial relations director E. G. Mattison, was serving a year as a loaned executive with the national office of the Plans for Progress Advisory Council. PFP companies had participated in a vocational guidance institute in Detroit in 1964, bringing together high school guidance counselors and business leaders to discuss the pragmatic challenges in the employment of inner-city youths. Mattison and others in the PFP national office believed that the Detroit program could serve as a model for an Atlanta-area effort, and he directed Gordon to work toward setting up such a program.[3]

Gordon contacted colleges, business leaders, and school systems and hosted a July 19–30, 1965, seminar for high school guidance counselors and administrators on the "Employment Problems of Disadvantaged Youth in the City of Atlanta." Representatives of Coca-Cola, Lockheed-Georgia, Trust Company of Georgia Bank, Southern Bell, Mead, and Rich's, the Atlanta department store that had been targeted by sit-ins in 1960–61, participated in panel discussions, along with leaders from Atlanta's black—and white—institutions of higher education. Hobart Taylor, executive vice chair of the PFP initiative and adviser to President Lyndon Baines Johnson, addressed the meeting. Shortly thereafter, Gordon began pulling together the corporate sponsors as well as other local businesses to form an MEA, and in March 1966, he incorporated the nonprofit Atlanta Area Voluntary Merit Employment Association.[4]

The concept of "merit employment" in relation to equal employment opportunity dated back to the 1940s, when the American Friends Service Committee (AFSC) launched such a program. The concept bore some resemblance to the quiet strategy pursued by the Urban League. AFSC-affiliated "'merit employment' advocates put a lot of energy into symbolic hires of usually overqualified black workers," an approach based on the assumption that working with limited numbers of highly skilled and educated blacks would lead whites eventually to accept blacks as equals. The program's chief goal seemed to be to win the "hearts and minds" of local employers, but "the placement of token blacks in high visibility positions did little to change the stark realities of postwar black employment." This approach also failed to define *merit*, a fluid concept that allowed for a maximum of managerial discretion in interpretation.[5]

In spite of such weaknesses, the AFSC program persisted into the 1960s, establishing a number of local branches. In January 1962, members of the National Urban League, Atlanta Urban League, the AFSC, and the Anti-Defamation League met to form an Atlanta Merit Employment Coordinating Committee. The committee heard from a speaker on "Methods of Securing Equal Opportunities in Industries with Government Contracts." The AFSC pledged to provide information on firms in the Atlanta area that had government contracts worth more than $50,000. In early February, Tartt Bell, executive secretary of the AFSC's southeastern regional office, addressed the Hungry Club at Atlanta's Butler Street YMCA on the subject of merit employment. But the organization gained little in the way of public attention. The *Atlanta Daily World* published articles on merit employment with some frequency in the 1950s and early 1960s, generally using the term in much the same way as *equal employment opportunity*.[6]

The key difference between the AFSC's merit employment committees and those established under PFP auspices was membership. While the AFSC committees appeared to have been composed generally of members of reform-oriented organizations, the MEAs consisted of representatives from the business community. By January 1967, the Atlanta MEA had seventy member companies, a "large number" of which, Gordon reported, were "non–Plans for Progress companies." The members ranged in size from Lockheed, with twenty-five thousand workers, to a branch office of a national brokerage firm with thirty employees. The "membership dichotomy" of PFP and non-PFP companies had "both its pros and cons." Non-PFP companies were "quite sensitive about a need to maintain a local, more-or-less *independent* image in the programs we undertake and in our community, or public, relations." Gordon's statement implied that many firms wanted to avoid public connections to national organizations and the perception of outside interference.[7]

Gordon also reported to the PFP's national meeting about the Atlanta MEA's Vocational Guidance Institutes, Technical Assistance Committee (formed to offer advice to member and nonmember companies on implementing affirmative action plans), and Living Witness program, which Gordon may well have considered the group's most valuable programming. Twice each year, young workers from disadvantaged groups spoke to more than eleven thousand students at seven predominantly black Atlanta high schools, putting into practice the theory that "nothing gives the student more inspiration" than firsthand testimony from people of similar backgrounds. In the spring of 1970, about 180 workers participated, discussing the educational requirements for their jobs and responding to questions about "their personal employment experiences." By that point, more than sixty-five thousand high school students had taken part. Fifteen years later, a total of ten thousand motivators, more than 80 percent of them black, had spoken to upwards of six hundred thousand students, most of them from minority backgrounds, and the program, which had been renamed Youth Motivation Day, was "understood to be the oldest, largest, and longest ongoing motivational program of its kind in the United States." It was among Gordon's proudest accomplishments.[8]

In 1982, the NAB funded a study of the effectiveness of the program. Among the 822 student participants who went on to complete high school but received no further education, 410 had little memory of the program, while 113 recalled it negatively. In the words of a nineteen-year-old construction worker, the experience constituted "a waste of time." However, participants who had attended technical school or college or had earned college degrees were much more likely to have positive memories, as in the case of the twenty-year-old college student who recalled, "It was nice to see so many black people in jobs like those. We liked that part the best." But the study did not attempt to explain this correlation. The most successful students may have more effectively internalized the motivational message and used it as a springboard to further education, or they may simply have viewed the experience more positively in hindsight.[9]

The young workers who shared their experiences with the students also offered mixed responses, though none offered negative evaluations. Fifty-seven of the fifty-nine respondents who held only high school diplomas as well as ten of the thirteen with graduate school experience had positive views of the program. But of the forty-eight motivators who had four-year college degrees—the middle group in educational terms—twenty-eight expressed neutral views. Many of the workers found a one-day program simply too infrequent and isolated from the students' daily experiences to make much difference. As one man wrote, "If these companies neglect to hire and train these students once they finish, then I feel that this program is only a 'song and dance' routine. What black students need are more affirmative commitments [of jobs] and less talk."[10]

Gordon and the Atlanta MEA went beyond the vocational guidance seminars. In 1967, the Georgia Department of Education provided funding to set up the Occupational Information Center for Business and Industry, through which the MEA and its member firms provided summer work experience to counselors and teachers from inner-city high schools. This work experience was intended to enable the educators to go back to their schools and help their students prepare for actual jobs. Gordon saw these efforts as a public-private partnership that enabled schools and the business community to respond to mutual needs.[11]

Gordon traveled the South and occasionally beyond, evangelizing for equal employment plans. Speaking at a PFP seminar in New Orleans in 1966, Gordon reported that managers commonly expressed fear that if a company publicized the goal of hiring without discrimination, it would be overwhelmed with applications from unqualified minority job seekers. The reality, Gordon explained, was that "the best qualified Negroes tend to apply first for the jobs." Equal employment opportunity was "a human problem" that had to be "solved in a human way"; otherwise, "it will be done in a legalistic way." Gordon urged personnel managers to develop positive plans for affirmative action and cautioned that government intervention might accompany inaction.[12]

In February 1967, Gordon traveled to Richmond, Virginia, to encourage the formation of a merit employment group there. He argued that because the Civil Rights Act had effectively made merit-based employment the law of the land, "constructive action" (a phrase he underlined) was necessary. Gordon seemed to have made a conscious choice to use this wording rather than the term popularized by Executive Order 10925, affirmative action, but he meant the same thing. "Speaking for my own company," Gordon told his audience, "we don't cherish the idea of having minority members apply at our employment office only to be turned away because they are unqualified, because they have not seen the need for a high school education." Lockheed personnel managers "also don't feel comfortable in turning away minority members or anyone else who have a high school education but still don't have the necessary training or skills ... for work opportunities open to them, often even entry level training jobs." Gordon and his colleagues were "not satisfied as businessmen that a sizable segment of the Negro community is not in the economic mainstream of life. We are not sure the Negro community and others understand our position as employers on all these points, and consequently, the threat of poor race relations hangs over our heads." Gordon thus implicitly accepted the idea that many of the South's prospective black workers would be unprepared and unmotivated and that the business community needed to help with educational and motivational efforts.[13]

In April 1968, Mattison clearly stated what he saw as the ultimate purpose of such programs. After reading the Atlanta MEA's second annual report, Mattison viewed the organization's actions as "a good example of what the right amount of good will and determination can do to bring about the genuine cooperation of the real business community in solving one of our major national problems." Gordon's "efforts to build" the MEA had brought "great credit to Lockheed and yourself, but more than that, you and your colleagues in the MEA have made a lasting contribution to Atlanta and all its citizens, black and white." When H. L. Poore, the production supervisor who had told Harry Hudson that no African American could function as a department manager at Lockheed-Georgia and now the man in charge of the company's C-5 program, saw the annual report, he thought it "Great."[14]

Such efforts appeared increasingly insufficient by the late 1960s. The stylized narrative of the U.S. civil rights movement moves from peaceful protest for inclusion in the 1950s and early 1960s to more radical demands for economic equality in the second half of the 1960s. As the U.S. economy lurched toward a crisis point—more demands from more groups for a larger share of the fruits of economic growth—even mainstream consensus liberals like Dr. Martin Luther King Jr. demanded much more vigorous actions than those that formed LBJ's War on Poverty. The proposed Freedom Budget was just one of those efforts.[15]

In the wake of the Detroit riot and others in the summer of 1967, President Johnson appointed the National Advisory Commission on Civil Disorders (generally referred to as the Kerner Commission), which famously concluded that the United States was "moving toward two societies—one black, one white—separate and unequal." But rather than making a massive financial commitment to new programs, LBJ chose to devote limited, targeted funds to private-sector job training, primarily through the NAB. Most members of NAB metros opted to pursue noncontractual programs geared to finding jobs for what were commonly known at the time as the "hard-core unemployed." Such efforts were unverifiable: companies could devise whatever "fictitious numbers" they wanted for their "voluntary pledges," garner positive media coverage, and avoid the paperwork and potential intrusions of a government contract.[16]

Gordon's work with NAB brought him into contact with a wide array of personnel professionals, including Detroit native Richard Drabant. After spending two years at the University of Michigan in Ann Arbor, Drabant went to the university's Dearborn campus for a co-op program with Ford, becoming the company's youngest line foreman while earning a degree in business administration.[17]

While growing up in the Detroit suburbs, Drabant knew "no people of color," and virtually the only African Americans in his college classes were scholarship athletes. But the resident adviser in Drabant's dorm was African American, and he provided "civil rights literature upon request" and discussed such issues with Drabant, influencing much of his later life and work. In 1966, Drabant left Ford to enter Chrysler's two-year management training program, which included evening graduate courses that led to a master's in business administration. Drabant's group of twenty-five trainees included "two or three blacks," one of whom became a friend of Drabant's. His relationships with these two African American men taught him that segregation was as much a northern phenomenon as a southern one.[18]

In the late 1960s, Drabant became involved with a civil rights group promoting open housing in the Detroit suburbs, an experience that left him "discouraged" and "battle weary." Drabant and other members of the group conducted a 1968 survey of white attitudes toward housing integration that seemed to show some improvement in white attitudes, but many householders refused to respond to the door-to-door survey. In addition, written comments included "I'd probably shoot 'em" and "I wouldn't have the courage to sell [my house] to a Negro," though other respondents were more positive, declaring, "The soul has no color." The experience left Drabant "bitter about suburbia," "sick and tired of the mentality that sees crabgrass as Public Enemy Number One," and considering moving into the city itself.[19]

After completing the training program, Drabant joined the personnel department at Chrysler's Highland Park machining plant. It was a "fascinating experience." The workforce of thousands had only three black foremen and one black department manager. The skilled trades workforce was

90 percent white, while the unskilled/semiskilled workforce was 90 percent black. Consequently, "if an assembly line with all black workers went down, . . . white skilled workers . . . would come in to fix it."[20]

Drabant moved into Chrysler's training department in 1969 to work in the automaker's version of the NAB Hire First program. Contracting companies could hire the hard-core unemployed, with the NAB using its federal funding to pay their training wages as well as to subsidize wages for a time thereafter. Plant employees labeled the program *hard core*, "stigmatiz[ing] the program" as benefiting a group that "was referred to throughout the corporation as people you would not hire." Upset about this poor image, Drabant identified the job qualifications of the hard-core people who were rejected at the plant gate as well as of the non-hard-core who were accepted and found "not much difference at all. But there was always somebody with a university degree who wanted to buy alarm clocks for the hard core to help them get up on time." Program participants faced intense scrutiny and the expectation that they would fail because they lacked the work ethic or cultural values that would support regular attendance and quality work. In Drabant's view, the Hire First program offered "the kind of training that should have been provided to everybody who went to work at Chrysler," and participants consequently developed a lower turnover rate than plant-gate hires. The training included explanations of the plant rules and their history and hands-on training with full opportunity to ask questions. Participants ultimately entered the workplace with at least rudimentary knowledge of processes, tools, and materials, so that "even if they went to work for a bigoted, 'Let's wash 'em out in 90 days' mentality foreman, they could succeed because they knew more about the job than the person working next to them." Some of "the more enlightened plant managers" adopted aspects of the training, but making such training universal proved too expensive in the absence of NAB funding.[21]

Impressed by Chrysler's program, NAB leaders invited Drabant to spend a year in Washington as a loaned executive. Chrysler agreed, and Drabant became NAB vice president of disadvantaged and support programs. He hit the "rubber chicken circuit," selling NAB's training mission to business groups around the country, extolling the virtues of NAB seminars and its jobs program. He had expected to be working on "the promulgation and expansion of contract programs" like Chrysler's but instead discovered that "the preponderance of the NAB effort across the country was voluntary" and that "a lot of locales and companies wouldn't even touch contracts" because they "viewed them as difficult, red-tape ridden."[22]

"Convinced that contractual programs were the only way to go," Drabant criticized Ford and General Motors during the 1970s, labeling them "gutless" for refusing to initiate contract programs.[23]

NAB metros also cooperated, or were expected to cooperate, with other federally funded, locally administered job training/employment programs such as those conducted under the Comprehensive Employment and Training Act (CETA). Beginning in 1973, CETA provided federal block grants to state and local governments to hire and train workers in public jobs with the long-term goal of moving the workers into the private sector. The program also funded summer jobs programs for disadvantaged youth, classroom training programs, and on-the-job training within the private sector. By the end of the 1970s, CETA had become the largest federal job training program of the post–World War II era.[24]

Just as Congress enacted the CETA legislation, Maynard Jackson won election as the first black mayor of Atlanta—indeed, the first African American mayor of a major southern city. Atlanta's African American population was booming, and between 1955 and 1973, the number of black students in the city's public schools rose from just over thirty thousand to about seventy-five thousand, while the white student population fell from just over sixty thousand to a little more than twenty thousand. "White flight" profoundly reshaped the city's politics in the 1970s. William B. Hartsfield and Ivan Allen Jr. had presided over political coalitions that included the business leaders and upper middle class of both races, increasingly accommodating rising black demands for representation. In 1969, Sam Massell, a successful real estate agent and a liberal, was elected the city's first Jewish mayor, while Jackson won the post of vice mayor. In 1973, the thirty-five-year-old Jackson challenged Massell for the city's top post and won.[25]

The civil rights movement had played out through the 1960s against a backdrop of white racial anxiety, which manifested in Lester Maddox's 1966 gubernatorial victory as well as in white flight. Such anxiety was also evident at Lockheed, with its dwindling workforce and management efforts to protect at least some of the black progress of the 1960s.[26]

In this atmosphere, Mayor Massell visited the Butler Street YMCA's Hungry Club in October 1971 and urged black leaders to "THINK WHITE"—a phrase that the *Atlanta Daily World* printed in capital letters to reproduce Massell's emphasis. The mayor argued that the time had come for "blacks to learn the needs and fears of the whites if we are to mutually benefit from co-existence." Otherwise, white capital would follow white homeowners out of the city, leaving behind an empty shell, Massell observed, echoing NAACP executive director Roy Wilkins's statement that white flight nationally threatened to leave black politicians holding office in "shells of cities."[27]

Massell's appeal implicitly invoked the "good Negro"/"bad Negro" dichotomy. Although the moderately conservative *Daily World* cautiously agreed with the mayor, most black leaders preferred former SNCC activist John Lewis's argument that black Atlantans "should have an interest in controlling this city. We are a majority of this city, and we should control it." And African American alderman Henry Dodson responded that "thinking white" was not necessary: "I can think black and get along in this society."[28] That idea, however, was precisely what management officials at Lockheed and at other U.S. corporations feared as a disruptive force.

Massell returned to these themes in a September 1972 speech at Emory University. In "From Fear to Eternity," a title almost certainly chosen by the mayor himself, he doubled down on his earlier remarks and signaled a main theme of the upcoming campaign: "The young, the poor, the black have a heavy responsibility. Adjustment to the use of rights long denied is in and of itself taxing of mind and body, but conquering that alone is not enough. Those who move into formerly forbidden territories must take care lest they rush the entire structure.... If you are black and have become powerful, you must be able to think white to understand their needs. To do less will destroy all that has been gained by the struggles up to this point." The speech drew virtually no coverage in the Atlanta media: Massell gave a major speech on the topic of crime the same day, and two Atlanta television stations carried it live, while the other two showed it on tape delay. Neither the *Atlanta Constitution* nor the *Atlanta Daily World* printed any references to the Emory speech, but both papers printed stories on the crime address. But although crime initially appeared more salient, the issue of black political control and African American sensitivity to white concerns dominated the 1973 mayoral election.[29]

As the campaign neared its conclusion, Massell came closer and closer to simply echoing the fears of the city's middle-class whites, on one occasion telling an audience, "One can almost see them dancing in the streets in anticipation of a black takeover." A Jackson victory, he warned, would lead whites to "flee the city in greater numbers, and 'real estate would really drop to the bottom.'" Massell's campaign slogan summed up his message—"Atlanta—Too Young to Die." For his part, Jackson positioned himself as the candidate of both the black poor, advocating increased city investment in services to impoverished neighborhoods, and the black upper and middle classes, promising "a proportional share of political and economic power" for the black elite.[30]

Massell had previously been an ally of the black community in many respects, and he, like many other whites, was no doubt truly taken aback by what he perceived as the speed with which change had come, genuinely fearing the economic and social disorder that might follow black ascension to power. Not surprisingly, however, the African American community had a vastly different perspective.

Jackson won the nonpartisan city election with 60 percent of the vote, winning support from 95 percent of black voters and 18 percent of whites. Jackson set about trying to fulfill his promises to the black poor. He proposed raising city taxes by about $6 million to improve services, but the city council rejected this proposal. Jackson then "redirected" federal community development block grant funds "toward revitalizing the city's poor black neighborhoods, including housing construction and rehabilitation, improving sanitation, street maintenance, recreation facilities, and social services." Jackson also engaged in a long and politically costly fight to replace the Atlanta police chief over issues of police brutality, responding to the concerns primarily of inner-city African Americans. The mayor's "bold city leadership, weighted toward the concerns of poor local blacks," "brought a hostile response from the city's white business elite and their allies throughout" 1974.[31]

CETA, like the community development block grant initiative, was a federally funded but locally administered program that seemed to offer a perfect tool for aiding poorer blacks through job training and public employment. Gordon and his local NAB organization also had an interest in CETA, and the new city administration and NAB came into contact and eventually conflict.

The NAB and Gordon played a major role in revising the CETA program in the late 1970s and early 1980s. Many people within the business community came to view CETA, "hampered by accusations of mismanagement" and "subject to charges of fraud and abuse," as a tool primarily used by local politicians as a boondoggle to reward supporters. Few CETA jobs involved meaningful work experience, and even fewer led to jobs in the private sector. Gordon's personal experiences with the program reinforced his conviction that despite CETA's laudable goals, it was not even coming close to achieving them.[32]

According to Gordon, at a late 1977 Labor Department briefing, one official observed that CETA was not working for jobs in the private sector, to which Gordon responded, "You know, we need to do something about that.... The legislation needs to be changed." When the official noted, "Well, you know, we can't change laws just like that," Gordon replied that the Carter administration already had "people over there right now that are working on amendments to CETA." The law was up for renewal in

1978 and faced an uphill climb. NAB leaders, others in the business community, and conservatives had become deeply dissatisfied with the program's emphasis on public employment and with its corruption. Atlanta-area media had begun reporting allegations of widespread theft of CETA funds by low-level administrators, former workers receiving checks long after their employment ended, false and exaggerated work hours, and other abuses. Eleven city employees eventually were indicted for embezzling or misapplying about $31,000 in CETA funds, but tales of much more extensive malfeasance circulated widely.[33]

Atlanta's CETA director, Aaron Turpeau, nevertheless defended the program and attested to its value. In March 1978, as the Carter administration and NAB prepared to introduce significant changes to the program, Turpeau told an audience that "over 35,000 Atlantans have been either trained or employed under CETA." While CETA had placed about forty-five hundred workers in private-sector jobs following training, the bulk of the program's beneficiaries worked in the public and nonprofit sectors. The Atlanta Police Department, for example, used CETA workers for parking enforcement. The Atlanta public schools and the Chamber of Commerce also numbered among the 160 agencies and nonprofits that utilized CETA workers. Turpeau also observed that "the Bureau of Cultural Affairs is really staffed by CETA." That agency was among Mayor Jackson's signature innovations, providing government support and funding for art projects in public spaces, outreach programs for schools, and more.[34]

The Jackson administration and Turpeau saw CETA as playing a vital role in providing public employment to disadvantaged groups and enhancing the city's ability to provide services to its citizens. Later studies, however, offered mixed reviews of CETA's effectiveness. Atlanta's deputy CETA director, H. Wynn Montgomery, argued that the private-sector job training opportunities contemplated by the program's architects required close coordination between local government and the business community, yet businesses were slow to participate in CETA job training programs. A late 1973 recession caused unemployment to nearly double from 4.8 percent to 9 percent by March 1975, meaning that qualified workers were available and thus limiting interest in a major new training program. The business community's less-than-enthusiastic response reinforced local officials' commitment to the public-employment mandate, which many saw as urgent.[35]

Jackson's election threatened the close business-government collaboration that had characterized Atlanta since World War II. Jackson was an outsider, a relative unknown who came into office with a progressive agenda that included controlling development, affirmative action, and black political empowerment. Jackson struggled to gain business support because he and many of his administration's top staffers (including Turpeau) were not members of the governing elite and did not favor the traditional Atlanta strategy of negotiation and compromise. The emergence of a tangible representative of black political power with an agenda that included some significant redistribution of economic resources clearly changed the game. Despite its shortcomings, Jackson's affirmative action program certainly redistributed jobs and contracts to minority workers and businesses, dramatically altering Atlanta's status quo.[36]

The easing of the recession after mid-1975 led to increasing calls from the national business community, led by the NAB, to reform CETA to deemphasize public employment and increase on-the-job training, shifting funds toward subsidizing private-sector employment. In fiscal 1977, CETA had more than 550,000 public-service employees and more than 536,000 people involved in classroom training totaled. In contrast, only 176,000 participants were engaged in on-the-job training, most of them in the private sector. NAB aimed to reverse those numbers. The move to reduce public employment fit nicely with the budding deregulation movements in Congress.[37]

NAB leaders were looking for ways to revitalize their program, and business leaders sought to return to an emphasis on private-sector initiative similar to the PFP approach. NAB had begun as a public-private partnership, but the agency's Job Opportunities in the Business Sector program offered a subsidy of only around $800 for hard-core hires, which simply did not offer businesses enough incentive to participate. Moreover, whatever tepid enthusiasm had existed for NAB's training program all but disappeared during the recession of 1974–75. In the interim, CETA's government and nonprofit managed training programs and large public-service employment initiative seemed to push the private sector to the sidelines. Reforming CETA and gaining a seat at its table for NAB offered the prospect of influencing the greater funding available under the CETA umbrella.

As the Carter administration prepared for the fight to reauthorize CETA, the NAB president asked Gordon to put together a task force to draft proposed revisions. Gordon assembled a team of personnel managers with whom he had worked in NAB-related activities over the preceding decade and devised suggestions for reforming CETA's job training offerings under the rubric of the Private Sector Initiative Program (PSIP). Under the reforms, CETA prime sponsors (generally, as in the case of Atlanta, municipal governments) were required to form private industry councils (PICs). A majority of the members of each PIC had to come from the private sector, as did the chair of the PIC. The PICs would gain substantial control over the block grant funding for job training.[38]

NAB executive vice president Matthew Coffey sent a copy of Gordon's NAB proposal to Lockheed-Georgia president (and NAB board member) Bob Ormsby in March 1978, as Congress prepared to hold hearings on CETA reauthorization. Coffey reminded Ormsby that at its most recent board meeting, the NAB had "directed the staff to expand its existing efforts and work with the Administration in shaping the President's new $400,000,000 Private Sector Initiative Program." "In agreeing to our request for an expanded voluntary" private-sector on-the-job training program, the Carter administration "has also asked NAB to play a leadership role ... in developing local business-led councils that would plan and approve employment programs such as on-the-job training," the crucial step in moving the unemployed from public employment to the private sector.[39]

That same month, Gordon wrote to Ormsby to elaborate on some of the details of the new CETA guidelines. The Labor Department had accepted the majority private-sector representation for the PICs but had insisted that prime sponsors appoint the PIC members. The guidelines strongly suggested that NAB metros, where they existed, should form "the core of support" for the new PSIP and its PICs. Lobbying efforts continued, Gordon told Ormsby, though NAB officials had "made progress but not obtained NAB autonomy in setting up local Private Industry Councils." In many cities where "strong local business manpower programs exist," the influence of prime sponsors would not be a problem. But, Gordon cautioned, "Atlanta will be a problem. Unless something is done, Maynard Jackson and other public officials would appoint and control the PIC. Knowing this, I set up a meeting last week with Jesse Hill/Tom Hamall of the Chamber and Jack Fitzpatrick/Matt Coffee [of NAB]. NAB agreed to fund a full-time Metro director and the Chamber is very interested in taking a leadership role." Gordon had proposed the creation of a nonprofit corporation, the Private Industry Council of Atlanta, and had already arranged for an official group of past Chamber of Commerce presidents to consider the proposal.[40]

According to Montgomery the most important change wrought by the PSIP was that "unlike existing CETA advisory councils that are empowered only to make recommendations to Prime Sponsors, the PICs have joint planning and approval power." That is, the PICs, which would be dominated by the business sector, would have veto power over any proposal from prime sponsors to spend money on training programs. The PIC also had the "right to review and comment on all other parts of the Prime Sponsor's annual CETA plan," although the council would not have a veto in this area. Montgomery characterized these provisions as "the first real effort to establish a partnership," albeit limited, between prime sponsors and the private sector. While authority would be shared, "accountability remains solely with the prime sponsor." In other words, while the private sector representatives on the PICs could agree to allocate or refuse funds for any proposal, the prime sponsor—in Atlanta's case, the mayor's office—bore full responsibility for management of funds. Montgomery noted that the U.S. Conference of Mayors had objected to this portion of the reform, declaring that it "contradicts all notions of sound management." In addition, the PIC members would elect the chair, heightening the contradiction. In essence, business groups would control the programs and distribution of funds, but municipal governments would suffer the consequences if programs failed or if funds were mismanaged.[41]

Congress did not act on the CETA reforms until October 1978, but the Department of Labor, confident of passage, moved forward in May to urge the formation of the PICs and used contingency funds to give thirty-four prime sponsors, including the city of Atlanta, $25,000 planning grants to fund pilot activities. Congress eventually approved the changes but provided no funds, and the Labor Department doled out additional $25,000 planning grants. Prime sponsors, however, felt little urgency to move before more substantial appropriations were forthcoming.[42]

Atlanta used its planning grants to improve the connection between public-service employment and the private sector by establishing a job referral service for persons leaving the employment program. Nevertheless, further coordination between the city and the private sector was severely limited as a consequence of what Montgomery labeled "a lack of mutual understanding and, in some cases, respect." Atlanta's CETA officials had "made several pre-PSIP attempts to increase private sector involvement," including the 1974 formation of a Labor Market Advisory Committee made up principally of business representatives. "Several meetings made it clear," however, "that declining business conditions were not conducive to business interest in training programs." CETA staff members increasingly focused on the rapidly growing public-service employment component, and the Labor Market Advisory Committee "atrophied," "disillusion[ing] Prime Sponsor staff." Though staff members acknowledged that they bore some responsibility for occasional failure to "follow through," they developed an impression that the business community was disinterested.[43]

The lack of business involvement in CETA also meant that "the Atlanta business community knew very little about" the program. With the "negative publicity" surrounding the program and the charges of mismanagement and corruption, along with a more generalized revolt against the public sector, especially programs that appeared to serve minorities, CETA cheaters took on something of the aura of the "welfare queen," a term popularized by Ronald Reagan in 1976. "Thus," Montgomery observed, "the situation in Atlanta was not conducive to establishing a public-private partnership."[44]

Into this less-than-ideal situation, Gordon and others within the Atlanta NAB metro tossed an incendiary device. "Prior to the award of the initial planning grant" in June 1978, Gordon contacted Turpeau "and advised him that an organization, the Private Industry Council of Atlanta, had been incorporated to administer NAB activities." Given the name of the new body, Gordon "suggested that this organization should serve as the City of Atlanta's PIC." Not surprisingly, "this offer was greeted with less than enthusiasm by CETA staff." Gordon and his NAB colleagues had blindsided Turpeau and the mayor's office. Though the Carter administration expected the NAB to play a "leadership role" in the PSIP, it was not a requirement, and the Atlanta NAB metro had formed a PIC and selected the private-sector members without consulting with the prime sponsor. Turpeau was outraged that NAB had jumped the gun and seized control of the new body.[45]

Turpeau and the mayor's office pointed out that the membership of the new PIC violated the mayor's policy that required all members of advisory bodies to his administration to reside within Atlanta's corporate boundaries: Gordon and a few other members of PIC board lived in the overwhelmingly white suburbs. Despite their protests, however, city officials had no power to force changes to the board, and Jackson reluctantly revised the policy. Though a few changes were made to the PIC board, Gordon and the NAB had made their point. Business influence had helped change CETA. The local business community, leveraging connections with national business organizations, the Labor Department, and the emerging conventional wisdom about government waste and private-sector efficiency, had established control.[46]

By the time the CETA reforms were enacted, however, Jackson was well on his way to reaching an accommodation with the business community, as evidenced by the changes that took place between a 1970 strike by Atlanta's sanitation workers and another one seven years later. When the city's mostly black sanitation workers, represented by the Association of

Federal, State, County, and Municipal Employees, went on strike in 1970, Mayor Massell fired them and Jackson vociferously defended them. After thirty-seven days off the job, the workers were rehired but failed to get the pay raise they had demanded. When the workers struck again in March 1977, in the midst of Jackson's reelection campaign, the mayor acknowledged that they "need a pay increase. The employees deserve a pay increase." But, he said, "we don't have" the money. Union officials and several city council members disputed that assertion, claiming that the city's finances were strong, property tax revenues had exceeded expectations, and several million dollars could be redirected to the sanitation workers from other city agencies and the massive project to construct a new airport. That endeavor was Jackson's signature achievement, blending affirmative action and minority set-asides that aided black-owned businesses with his commitment to making Atlanta more attractive for business.[47]

According to a *Washington Post* article, "There are some close to Jackson who agree the mayor could try to" scrape together the funds. "But they argue that the politics of the city, including strong antiunion feelings, the possibility of a 12-to-6 defeat by the city council on requests for money transfers, and howls of protest from Atlanta whites if airport or water funds are tampered with, make those choices even less acceptable politically." Jackson instead fired the strikers, just as his predecessor had. Union officials pointed out the irony, which was not lost on Jackson himself: When Jackson heard protesters singing "We Shall Overcome" outside his office, he "turned to an aide and said, 'If anyone had told me four years ago that today I'd be on the wrong side of that song, I'd have called them a liar.'"[48]

After the initial shock of being blindsided by Gordon and NAB, Turpeau and much of the CETA staff swallowed their frustration and found ways to work with the PIC. Nevertheless, Turpeau later took a dim view of Gordon; Gordon, too, acknowledged that he and Turpeau never got along. Despite his general distrust of Jackson and his administration, however, Gordon served on the PIC for the entirety of its existence and remained involved after it became part of the apparatus of the 1982 Job Training Partnership Act.[49]

CETA's public-service employment component was originally conceived as a countercyclical measure in the recession of 1974–75. After the recession subsided, the job creation element remained. Particularly under the Carter administration, public-service employment shifted its focus "from countercyclical efforts to an attempt to create jobs for the disadvantaged and especially minorities. By 1978, [public-service employment] was funding year-round jobs for nearly 1 million adults and youth, and summer jobs for another 1 million youth." CETA's total funding topped out at $18 billion (in 2011 dollars) in 1979. "Even excluding the costly" public-service employment program, one analyst observed, "real expenditures on CETA programs were approximately 50 percent greater than those for similar MDTA and EOA programs during the late 1960s, and nearly double the real expenditures during the early 1990s on similar services under" the 1982 Job Training Partnership Act (JTPA). CETA clearly represented the high tide of federal job training programs and expenditures. Moreover, in the late 1970s, economists developed new techniques for evaluating the success of such programs, generally obtaining disappointing results. Critics argued that job training and public-service jobs had a negligible long-term impact on the earnings of the poor and disadvantaged and that some jobs may have duplicated and diminished private-sector opportunities. Analysts increasingly downplayed job training and job creation and advocated education as a more effective means of increasing the skills, job prospects, and earnings of the poor, and the federal government began to focus on such policies as No Child Left Behind and on increasing student loans and Pell Grants to support college attendance.[50]

After Ronald Reagan's 1980 election, the pace of business reaction against the perceived excesses of the previous decades quickened. In 1981, Congress terminated CETA's public employment activities. A year later, Gordon headed another NAB task force working to draft a replacement, the JTPA. Reflecting the Reagan administration's increased focus on private-sector control of jobs and job training, the JTPA even more fully embraced the NAB's approach. Private-sector employers were put in charge of designing and implementing job training programs with federal funds, creating a public-private partnership in which the private sector called all the shots.[51]

CETA had always been a hybrid, seeming to attempt to satisfy two distinctly different interests. It was, on the one hand, part of Nixon's new federalism, granting significant authority to state and local governments to craft the details of employment and training programs. Yet it was federally funded, with the U.S. government taking responsibility for generating the revenues. It was a sort of Great Society program by way of devolution. And it no doubt encouraged a great deal of corruption and questionable activities at the local level.

Yet the program contained within it what Judith Stein might have referred to as a bit of "the old time religion," using the power of the state to directly address the crisis of unemployment and slowing growth. The economic surpluses of the 1950s and 1960s had generated if not enthusiasm then at least tacit acceptance of large federal programs aimed at reducing the extreme levels of inequality in American society. Those efforts included public-private partnerships to promote desegregation of labor markets and more emphasis on training. Business had participated in many of these efforts. By the 1980s, however, the position of NAB and the business community reflected the new prevailing mood among wealthy elites: the system had gotten out of control and become overly generous, and the "excesses" of the Great Society and the 1960s had to be reined in. The emerging set of "neoliberal" policy prescriptions clashed with the emergence of black political power, and the struggle over CETA was a prime example. Jackson and Turpeau reached an accommodation with the business community, just as business leaders accommodated to the new reality of minority set-asides and affirmative action. Atlanta's growth coalition teetered and cracked but eventually pulled itself back together after incorporating larger portions of the rising black middle class. The CETA controversy, at least in the Atlanta context, appears to reflect what James Jennings has described as "a general refusal to allow Blacks use of the system's resources on an equal footing." Indeed, most scholars argue that Jackson's agenda never included anything more than improved black access to the existing structure of development in Atlanta. CETA represented an excellent example of the reaction of white elites to black demands for control over resources.[52]

President Johnson's Council of Economic Advisers had urged a strategy focused on addressing the needs of different groups that faced structural barriers to employment via modest expenditures on training, education, and antidiscrimination enforcement. Congress and the Nixon, Ford, and Carter administrations had subsequently opted for the path not taken by Johnson in the 1960s—public-service employment. CETA's high-cost job creation program drew vociferous criticism and was eventually abandoned in the face of business opposition and advocacy of a return to the earlier alternative. Harry Holzer finds much merit in the Johnson administration's analysis and approach, though he questions its scale. On another level, however,

> the optimism of President Johnson's economists that a series of new and modestly funded programs in a growing economy could greatly reduce or even eliminate poverty proved unfounded. For instance, technical change along with globalization proved much more costly to the poor than they envisioned, as the growth of earnings among the less-educated stalled or was even reversed. For less-educated and especially black men, these forces were devastating—and resulted in falling employment, falling marriage rates,

increasing births outside marriage, and rising crime and incarceration—much as Pat Moynihan feared they would.

Holzer carefully avoids wholesale endorsement or rejection of public-service employment. Econometric analyses of the cost-effectiveness and long-term benefits and costs of such programs were necessarily qualified. Holzer's characterization captures the nuances and potential of job creation programs: "When the workers are generating services that are not available in the private sector but which local residents seem to value, the estimated benefits of the programs can rise as well." In other words, the value of public-service employment could to a great extent reside in the eye of the beholder.[53]

Jackson, for his part, believed that the loss of the CETA program, especially the public-service component, was a great loss to the nation's cities. In March 1995, President Bill Clinton and Vice President Al Gore convened the Southern Regional Economic Conference at Emory University, bringing together business, educational, and community leaders to hear from a series of speakers that included BellSouth chair John Clendenin and Atlanta public school superintendent Benjamin Canada. Perhaps the liveliest address came from Jackson, fresh off his third term as mayor (1990–94), who advocated a vigorous new program of government activism and declared that constructive solutions to continuing problems of urban poverty had been abandoned too soon.[54]

Jackson's views echoed those expressed by the Reverend Jesse Jackson in his 1988 speech to the Democratic National Convention. As Jackson passionately critiqued what he perceived as the failed policies, lack of employment opportunities, and lack of hope that had settled over much of inner-city America, he declared, "They displaced CETA, they did not replace CETA."[55] Both men viewed a sort of bait-and-switch as having occurred. CETA was replaced by the JTPA in 1982, but it included no public-service employment component, and many urban advocates and civil rights leaders believed that JTPA failed to deliver significant results. In 2009, Turpeau advocated reviving a CETA-style program to combat the Great Recession: "If you want to stimulate the economy, give poor people some meaningful jobs, and they will work and circulate the money as fast as they get it."[56]

As was the case for many personnel professionals during this period, Gordon's experiences at Lockheed had thrust him into the role of civil rights reformer.[57] Gordon played a lead role in developing, implementing, and later evangelizing for an approach to the problems of racial discrimination, structural unemployment, and poverty based on public-private partnerships, with the private sector taking the initiative. Lockheed's management thus helped desegregate its own workforce and those of the South and the nation during a period of regulatory uncertainty. As that environment evolved in the 1980s, however, progress toward more integrated workplaces slowed.

CONCLUSION

Business, civil rights groups, and government may have made the best of the inclusion approach, but they nevertheless recoiled from the deeper transformation that was the implicit goal of the movements of the 1960s and from a full commitment to creating a vigorous public sector. Indeed, the tide turned against massive public investment everywhere in the West in the late 1970s and 1980s.

By the 1980s, the business response to active government regulation of business and intervention in the labor market transformed the corporate liberalism of the 1960s into neoliberalism.[1] Many of the poor and working class, black and white, in Atlanta and other metropolitan regions were left behind. Rising expectations led to a backlash from the business community. Both federal job training programs and public employment as a viable option fell by the wayside, though corporations made significant commitments to policies of diversity and inclusion. The rise of economic inequality since the 1970s may be related in part to the balance of forces around that tension.

What remained of the old corporate liberalism that characterized much of the Cold War era? Diversity management emerged beginning in the 1980s. Equal employment opportunity and affirmative action, as concepts and programs of action, arose from the dynamic interplay of government regulation and corporate response, forming one important aspect of the sense of corporate social responsibility that emerged in the postwar era. Diversity, as Jennifer Delton puts it, was "almost wholly a corporate creation." "As accepting of affirmative action as companies were," she writes, "it was not completely their own policy. Diversity, however, is." In the formulation developed by human resource professionals, "diversity goals" were tied to "business objectives," and recognition and celebration of diversity was good for productivity. The new ethos lost not only equal employment advocates' earlier emphasis on "individualism and merit" but something more. As Kevin Stainback and Donald Tomaskovic-Devey argue, without pressure from government regulators and social movements, the new ethos lacked the historical sense that led Hugh Gordon and others to insist that affirmative action policies were necessary to redress imbalances created by the weight of centuries of slavery, Jim Crow, and policies that acted as affirmative action for whites.[2]

So what did Lockheed-Georgia achieve in the EEO arena between 1951 and 1972? Tables 1–5 help illuminate some broad trends.[3]

Prior to the Civil Rights Act, Lockheed made some tentative progress toward racial integration with its targeted hiring of African American men and goal of promoting at least a few of them into supervisory positions. Lockheed-Georgia performed at least as well as others in the aircraft industry, with six black supervisors—of all–African American crews—as of October 1955. Black employment reached its peak during the decade in 1957, when Lockheed-Georgia employed 1,350 African Americans (7.8 percent of all workers). By March 1961, employment at Lockheed-Georgia had sunk to just over half its mid-1950s peak, and black employment fell to just 474 individuals (4.5 percent of all workers). By July 1966, Lockheed's total employment had rebounded to 23,365, and African Americans made up about 6 percent of the workforce, still well short of the area's overall black population of about 21 percent.

Between 1964 and 1970, the era when the Civil Rights Act went into effect, Lockheed-Georgia made rapid EEO progress. In 1966, less than 1 percent of "officials and managers" (the EEOC category for personnel with supervisory responsibilities) were African Americans. By 1970, that proportion had more than doubled, though it remained much too low. From fewer than 500 of more than 10,000 employees in early 1961, Lockheed-Georgia increased African American employment to 3,263 of 32,793 in August 1969, when affirmative action had reached its high point. In 1968–69, African Americans constituted 11.4 percent of all of Lockheed-Georgia's new hires and nearly a third of those hired for entry-level positions. In addition, African Americans accounted for 19 percent of promotions of hourly workers in 1968 and 24 percent the following year. Consequently, African

TABLE 1 African Americans in the Workforce, Select Aircraft Manufacturing Facilities, mid-1950s

	Number of African American Workers	Total Site Workforce	Percentage	Number of African American Supervisors
Lockheed, Marietta, Georgia	1,297	19,443	6.7	6
Chance-Vaught, Dallas, Texas	134	18,000	0.7	1
Boeing Aircraft, Wichita, Kansas	749	30,368	2.4	

TABLE 2 Lockheed-Georgia Total Employment and African American Employment, 1951–1974

	December 1951	December 1952	October 1955	February 1957	March 1961	December 1965	July 1966	December 1966	December 1967	August 1969	August 1971	August 1972	October 1972	June 1974
Total Workforce	10,700	11,152	19,443	17,350	10,484	22,000	23,365			32,793	19,000		12,000	10,000
Number of African American employees	< 100*	457	1,297	1,350	474		1,402			3,263				
Percentage total		4.1	6.7	7.8	4.5		6.0	5.7	6.9	10.0		6.8		
Percentage of African Americans in supervision			0.05				0.9			2.0			3.1	

*No black workers in production jobs.

Note: In 1969, the seventeen-county area from which Lockheed drew employees was 21 percent African American (Jim Mercer to Hugh Gordon, April 8, 1970, Folder 29, Box 2, Gordon Papers).

TABLE 3 African American Employment at Lockheed-Georgia, 1968–1969

	1968	1969
African American hires as percentage of total hires		13.9
African American entry-level hires as percentage of total entry-level hires	30.8	32.9
African Americans as percentage of total hourly workforce		12.0
Promotions of African Americans in hourly positions as percentage of total promotions	19.0	24.0
Total number of African Americans in supervisory positions		61 (2.0%)

TABLE 4 Hires and Promotions, Lockheed-Georgia, 1968–1969

	Total Number	Number of African Americans	Percentage
Hires	49,852	5,662	11.4
Promotions	44,040	5,291	12.0

TABLE 5 African Americans by Employment Category, Lockheed-Georgia and Select Other Large Firms

	Lockheed-Georgia (%), July 1966	Lockheed-Georgia (%), 1970	Other Large Firms (%), 1970	Lockheed-Georgia (%), 1972
Supervision	0.9	2.0	0.4–3.4	3.0
Salaried nonsupervisory	0.8	1.72	0.6–3.6	
Office-clerical	3.4	7.3	2.0–10.3	
Skilled	5.8	7.0	1.0–9.2	
Semiskilled	12.6	17.0	7.2–29.1	
Laborers	44.1	36.4	5.6–63.4	

NOTE: The largest job categories were skilled workers and semiskilled workers. Laborer was a very small category at Lockheed-Georgia, with only thirty-six persons in July 1966 and the number apparently never topping four hundred. In 1970, the company seems to have combined this category with the EEOC's Service Workers category.

American representation in semiskilled positions increased by about 26 percent in just two years. As of October 1972, blacks comprised 3 percent of supervisory personnel.

Despite such progress, some other large firms did better, and by 1970, Lockheed-Georgia's record placed in the middle of the pack among large firms, trailing the leaders by significant margins. In 1972, after two decades of efforts to promote equal opportunity employment, Lockheed-Georgia's workforce was 6.8 percent African American—roughly the same percentage as in 1955.

Both Harry Hudson and Clarence Sinkfield, however, saw real progress. Despite the discrimination they experienced, they had long careers with Lockheed and on balance judged those careers successful. Sinkfield proudly wore his Lockheed badge after hours and enjoyed the tangible benefits such as credit that accrued to company employees. Hudson, too, felt tremendous pride in his work and was angry at criticism of Lockheed during the 1970s, defending the significance of the company's—and his— work for the nation's defense.

In 2009, Hugh Gordon, normally reticent about discussing politics directly, recalled that his boss, E. G. Mattison, had described Hubert Humphrey, who served as vice president under Lyndon Johnson and who was the 1968 Democratic presidential candidate, as "the most dangerous man in this country." Gordon went on to explain that Humphrey would have done "what Obama's trying to do. . . . He tried to socialize everything. He was about as far left as you could get." Gordon and other Lockheed executives apparently were extremely conservative politically. Yet as Johnson adviser Hobart Taylor observed in 1967 of the men who formed the initial Business Advisory Council for Plans for Progress four years earlier, "Although most of them were not necessarily liberal, and 90 per cent of them were Republicans, and probably conservative Republicans at that, [they] still were committed to this particular project, which was what I wanted." In fact, according to Taylor, "the more conservative they were, the better I liked it, in a way, because I knew that they would be able to protect this project better than anybody else."[4]

A fierce champion of free enterprise, Gordon was horrified by anything that smacked of collectivism. His conservative instincts led him to distrust government initiatives. But he internalized the idea that discrimination, poor education, poverty, and other barriers harmed and restricted individuals' life chances and slowly embraced a broader conception of structural barriers to employment. He came to believe that justice required that these barriers needed to be reduced or eliminated so that people could rise according to their merit, to use the term most often deployed by both proponents and opponents of affirmative action in the 1950s and 1960s. Indeed, the personnel profession as a whole embraced equal employment and affirmative action at the same time that the older purpose of industrial relations, dealing with unions or avoiding unionization, declined in significance.

Gordon and many of his business colleagues came to support subsidized job training and employment in the private sector through various federal programs but became deeply uneasy when the U.S. government turned over control of massive amounts of money for those programs to local politicians, fighting to restore that control to the private sector. They believed that large-scale public-service employment threatened the free enterprise system as a whole and had to be stopped. Eventually, they accomplished that goal as well. The affirmative action and diversity programs pioneered by Lockheed and implemented by many large firms in the 1980s and beyond opened opportunities that had been effectively closed to African Americans, members of other minority groups, and especially women. Those programs often did not reach into the working class or draw in people who were only loosely attached to labor markets. Programs such as CETA held that promise, though how an expanded and longer-lasting CETA might have fared remains unclear. But the implicit job guarantee that CETA might have implemented would have constituted a major structural transformation of the U.S. economy. In the end, national policy and business preferences settled on less ambitious policies that offered some inclusion in the existing system.

In spite of the business community's general opposition to government mandates, those mandates—often vague and open to interpretation—helped shape an environment in which discrimination became increasingly intolerable. At those critical points in Lockheed's history when the company acted to reduce discrimination and promote equal employment, those actions resulted from government pressure and black protest of one form or another—in California in 1941 and in Georgia in 1951, 1961, and 1966. While the early government mandates against discrimination were almost totally unenforceable in any legal sense, they began a process—slow and painful—of setting new standards that businesses were expected to meet. The prospects for black workers seemed to flow with Lockheed's contract fortunes. Robert Weaver had formulated the hypothesis that government mandates combined with strong overall employment growth could be successful in breaking down racial barriers. Though Weaver was not thinking in terms of employment growth at individual firms, at Lockheed it seemed to work that way.

The obverse of Weaver's formula for progress in racial integration came to the fore in the 1970s and 1980s throughout the U.S. economy. When

Lockheed first confronted discrimination complaints in 1951, company officials had noted International Harvester's Memphis plant as a potential model. By 1969, however, "Harvester's experiment in biracial industrialism in a southern city bears all the earmarks of a failure." Although Harvester had a pioneering industrial relations department and represented the leading edge of racial integration in southern industry in the early 1950s, the energy faded with the departure of top management figures who were deeply invested in antidiscrimination policies and practices. "In the 1960s," Jennifer Delton concludes, the company's "leadership chose to ride on the reputation for racial fairness" established earlier "rather than live up to it." However, the main significance of International Harvester's efforts in Memphis "resides less in its ultimate results than in its early efforts."[5] International Harvester, like Lockheed, introduced and explored key strategies that other firms later applied in affirmative action and diversity plans. Significant, lasting progress proved slower and more halting than civil rights groups, workers, and even some human resource management professionals would have preferred.

International Harvester, again like Lockheed and other large corporations, faced economic crisis in the 1970s. Lockheed barely survived, and employment at the Marietta, Georgia, plant was dramatically reduced, limiting the direct potential for black advancement. International Harvester's Memphis plant was even less fortunate. Desegregation efforts stalled as a result of management apathy and "a segregationist faction in the UAW local." Large, union-organized plants owned by Harvester and Firestone Tire and Rubber closed in the early 1980s as corporations fought unions and relocated production to cheaper labor markets.[6] Memphis and traditional manufacturing fared decidedly less well in the 1980s and 1990s than did the Atlanta region and its more diversified economy. In both places, however, working-class and poor African Americans struggled. Frank Dobbin and Jennifer Delton credit Gordon and Lockheed with leading the development of affirmative action programs that helped reduce employment discrimination. That their leadership largely resulted from the federal government's entreaties, informal pressure, moral appeals, and finally mandates does not diminish the accomplishment. Delton acknowledges that problems remain and that race has not vanished as a limiting factor for many Americans, but "it is equally important to not let these problems prevent us from seeing that corporations have been a real and powerful force for racial progress in the United States." Within the confines of the U.S. economic system, few alternatives existed. But the social transformation for which many reformers and radicals of the 1960s hoped remained elusive.

Lockheed-Georgia's experience with equal employment opportunity could perhaps support the findings of scholars such as Manning Marable and Glenn Eskew that the black masses were left behind by the emphasis on programs such as affirmative action and the abandonment of a larger public role in guaranteeing employment. At the same time, however, the story told in this book can also be seen as evidence for Gavin Wright's more positive view of the civil rights movement's impact on the economic fortunes of African Americans, especially in the South.[7]

Lockheed-Georgia's leaders took seriously the challenge of building an equal employment opportunity program that could truly include disadvantaged minorities. Taking into account both internal practices and the shaping of government-funded job training programs, the company's approach emphasized private-sector initiative. And it recorded tangible achievements. Mattison, Gordon, and other personnel professionals sought to open the U.S. and southern business worlds to groups that had previously been almost completely shut out, recognizing early on that simply removing *White* and *Colored* signs and declaring Lockheed an "equal opportunity employer" was not enough. These officials struggled to move beyond the simplistic notion that discrimination consisted only of individual, intentional acts and to incorporate the concept of structural barriers to opportunity. Through what John Sutton and Frank Dobbin label an "iterative process" of conflict and negotiation with government agencies and the courts, Lockheed's personnel managers groped their way toward creating effective equal opportunities.[8]

Recent events—from the emergence of Black Lives Matter to the emboldening of groups advocating both thinly veiled and unveiled versions of white supremacy—have demonstrated that issues of race have not disappeared from the American social and political landscape, but few would deny that the 1960s and 1970s saw significant progress in expanding opportunity and improving the well-being of the poor and minorities, with carryover effects through the ensuing two decades. Acknowledging the imperfections of antipoverty and antidiscrimination efforts, Wright has marshaled substantial evidence that white and black Americans, especially southerners, "shared the prize" of improved material conditions as a result of the strands of civil rights protest and reform, including improvements in education, the ability to use political power to provide tangible benefits such as employment, and the desegregation of labor markets. Though these gains did not lift everyone equally, most Americans found their lives at least somewhat improved. And as Wright emphasizes, the era's gains must be considered "relative to conditions and trends prior to the protests of the 1960s and the legislation of 1964 and 1965. By this standard, the economic advances of black southerners were remarkable and have largely been sustained. By contrast, reduction in the regional poverty rate largely came to an end after 1980. Thus the South has been the locus of both the movement's greatest economic success and its greatest disappointment."[9]

Recent work by Thomas Piketty, Walter Scheidel, and other scholars also points to the 1970s as a turning point for economic inequality. From the Great Depression through the early to mid-1970s, the gap between the very rich and everyone else shrank and then stabilized at historically low levels. By 1980, however, that gap had begun to grow again, and on the eve of the Great Recession of 2007–9, inequality had climbed back to predepression levels. With neoliberalism ascendant, public investment, public employment, and the regulatory state became special targets of reformers intent on privatization and creating the maximum freedom for capital flows.[10]

The Lockheed story illustrates the difficulty of creating programs and policies to address deeply rooted poverty and inequality. Though it is important, as Tom Adam Davies and Maurice Hobson, among others, emphasize, to pay attention to those left behind, it is equally important to recognize the accomplishments of Hugh Gordon, Harry Hudson, and their colleagues.[11]

They worked to improve the existing system rather than to radically reform it, in the process helping to move the South and the nation away from racial discrimination in employment.

EPILOGUE

As Lockheed's Georgia division—since 1995 part of Lockheed Martin—approached its fiftieth anniversary, race remained a potent issue, both within the plant and in the broader metropolitan Atlanta community. On May 10, 2000, a group of Lockheed employees filed a pair of class-action lawsuits alleging that the company discriminated based on race. Two days later, Lockheed Martin announced that Lee Rhyant, an African American currently serving as vice president for production at Rolls-Royce Aerospace in Indianapolis, had agreed to become a corporate vice president and site manager for the Marietta location. Lockheed Martin spokesperson Sam Grizzle insisted that Rhyant's hiring reflected his twenty-five years of experience in aviation manufacturing, not his race, although outgoing Lockheed Martin president Tom Burbage acknowledged that the company had been "working hard to find qualified African-Americans to put in senior management positions." The months-long search for the vice president's position had included about fifteen candidates, but Grizzle and Burbage could not say how many of those candidates had been black, though "there 'must have been a few.'" An attorney for the plaintiffs in the new lawsuit, Josie Alexander, found Rhyant's hiring "interesting" but declared, "'Merely replacing the site manager at one plant' will not compensate mistreated workers or prevent future occurrences."[1]

The lawsuits included more than a hundred "complaints of discrimination from current and former employees in plants from South Carolina to Texas." Among the charges were discrimination in rates of pay and promotion, harassment, and the creation of a "hostile work environment" that included racial slurs, the circulation of "Back to Africa" tickets, and a noose hung in a black employee's work area. Burbage argued that such incidents could not be blamed on the company: "We're a mirror of society and like you have in any group, you'll have people with different prejudices." The company, he insisted, was doing its best "to let people know that we won't tolerate it at the workplace."[2]

Clarence Sinkfield was among the lawsuit's plaintiffs. Sinkfield was an Atlanta native whose father was a cook for a railroad and whose mother was a silk finisher for a dry cleaner. When Sinkfield graduated from high school in the late 1950s, Georgia Tech remained an all-white institution, so the state of Georgia paid for him to attend Virginia's Hampton Institute, where he earned a degree in business in 1963. After working as a substitute teacher in the Hampton area for two years, Sinkfield returned to Georgia, where he found a job as an assembly helper at Lockheed in May 1965. The facility "was huge, and he "got lost a couple of times." He received his training on the job, "with someone who knew what they were doing." He found some racial tension: "Whites sort of kept to themselves, and blacks kept to themselves." After ninety days, he was promoted to assembly installer, a position he held for about a year, or roughly until the same time that Lockheed was served with the charges that ultimately led to the Banks case.[3]

At that point, according to Sinkfield, "they made me a lead man undercover. No one knew I was a lead man and getting lead man's money. There were other people in that crew who had been making more money than I was. As a lead man, I got twenty cents more [an hour] than the highest-paid person in the crew." Sinkfield's promotion could not be publicized because the lead man was supposed "to be the most senior qualified person" on the crew, but his crew included qualified whites with more seniority. Not until months later, when the more senior whites had moved to other areas or had left Lockheed, did Sinkfield publicly assume the job. Sensitivity to racial etiquette continued to influence Lockheed's management of the shop floor.[4]

In late 1968, Sinkfield took the management selection test. More than a month later, he had heard nothing about whether he would be considered by a selection committee for a promotion into management, and like some of the plaintiffs in the Banks case, he was never told his score. After he "raised a little hell," he was soon promoted to supervisor on the aft section of the C-141, an assignment he described as "an odd deal." The crew was about two-thirds white and one-third black. "The whites didn't want the blacks telling them what to do," while the blacks envied Sinkfield, and he "had more problems getting them to do what they were supposed to do because they were black and I was black and they thought they were supposed to receive some kind of special treatment." Over time, however, Sinkfield "gained the respect of both" groups by avoiding playing favorites and treating everyone fairly.[5]

Sinkfield piled up awards and commendations; his performance reviews were "always top-notch." He moved from the C-141 to the C-5 line and then to the C-130 work area, where he encountered another odd situation. A few hours after he was introduced to the lead man in the area he would be supervising, the man "told me he was giving up the lead man position," claiming that "he had been planning on it for some time." Sinkfield never knew the truth of the situation. The man may not have wanted to serve as lead man under a black supervisor. Or he may have been upset because he was passed over for the supervisor's position. Whatever the case, Sinkfield described his time in the area as "an ordeal."[6]

More than two decades passed before Sinkfield was promoted to assistant department manager in 1994. During that time, he recalled, "I had seen guys make manager who came in long after I did." After four years as an assistant manager in several departments, "my manager retired, and . . . everybody in the department thought I was going to be the manager. You know what they did? They merged the two departments" and put the manager of the other department at the helm, making Sinkfield one of three assistant managers. After the merger, a management official said to Sinkfield, "I want to apologize for the white race." Though the official provided no further information, that comment "told me something." And then in 2000, when Sinkfield retired, "they split the departments back up."[7]

Just prior to his retirement, Sinkfield joined the *Reid v. Lockheed Martin* lawsuit. It was one of a handful of such cases filed against high-profile Atlanta-area companies, including Coca-Cola and Georgia Power, in 1999–2000. Sinkfield, Melvyn Reid, and other plaintiffs formed Workers against Discrimination, to promote the cause, sending a delegation to visit Atlanta congressman and civil rights icon John Lewis in September 2000 and drawing vocal support from Atlanta congresswoman Cynthia McKinney. Alexander recruited Johnnie Cochran, who had leaped to fame in the O. J. Simpson case a few years earlier, to add clout to the plaintiffs' legal team. Prominent members of the black clergy pledged support, and the Equal Employment Opportunity Commission (EEOC), which had found evidence of discrimination in most of the individual cases, tried to join the lawsuit.[8]

Unlike the Banks case, *Reid v. Lockheed Martin* never made it to trial, nor was there a settlement. U.S. district judge J. Owen Forrester denied the EEOC's petition to join the case in January 2001, and on August 2, he ruled that the charges contained in the multilocation lawsuit did not constitute a class action. Individual plaintiffs were free to continue their cases separately, but the tenor of the judge's ruling and the difficulty and expense of proceeding in this manner made such a course unattractive.[9]

Forrester's ruling included a commentary on evidentiary disputes between the parties and detailed his reasoning. The plaintiffs had used an expert statistician to analyze pay rates in search of racial differentials. The judge found the expert's report "troublesome." The statistician "admitted in his deposition that his reports contain numerous errors including mathematical mistakes, the inclusion of wrong and misleading tables," and more. Inconsistencies between the affidavits and deposition testimony from some plaintiffs also were an issue. But Forrester's decision to deny class status came down to two crucial points. First, the plaintiffs had attempted to sue on behalf of all black employees at all Lockheed Martin locations on the basis that the various plants used inconsistent and arbitrary policies and procedures for promotions and pay rates. The judge was persuaded that whatever inconsistencies existed had resulted from the 1995 Lockheed–Martin Marietta merger and that the new company should be given time to standardize its personnel departments and policies. Not until January 2001 had Lockheed Martin declared, "We are now operating as one company," and the judge accepted this statement, at least in broad terms.[10]

More significantly, Judge Forrester ruled that the social conditions that made class-action lawsuits permissible under the Civil Rights Act had changed:

> In contrast to the early days . . . , it is now more uncommon to find an employer that overtly encourages wholesale discrimination on the basis of race; race discrimination today usually comes in more subtle forms. It is perhaps more unusual still to find an employer such as a federal defense contractor—required by Executive Order 11246 and 41 C.F.R. § 602.1 to create and implement affirmative action programs, and whose employees are represented by a number of different unions—that can manage to engage in discrimination on a class-wide basis in the face of executive branch oversight and collectively-bargained grievance procedures through which issues of discrimination can be brought to light.

Class-action discrimination suits, he implied, were more difficult to justify than in the days just after segregation. One might quibble with the judge's confidence in government oversight and collective bargaining, but there was no denying that regarding issues of diversity, to use the more modern parlance, the business environment had been transformed, in the South as well as elsewhere. The judge's ruling effectively ended the lawsuits, and in August 2003, Forrester "dismissed the case without prejudice for lack of prosecution." Although Sinkfield and the other plaintiffs opted not to pursue individual cases, he heard from friends who still worked at Lockheed that "things are better now: blacks are put into salaried positions that they hadn't been before."[11]

The failure of the Reid case to gain class certification did not necessarily indicate a general trend. Shoney's, owner of several restaurant chains, settled a class-action racial discrimination suit covering about twenty-one thousand employees for $132 million in late 1992. The case in many ways exemplified the atmosphere at the EEOC under the Reagan administration—the agency never issued a finding of "reasonable cause," which would have helped the plaintiffs pursue the case. Nevertheless, the plaintiffs' attorneys accumulated such overwhelming evidence against Shoney's that the company settled. Texaco agreed to pay $176 million to settle a race discrimination suit in 1996. The following year, Atlanta-based Home Depot settled a gender bias suit involving twenty-five thousand current and former employees for $87.5 million. In 2000, Coca-Cola settled a racial discrimination suit for $190 million. And in 2004, aircraft manufacturer Boeing settled a gender discrimination suit covering eighteen thousand workers for $72 million. These settlements generally included company pledges to change practices and a period of monitoring by court-approved bodies, just as the Banks case settlement had in 1972.[12]

In many ways, Sinkfield's attempt to climb Lockheed's corporate ladder was reminiscent of Harry Hudson's. After becoming the first African American buyer in Lockheed-Georgia's history in 1961, Hudson had to wait eight years for his next promotion, and it was to semisenior buyer, a classification he did not even know existed. He had his sights set on moving up to senior buyer and eventually to subcontract administrator and purchasing agent, the top classifications in his department, but ten more years passed before he received the promotion to senior buyer. And even then, he only received the upgrade after he complained to his supervisor that a young—white—buyer he had trained a few years earlier was now a senior buyer. Hudson demanded a raise and promotion, and he got them. Even though "it was late as hell, I felt good that I had finally gotten an upgrade." But he also recognized that he would never rise any higher in the Lockheed corporate universe. For the rest of his career, he would help and train younger buyers as they came into the department and watch them advance while he remained where he was.[13]

Hudson still held the title of senior buyer when he retired in December 1987, thirty-six years after joining the company. Racism remained "prevalent . . . right up to the end," and the company made "only those changes necessary to meet the government's defense contract demands." Nevertheless, Hudson believed that "individuals of all groups were able to make improvements in their status because of their enthusiasm, training, ability, and efforts. . . . [H]iring practices changed for the better for individuals having these capabilities"—that is, for those who merited advancement. But, as Hudson asked rhetorically, "What's merit?" As economist Robert Frank points out, merit rarely if ever solely determines a person's fate—

luck plays a generally underappreciated and sometimes primary role. Race, gender, and class helped shape outcomes as well. Hudson would have appreciated Frank's analysis.[14]

After his retirement party, Hudson recalled,

> I slowly strolled through the department, caught the elevator and went down.... I walked out to my van and slowly got in, drove around the parking lot for the last time as an employee. I went up to the main parking lot and parked by the [recreation] building. I got out and stood looking at that big plant for about ten minutes. All of the almost thirty-six years rolled through my mind. The good and the bad. The good overruled the bad. I had first seen that place when I was twenty-seven years old. Now I was sixty-two years old and ... I no longer worked at the bomber plant. It sure didn't seem that it had been that long. The sun seemed to shine brighter and I realized that the days of getting up early, meeting schedules, writing documentation, negotiating, trying to be diplomatic, being congenial yet hardnosed when necessary, the personal responsibility I always felt when trying to satisfy our customers, getting along with all of those other grunts and the stress of keeping up with changing technology ... it was over! Gone! Not required anymore!
>
> A feeling of peace came over me. It was wonderful. I got back into the van and pulled out of the lot onto the road in front of the plant. I took one last look and wheeled on home. To this day I have never looked back with regret (except one ...) nor missed ... being at dear old Lockheed (The Bomber Plant). All in all I guess it was a wonderful time.

Hudson's one regret: "Why in hell didn't I get the promotions that I had earned?"[15]

A great many men and women have gone through long careers negotiating paths through corporate bureaucracies and have retired feeling somehow cheated or denied advances or recognition they believed they had earned. For Hudson, and no doubt for many like him, race made the regret all the harder to shake: "I try not to feel that it was other than out and out pure rotten prejudice. I couldn't get that thought out of my mind."[16]

In his final years, Gordon researched the history of workplace integration in an attempt to better understand the larger story in which he had played a role. He was particularly influenced by legal scholar Cynthia Estlund's *Working Together: How Workplace Bonds Strengthen a Diverse Democracy*, which argues that the workplace was an unrecognized arena of civic engagement, a place—for many, the only place—where people encountered others from diverse backgrounds and thus was a significant theater of social change, "one site of associational life where the law has both leverage and legitimacy." While the workplace was not a magical solution to the problems of deteriorating social trust that she and a host of other scholars and social critics have identified, "the unique potential that does lie in working together is more readily realized through the deliberate interventions of public policy" in the workplace than in most other spheres of public life.[17]

Gordon extolled the virtues of voluntarism and always insisted that Lockheed had accomplished most of its progress in diversity without compulsion. Yet he repeatedly emphasized Estlund's book as a frame for the business/civil rights story. Perhaps he realized the tension inherent therein. The dynamic that played out in the business community in the 1950s, 1960s, and 1970s represented, within the confines of the postwar consensus, a social working through of the problem of racial discrimination in the workplace. As Gordon wrote in 1970, "I think it's fair to say much integration (and consequently much acceptance of Negroes by whites) has come about by leadership which says it's the law, it's social responsibility, it's good personnel policy, it respects human dignity, it's fair, it's right. In my opinion, we have come a long way . . . on that approach. It's easy to forget just how segregated we were in this plant a few years ago."[18]

Though both Hugh Gordon and Harry Hudson spent nearly their entire working lives at Lockheed-Georgia between 1951 and 1988 and they knew one another, their paths never really intersected at Lockheed-Georgia. But both men attended the December 1996 funeral of John H. "Pat" Patterson, Gordon's longtime assistant. Gordon was one of few white people in attendance—perhaps the only one. He had composed a few words to say about his friend and colleague, but, he remembered, "I couldn't do it. I was too emotional." Gordon asked Hudson to read the tribute.[19]

Gordon and Hudson had traveled separately along the path toward racial integration. After that phase of their lives had come to a close, they came together in the common experience of the passing of a fellow traveler.

APPENDIX
Representative Documents

These excerpts from representative documents in the Gordon Papers in the Gordon, Kruse, Wentzel Collection at Kennesaw State University provide insight into internal management deliberations on matters pertaining to equal employment opportunity and affirmative action in the late 1960s.

DIVISION OF LOCKHEED AIRCRAFT CORPORATION
INTERDEPARTMENTAL COMMUNICATION
TO C. A. Jenkins
DATE February 12, 1969
FROM Hugh L. Gordon
SUBJECT: EMPLOYEE DISCIPLINE

To help clear the air on this subject, here are a few facts relative to discipline of our Negro employees.

1. In 1968 there were 121 Negro employees dismissed, thirty-one percent of all dismissals. This compares with a workforce which now includes 9.4% Negro, and year-1968 hires which included 18.4% Negro.
2. In the month of January 1969 there were 31 Negroes dismissed, an up trend.
3. Out of a total of 184 official EEO complaints or charges dating back to 1965, not one Negro dismissal has been reversed—none of the complainants have been reinstated.

Despite the above facts, there is a myth generating about the disinclination of supervision to discipline Negroes and a myth generating about lack of management support in discipline of Negro employees. No doubt too many of our supervisors shy away from rule enforcement of any kind, and many others shy away from personal face-to-face confrontations with their employees. Some are "gun shy" from previous bad experiences, and some don't have the stomach for it in the first place. The latter probably includes people who are misplaced in supervision and probably others who with some help could "gut-up" to the job.

Many of the "gun shy" are inept or clumsy in inter-personal relations. They too need some help because these are skills which can be taught or developed. I realize this is a sad commentary on personnel handling by supervision, but unfortunately there is much evidence that this is a serious problem. Not everyone knows how to constructively criticize or how to motivate. Our grievance procedure has produced hundreds of examples over the years of inadequate personnel handling.

It has been said, "If you don't want to do something—one reason is as good as another." The growing trend in lack of discipline is to blame it on the Negro. And the dangers of this are twofold-(1) excused lack of discipline stimulates no discipline and (2) in defaming a large number of our employees, racial prejudices are further polarized and the tinderbox becomes bigger, more explosive. . . .

GORDON PAPERS, FOLDER 27, BOX 2

LOCKHEED-GEORGIA COMPANY
A DIVISION OF LOCKHEED AIRCRAFT CORPORATION
INTERDEPARTMENTAL COMMUNICATION
TO C. A. Jenkins
DATE June 27, 1969
FROM Hugh L. Gordon
SUBJECT: EVALUATION OF EQUAL EMPLOYMENT OPPORTUNITY JUNE 1969

CHANGES IN THE WORKFORCE

Since January 1968 a total of 12,550 hires have been brought into the [Lockheed-Georgia] workforce, 11,580 of which were hourly, most of which went into Manufacturing. The heavy build-up in Manufacturing has demanded all-out recruiting to obtain skilled workers and to establish pre-hire training and [on-the-job training] programs. About 2,000 pre-hire trainees were hired during this period (out of 2,800 entering five weeks' pre-hire training programs during which they received no pay, but $40/week subsistence). Over 4,500 skilled aircraft workers have been added to the payroll. Since the build-up in the "front shops" of the C-5 assembly line and the flight line, skilled hiring has been accelerated. Pre-hire training has diminished substantially and was recently discontinued in our manpower planning. The ratio of skilled hires to prehire trainee hires has increased from 1.1:1 in 1968 to 7.2:1 in 1969.

Concurrent with our hourly build-up, we have promoted 398 employees into supervision including 103 new supervisors in the 26 BC (C-5 Assembly). About 90% of these had no prior supervisory experience. These new supervisors represent 16.8% of the total [Lockheed-Georgia] supervisory/managerial workforce. A survey made at the first of the year showed that 17.6% of Manufacturing first line supervision were under age 30. That figure is undoubtedly higher now with more recent promotions and portends to remain high. We know that by 1975 sixty-two percent of the nation-wide population will be under age 35. Our workforce, like the population and like available manpower, will become younger. It will also likely include more minorities and more people with disadvantaged backgrounds. (This was verbalized earlier by Corporate Industrial Relations.)

Negroes at [Lockheed-Georgia] now comprise 9.5% of the workforce compared with 9.4% at year-end 1968, 6.9% in 1967, and 5.7% in 1966. In Manufacturing the composition has changed from 9.5% Negro in 1967 to 12.5% in June 1969.

On the C-5 program there are currently 18.6% Negroes compared with 18.8% one year ago. The back shops (26-02 BC) have the heaviest percentage (24.6%) compared to 8.2% in the front shops (26-01 BC) where there are more experienced, higher classified employees.

In summary, our hiring needs have changed to more skilled types. The unemployment rate in Atlanta is 1.9%. We are now seeking more mature people for training which is made possible by newly created training programs to assimilate skilled non-aircraft workers. We are also recruiting in rural counties throughout Georgia seeking the combination of nonaircraft mechanical skills and motivation to work.

However, we must observe that the current [Lockheed-Georgia] workforce was secured without lowering of basic hiring standards. All trainees met careful screening tests and interview requirements. Our workforce is a normal one—there is a marked absence of hippie or weirdo types. Few of the Negro employees have the bush or Afro haircut, although we would not consider this indicative of performance potential any more than long hair or heavy side burns. We emphasize [Lockheed-Georgia] has a normal looking factory workforce.

The current workforce population of the younger generation, minorities, and disadvantaged presents a continuing challenge to a younger, relatively inexperienced supervisory workforce. Although we have modified our hiring requirements to include more mature, more experienced personnel, this challenge to manage and effectively supervise a changing workforce appears to be a continuing one with no quick solutions through discipline or other singular techniques.

OPTIMUM OBJECTIVITY

Cutting across all techniques of management is the principle of optimum objectivity, and "Double O" is the key to effective supervision in race related matters. A white supervising a black or vice versa is generally race related—that is, it requires special understanding and special human relations skills.

We consider optimum objectivity something less than perfection certainly, but nothing less than the best in decision making that can be achieved. And most important it is something that favors a sound, lasting management decision—something that will weather the storm of appeal....

When optimum objectivity prevails, Negroes and whites are supervised, helped, trained and disciplined by the same standards. This, of course, is the policy, and the question is whether or not double standards are being applied.

We also need to ask the corollary question of whether or not optimum objectivity prevails in all race related decisions, a fair question for fair minded people. However, our human frailty often inhibits all of us as individuals to question our own objectivity. In brief, it's something we have got to work on.

DOUBLE STANDARDS?

A few militants are leading the way on federal charges and NAACP sponsored law suits alleging that Negroes are not hired, trained, and promoted by the same standards as whites. At present there are 153 EEOC charges outstanding and 11 lawsuits pending. Ten of the lawsuits represent class action charges that Negroes are given disparate treatment and have been harassed because of their race. The charges have been denied and the suits are being defended.

On the other hand, some members of supervision have expressed concern over "favoritism" accorded Negroes by our policies. The allegations of "favoritism" have been most difficult to pinpoint. Along this line, there has been a marked absence of specific complaints which Industrial Relations could investigate and deal with. The only specific complaint received by Personnel Services this year concerned a charge by an individual production department manager (1) that he could not get his job done because of excessive time spent answering EEO complaints and (2) that he and his supervisors were harassed by EEO investigators. Investigation revealed that (1) this foreman had spent less than 15 minutes this year answering EEOC charges and (2) all supervisors contacted asserted they had not experienced any harassment by the EEOC or Industrial Relations. The department manager's complaint to higher management, in this instance, was made at a time when an investigation was being initiated in his department concerning EEOC charges filed by three Negro employees, who were dismissed on the same day, all under the same supervisor. The record shows that 17 out of the last 25 unsatisfactory probation dismissals under this foreman were Negroes. This is the same department manager who was associated with the first EEOC complaint filed at [Lockheed-Georgia] under Title VII.

The EEOC is actively gathering facts to determine whether or not this unusual record is caused by racial bias. . . .

DISCIPLINE AND TURNOVER

Earlier this year we received a general charge that Industrial Relations was not backing up line management in the discipline of Negroes. Attached is an [interdepartmental communication] discussed in the President's Staff which threw some light on this subject. The record shows in 1968 that 31% of all dismissals were Negroes compared with a workforce of 9.4% Negro and 1968 hires which included 18.4% Negro. In 1969 there have been 132 or 42% Negro dismissals.

To date, there have been 236 federal charges alleging discrimination, 46 concerning dismissal. To this date not one single Negro dismissal has been reversed in resolution of these charges. The record thus shows that Negroes have been dismissed disproportionate to their number in the workforce. We are aware that some categorically feel Negroes are lazy, poor workers, prone to absenteeism, unresponsive to direction, and non-conforming. On the other hand the record also reveals 138 Negroes have been promoted this year, and Negro voluntary terminations comprise only 7.7% of the voluntary quits compared with 9.4% Negroes in the workforce. . . .

. . . [I]n the area of discharge . . . Negroes were released at a rate disproportionate to their representation in the plant population and at a rate greater than they are hired. Moreover in 1969, a year of declining Negro hires, there has been an increase in Negroes dismissed (42% compared with 31% in 1968). This could become attributed, if not properly interpreted, to management's express concern for discipline of Negroes in the workforce and be another "cause celebre."

A conclusion which may be reached from our statistics is that there is no hesitancy of [Lockheed-Georgia] management in dismissing Negro employees notwithstanding persistent rumors that Industrial Relations will not permit management to "get rid of" unsatisfactory Negro employees.

SUMMARY

Our summary observation is that the facts indicate no disinclination of [Lockheed-Georgia] supervision to discipline Negro employees nor is there any evidence of a double standard of discipline as applied to Negroes and whites. There is also no evidence to conclude that the relatively high percentage of Negro dismissals have been for anything but reasonable cause notwithstanding a number of race discrimination charges on file, but still being investigated. We recognize there are apprehensions among certain white supervision concerning discipline of Negro employees. We believe the dangers of encouragement of further Negro discipline, whether this be inadvertent or factually based, outweigh the advantages otherwise attainable.

The real problem lies in the challenge for supervision to relate to and supervise effectively an increasingly different workforce, one that includes more minorities, more young people, and people with different cultural and ethnic backgrounds. And right now better understanding of the unique human relations aspects of race differences, better understanding and application of basic supervisory skills in all personnel handling matters, and specific support and direction from management are imperative to resolution of the questions concerning management of the Negro in the workforce.

Our recommendation is to complete the planned development and implementation of a "Personnel Awareness" training program designed to provide supervisory awareness of human relations responsibilities inherent in providing equal employment opportunity. . . . Supportively [Lockheed-Georgia] management has committed itself to total involvement in a rededication to our affirmative action programs. We feel Corporate simply needs to reaffirm support of [Lockheed-Georgia] efforts to place this continued emphasis on the kind of "tough minded" management or decision making that encourages optimum objectivity in the supervision of Negroes and all other employees. . . .

GORDON PAPERS, FOLDER 27, BOX 2

July 25, 1969
Mr. Dwight Zook
Special Assistant to Vice President
Aerospace Systems Group
Executive Offices
North American Aviation—Rockwell
1700 East Imperial
El Segundo, California

Dear Dwight:

Enclosed are copies of the material we discussed relative to our EEO program. As I mentioned, we have not publicized our Conciliation Agreement by understanding with the Commission. However, the key elements of our program concern:

1. Development and use of promotional profiles (Hourly and Salaried).
2. Establishment of Special Employee Counseling Units (Hourly and Salaried).
3. Improved Management Selection Procedures. On promotion to salaried positions, where interview is required, we require an Industrial Relations Representative to interview as well as the line manager. In case of a difference in opinion, the decision is referred to a higher level line management selection committee.
4. Individual Development Programs. Copies of the forms used for this program are enclosed.
5. Ability Testing. This includes utilization guides, scheduled acceleration of test validation, cut score definition, and test administration guide—all compatible with the EEOC and OFCC testing guidelines.

In addition, we have established an Industrial Relations EEO Action Committee to periodically review and assure progress. One of the key functions of the Committee is to review tracking charts on minority representation in various sub-categories and take steps as necessary to implement upward minority representation.

As a result of the changes in our program initiated last year, we have increased the number and percentages of minority members in most all categories, especially in salaried jobs, and we feel that the changes have been beneficial to our people and our operations.

I hope that this information meets your needs and is helpful to you in your program.

>Very truly yours,
>LOCKHEED-GEORGIA COMPANY
>Hugh L. Gordon, Manager
>Personnel Services Division

GORDON PAPERS, FOLDER 28, BOX 2

NOTES

Abbreviations

AC	*Atlanta Constitution*
ADW	*Atlanta Daily World*
AUL Papers	Atlanta Urban League Papers, Woodruff Library, Atlanta University Center, Atlanta
NAACP Case Files	Legal Department Case Files, 1960–1972, Section II, Series A, Supplement to Part 23, Papers of the National Association for the Advancement of Colored People, microfilm edition.
Elkins Affidavit	Willie T. Elkins affidavit, March 27, 1961, Folder 33, Box 7, Joseph Kruse Papers, Gordon, Kruse, Wentzel Collection, Kennesaw State University Archives, Kennesaw, Ga.
Gordon Papers	Hugh L. Gordon Papers, Gordon, Kruse, Wentzel Collection, Kennesaw State University Archives, Kennesaw, Ga.
Kruse Papers	Joseph Kruse Papers, Gordon, Kruse, Wentzel Collection, Kennesaw State University Archives, Kennesaw, Ga.
LSS	*Lockheed Southern Star*
NYT	*New York Times*

Introduction

1. Hugh Gordon, "My Story of Historic Race Relations Change in the South," n.d., ten-page outline in possession of the author.

2. *LSS*, June 25, 1953, 1; "Atlanta Listed as Metropolitan," *Atlanta Constitution*, February. 4, 1949, 11; "Profile of Metro Atlanta, *Metropolitan Atlanta Chamber of Commerce*, https://www.metroatlantachamber.com/resources/reports-and-information/executive-profile; "About the Atlanta Regional Commission," *Atlanta Regional Commission*, https://atlantaregional.org/about-arc/.

3. Delton, *Racial Integration in Corporate America*, 176–91.

4. Dobbin, *Inventing Equal Opportunity*, 12–15.

5. Skrentny, *Ironies of Affirmative Action*, 139–42; Rubio, *History of Affirmative Action*, especially xiii–xv; Katznelson, *When Affirmative Action Was White*; *LSS*, September 14, 1951, 1.

6. Stainback and Tomaskovic-Devey, *Documenting Desegregation*, Kindle loc. 556.

7. Ibid., 595–600.

8. Ibid., 608, 620–22.

9. Ibid., 671–75.

10. Ibid., 674–78.

11. Stainback, *Documenting Desegregation*, Kindle loc. 688.

12. Marable, *Race, Rebellion, and Reform*, 84–85; Eskew, *But for Birmingham*,

333–37; Wallerstein, "1968, Revolution"; Stone, *Regime Politics*, 3. See also Hunter, *Community Power Succession*, 150–52.

Chapter 1. "Economic Necessity and Governmental Pressures"

1. Boyne, *Beyond the Horizons*, 243–44.
2. History Factory, *Innovation with Purpose*, 126–27, 62–63.
3. The standard history of Lockheed is Boyne, *Beyond the Horizon*. For a brief history of Lockheed, see the Lockheed Martin corporate website, http://www.lockheedmartin.com/us.html. For a critical appraisal of Lockheed's history, especially the firm's relationship with the federal government, see Hartung, *Prophets of War*.
4. Hartung, *Prophets of War*, 37–39.
5. Boyne, *Beyond the Horizon*, 55.
6. Rae, "Financial Problems," 110.
7. Boston, *Labor, Civil Rights*, 83; Hill, *Black Labor*, 102. For a detailed discussion of the civil rights community and the Wagner Act, see Hill, *Black Labor*, 101–5.
8. Biddle, *Barons of the Sky*, 258–60. See also Vander Meulen, "West Coast Aircraft Labor," 14–15.
9. Weaver, "Recent Developments," 242; Abel, "African Americans, Labor Unions," 622, 635–37.
10. Vander Meulen, "West Coast Aircraft Labor," 12–13; Boyne, *Beyond the Horizon*, 93, 112.
11. Lockheed, "Lockheed Electra-Fies the Airlines." This publication was serialized for distribution at the Lockheed Air Terminal and among employees.
12. Putney, "Revival of Apprenticeship." For a detailed overview of U.S. government training policies and programs in this period, see Dorn, "Investing in Human Capital."
13. *Los Angeles Times*, April 21, 1939, 11,
14. Hill, *Black Labor*, 177.
15. "Executive Order 8802: Prohibition of Discrimination in the Defense Industry (1941)," *OurDocuments.gov*, https://www.ourdocuments.gov/doc.php?flash=false&doc=72.
16. Collins, "Race, Roosevelt and Wartime Production," 283–84. See also Wright, *Sharing the Prize*, Kindle loc. 1186.
17. Weaver, "Negro Employment," 608–9. See also Wilson, *Segregated Scholars*, 230–45; Conrad and Scherer, "From the New Deal."
18. Weaver, "Negro Employment," 609–10.
19. Ibid.
20. Leonard, *Battle for Los Angeles*, 32–33.
21. Weaver, "Negro Employment," 610; Boyne, *Beyond the Horizons*, 131.
22. Quoted in Covington, "Democracy at Work," 162; *The Crisis* 48 (May 1941): 151.
23. Covington, "Democracy at Work," 162. For background on Covington, see Flamming, *Bound for Freedom*, 251, 299–300, 343–45, 363–64.
24. Weaver, "Negro Employment," 620–24.
25. Irwin, "Experience with Negro Workers," 65–72.
26. Ibid., 66; Dinero, *Training within Industry*, 24. For a brief summary and an

analysis of the management and labor responses to TWI, see Breen, "Social Science and State Policy." For a detailed description of the program, see *Training within Industry Report*. On TWI's postwar influence in Japan, Europe, and the U.S., see TWI Institute website, http://twi-institute.org/training-within-industry/. On Irwin's early work in training at Lockheed, see Carrington, "Skill to Order," 43, 56.

27. Irwin, "Experience with Negro Workers," 66.
28. Ibid., 67.
29. Ibid., 69.
30. Ibid., 70.
31. Ibid. On "good Negroes" and "bad Negroes," see Mixon, "Good Negro—Bad Negro." For just one modern example of the proliferation of the stereotypes, see Deadspin staff, "Russell Wilson."
32. Weaver, "Negro Employment," 620–24.
33. Scott, *Cobb County, Georgia*, 110–11. Scott's chaps. 5 and 6 detail the recruitment and development of the facility under Bell management. See also Holland, *Under One Roof*, 3–9.
34. Scott, *Cobb County, Georgia*, 110–11.
35. Ibid., 168–71. For a fuller discussion of the FEPC's efforts at Bell, see Merl Reed, "Bell Aircraft Comes South."
36. Boyne, *Beyond the Horizon*, 131; Hartung, *Prophets of War*, 48–50, 51.
37. Hartung, *Prophets of War*, 52–53, 54.
38. Ibid., 53–54.
39. Ibid., 59.
40. Kofsky, *Harry Truman*, 12; Biddle, *Barons of the Sky*, 293.
41. Delton, *Racial Integration in Corporate America*, 20–21.
42. Wright, *Sharing the Prize*, Kindle loc. 1166.

Chapter 2. "Lockheed Will Live in the Southern Tradition"

1. "Walls of Prejudice Falling, Career Conference Leader Says," *ADW*, November 20, 1951, 1.
2. Ibid.
3. Wright, *Sharing the Prize*, Kindle loc. 1128–37; Onkst, "First a Negro"; Turner and Bound, "Closing the Gap; Katznelson, *When Affirmative Action Was White*.
4. "Economic Status of Southern Negroes Shows Improvement," *ADW*, June 29, 1954, 2.
5. *ADW*, September 14, 1951, 1; *AC*, September 14, 1951, 6.
6. *AC*, September 14, 1951, 6. On McGill, see Teel, *Ralph Emerson McGill*; for a brief characterization, see Teel, "Ralph McGill (1898–1969)."
7. *AC*, September 14, 1951, 6.
8. *ADW*, September 14, 1951, 1; Sverdik, "*Atlanta Daily World*."
9. Harry Hudson, "Don't Stand behind the Fan (Jet, That Is)," Kennesaw State University Archives.
10. James V. Carmichael, "New Command Performance Calls for Old Teamwork," *LSS*, March 29, 1951, 1.
11. Ibid.; James V. Carmichael, "Labor Negotiations Begin with IAM," *LSS*, March 29, 1951, 1.

12. Betty Chandler, "People You Should Know," *LSS*, September 14, 1951, 2.
13. Ibid. On Georgia's 1946 gubernatorial election and its tumultuous aftermath, see Bullock, Buchanan, and Gaddie, *Three Governors Controversy*.
14. "Carmichael Writes Himself Out," *AC*, December 22, 1946, 11A.
15. Scott, "James V. Carmichael."
16. Talmadge quoted in Henderson, "M. E. Thompson," 64.
17. "Carmichael Says Lockheed Plant Will Not Discriminate," *ADW*, November 6, 1951, 1; "Executive Order 10210—Authorizing the Department of Defense and the Department of Commerce to Exercise the Functions and Powers Set Forth in Title Ii of the First War Powers Act, 1941, as Amended by the Act of January 12, 1951, and Prescribing Regulations for the Exercise of Such Functions and Powers," *The American Presidency Project*, https://www.presidency.ucsb.edu/documents/executive-order-10210-authorizing-the-department-defense-and-the-department-commerce.
18. Ibid.
19. "Memorandum: Lockheed Conference," January 30, 1952, folder 6, box 275, AUL Papers.
20. *ADW*, November 6, 1951, 1. For a discussion of International Harvester's racial integration policies and experience, see Delton, *Racial Integration in Corporate America*, chap. 5.
21. Delton, *Racial Integration in Corporate America*, 131.
22. Ibid., 137–38. See also Honey, *Going Down Jericho Road*, 38.
23. Delton, *Racial Integration in Corporate America*, 139–42.
24. *ADW*, November 6, 1951, 1.
25. C. L. Harper and C. W. Greenlea to James V. Carmichael, November 24, 1951, folder 6, box 275 AUL Papers.
26. C. L. Harper and C. W. Greenlea to Robert Gross, December 4, 1951, folder 6, box 275, AUL Papers.
27. *Notre Dame Alumnus* 35, 2 (February–March 1957): 41.
28. "Memorandum: Lockheed Conference," January 30, 1952, folder 7, box 275, AUL Papers. This meeting is also discussed briefly in the introduction to Hudson, *Working for Equality*.
29. Ibid.
30. Ibid.; "Committee Meeting, Lockheed Aircraft Company," January 24, 1952, folder 7, box 275, AUL Papers.
31. "Allegations of Discrimination Made by the National Urban League at Hearings before the President's Committee on Government Contract Compliance," July 9, 1952, Government Contract Compliance Case Files Re: Charges, box 9, Record Group 325, National Archives and Records Administration, Washington, D.C.
32. Ibid.
33. Ibid.
34. Ibid.
35. Ibid.
36. Gordon, interview by Scott and Patton.
37. "65 Top-Flight Consultants Set for Morehouse Career Meet," *ADW*, April 26, 1953, 1.

38. Hudson, "Don't Stand behind the Fan," 4, 8.
39. Ibid., 13.
40. Ibid.
41. Ibid., 14.
42. Ibid., 22–25.
43. *ADW*, December 19, 1952, 1.
44. Ibid.
45. Beatrice Murphy, "Fair Hiring at Lockheed," *Afro Magazine*, February 7, 1953, 10, clipping in folder 6, box 275, AUL Papers.
46. Scott, *Cobb County, Georgia*, 216–17, 223; "Dan Haughton," *National Aviation Hall of Fame*, http://www.nationalaviation.org/haughton-daniel-j/; Scott, "Impact of Bell and Lockheed."
47. *ADW*, December 2, 1954, 3.
48. Scott, "Impact of Bell and Lockheed."
49. Hudson, "Don't Stand behind the Fan," 22. On pull and networking, see Laird, *Pull*, chap. 5.
50. Hudson, "Don't Stand behind the Fan," 25–26; *ADW*, October 25, 1953, 1; *Jet*, November 12, 1953, 7.
51. *LSS*, October 29, 1953, 6.
52. Ferguson interview. See also Susan Reed, *Diversity Index*.
53. Hugh Gordon, "My Story of Historic Race Relations Change in the South," manuscript in possession of the author.
54. Hudson, "Don't Stand behind the Fan," 25.
55. Ibid., 26.
56. Ibid., 26–27.
57. Ibid.
58. Mintz interview.
59. Ibid.
60. Ibid., 30.
61. Ibid., 32.
62. Ibid., 32; Gordon Kemp interview.
63. McLendon interview.
64. Ibid.
65. Ibid.
66. U.S. Manuscript Census, 1930, 1940; *Milford Chronicle*, October 1, 1937, available at http://delmardustpan.blogspot.com/2008_09_28_archive.html?m=1; Hudson, "Don't Stand behind the Fan," 38.
67. Hudson, "Don't Stand behind the Fan," 7, 13, 38–39.

Chapter 3. "Progress to Be Permanent Had to Be Gradual"

1. *ADW*, February 2, 1954, 4.
2. Dewey, "Negro Employment in Southern Industry," 283–84.
3. Gordon, interview by Scott and Patton. On state fair employment agencies and laws, see Delton, *Racial Integration in Corporate America*, 27, 140, 158.
4. Delton, *Rethinking the 1950s*, 110–12.
5. Harry L. Alston to James C. Evans, October 20, 1954, Committee on Gov-

ernment Contract Compliance Case Files Re: Charges, box 9, Record Group 325, National Archives and Records Administration, Washington, D.C.

6. Hudson, "Don't Stand behind the Fan," 28.

7. James Evans to Harry Alston, December 1, 1954, Committee on Government Contract Compliance, Complaints File.

8. Charles Livermore to James Evans, December 8, 1954, Committee on Government Contract Compliance, Complaints File.

9. Boyne, *Beyond the Horizons*, 235, 255.

10. Ross interview.

11. Ibid.

12. Ibid.

13. Ibid.

14. Ibid.

15. Gordon Kemp interview.

16. Ibid.

17. Ibid.

18. Ibid.

19. Ibid.

20. J. O. Wyatt affidavit, April 5, 1961, folder 34, box 7, Kruse Papers.

21. *ADW*, March 2, 1948, 1; Elkins Affidavit.

22. Elkins Affidavit.

23. Ibid.

24. Ibid.; E. G. Mattison affidavit, March 28, 1961, folder 33, box 7, Kruse Papers.

25. Elkins Affidavit. Elkins's affidavit stated that Kennon had been fired in the summer of 1955; however, Lockheed's industrial relations director, E. G. Mattison, who was responsible for reviewing relevant personnel files and composing the company's responses to the complaints, reported that Kennon had "terminated his employment voluntarily in August 1953." The two accounts also differed on the timing of Kennon's replacement and on other matters. See Mattison affidavit.

26. Elkins Affidavit. Gene Mattison disputed the timing of Elkins's conversations with Hinds and denied that Hinds had been asked to sign any sort of confidentiality agreement.

27. J. B. Mabry affidavit, March 27, 1961, folder 33, box 7, Kruse Papers.

28. Ibid.

29. Ibid.

30. Elkins Affidavit.

31. Elkins Affidavit; Alfred Holmes, "Open Letter to Lockheed Employees," *ADW*, October 13, 1957, 4; Herbert Hill, "Status of Negro Workers," 148. See also "Merger Move Is Voted by Lockheed Local Union," *ADW*, October 18, 1957, 6.

32. Alfred Holmes, "Open Letter to Lockheed Employees," *ADW*, October 13, 1957, 4.

33. "Merger Move Is Voted by Lockheed Local Union," *ADW*, October 18, 1957, 6; "Committee Asks Negro, White Not to Merge at Lockheed," *ADW*, November 14, 1957, 1; Elkins Affidavit.

34. Northrup, "Negro in Aerospace Work," 23.

35. "Campaign Launched on Lockheed Plant Bias," *ADW*, March 29, 1961, 1;

Ross interview. Hollowell distinctly remembered warning the partially disabled Carmichael that he would have to climb twenty-five or so steps to get to Hollowell's office. Carmichael had replied to Hollowell that the meeting was important because "we need that contract," so he would get up the steps. Hollowell and Ross believed that the first production contract for the C-130 had prompted the African American complaints. Hollowell believed the meeting was in the early 1950s. Ross dated it to 1954 or 1955, since he did not go to work at Lockheed until 1953 and believed that it occurred after his marriage in April 1954. The precise date is unimportant, except that both participants remembered it specifically as related to the C-130 rather than the C-141, which prompted the better-known crisis in 1961. While the Georgia division received a contract for C-130s in 1954, numerous additions and revisions were made to the contract in later in the decade, and the meeting may have been related to one of these follow-up deals.

36. Ross interview.
37. Hudson, "Don't Stand behind the Fan," 34.
38. Laird, *Pull*, chap 5.
39. Mintz interview.
40. Herbert Hill, "Status of Negro Workers," 146–47.
41. Ibid. Hill placed the word *accidental* in quotes, indicating that someone else—probably a local white union leader—had used that term.
42. Hudson, "Don't Stand behind the Fan," 37.
43. Ibid., 38.
44. Ibid., 39–40.
45. Ibid., 43.
46. Mangum and Parcell, "Pet Milk Company 'Happy Family' Advertising Campaign," 71. The Fultz campaign had the dubious effect of promoting the substitution of Pet Milk and infant formula for breastfeeding. On marketing to the African American community, see Delton, *Racial Integration in Corporate America*, 47–53; Chambers, *Madison Avenue*; Moss Kendrix pages, *Museum of Public Relations*, http://www.prmuseum.com/kendrix/moss1.html; Capparell, *Real Pepsi Challenge*; Warren Goldstein, "The Color of Cola," *NYT*, February 4, 2007, 3D.
47. Hudson interview; *Washington Afro-American*, October 19, 1957, 18.
48. Hudson, "Don't Stand behind the Fan," 46.
49. Ibid.
50. Ibid., 46–47.
51. Ibid., 60–61.
52. E. G. Mattison, "General Non-Discrimination Policies and Practices of the Georgia Division, Lockheed Aircraft Corporation," May 1, 1961, folder 35, box 7, Kruse Papers. For slightly different employment numbers that fit the same general pattern, see Holland, *Under One Roof*, 54.
53. "C130s Help Hiring by Lockheed," *AC*, February 8, 1961, 8.
54. Mattison affidavit.

Chapter 4. "A Problem That Was Already Here"

1. Huff, "Sibley Commission."
2. Bartley, *Creation of Modern Georgia*, 215.

3. Huff, "Sibley Commission"; Roche, *Restructured Resistance*, 148–50.

4. Albert Riley, "Lockheed Given $1 Billion Order Providing 5,000 Jobs at Marietta," *AC*, March 14, 1961, 1.

5. Marion Gaines, "Georgians Hail Boost in Economy," *AC*, March 14, 1961, 1; *LSS*, March 17, 1961, 1.

6. Gordon Roberts, "'Brand-New Era' Seen for State: AIG Head Says Economic Good Tidings Not a 'Windfall,'" *Atlanta Journal*, March 19, 1961, 1.

7. "Schools Accent Lockheed Pact," *AC*, March 17, 1961, 11; "Lockheed Gets a Nice Nod," *ADW*, March 16, 1961. This fits well with Gavin Wright's general analysis of the relationship between civil rights reform and the business community. See Wright, *Sharing the Prize*.

8. "Pulse of the Public," *AC*, March 24, 1961, 4.

9. William Fowlkes, "Mayor Yet Doesn't Know about Race," *ADW*, March 16, 1961, 1.

10. Brown-Nagin, *Courage to Dissent*, 168–71; Hatfield, "Atlanta Sit-Ins."

11. Panel IV of Rockefeller Brothers Fund, *Challenge to America*, 25; Hodgson, *America in Our Time*, chap. 4; Delton, *Rethinking the 1950s*, especially chap. 3.

12. "Executive Order 10925: Establishing the President's Committee on Equal Employment Opportunity," *Equal Employment Opportunity Commission*, https://www.eeoc.gov/eeoc/history/35th/thelaw/eo-10925.html. For an analysis of the order, see McLaury, "President Kennedy's E.O. 10925."

13. Graham, *Civil Rights and the Presidency*, 37–38.

14. "Say Vending Machines Set for Lockheed Food," *ADW*, March 28, 1961; *LSS*, March 17, 1961, 1; E. G. Mattison, "Memorandum for File, Subject: Meeting with Negro Attorney Donald L. Hollowell Re: Colored Problem in the Plant," March 27, 1961, quoted in Reed, *Diversity Index*, 69.

15. Harmon Perry, "Campaign Launched on Lockheed Plant Bias," *ADW*, March 29, 1961, 1.

16. "Billion for Lockheed Protested by NAACP," *AC*, April 1, 1961, 1; "Re-Examination of Lockheed Plant Contract Urged," *ADW*, April 1, 1961, 1.

17. "Billion for Lockheed Protested by NAACP," *AC*, April 1, 1961, 1. See also "Re-Examination of Lockheed Plant Contract Urged," *ADW*, April 1, 1961, 1.

18. "U.S. to Act to End Segregation at Lockheed," *ADW*, April 12, 1961, 1.

19. Feild interview.

20. 1940 U.S. Census; "Labor Day Forum," *The Voice: Weekly Publication of the Diocese of Miami*, August 26, 1966, 3.

21. E. G. Mattison, "General Non-Discrimination Policies and Practices of the Georgia Division, Lockheed Aircraft Corporation," May 1, 1961, folder 35, box 7, Kruse Papers. Mattison had access to company personnel records in preparing his affidavit, so the document offers some revealing information. However, Mattison also was explicitly countering the complaints and presenting support for company management's position that it was dealing with "a problem that was already here."

22. Ibid.

23. Ibid.

24. Ibid.

25. Ibid.

26. R. H. Hudson affidavit, April 21, 1961, folder 35, box 7, Kruse Papers; obituary, *Anderson Independent-Mail*, October 20, 2015.

27. Hudson affidavit.

28. Ibid.

29. Ibid.

30. Ibid.

31. Ibid.

32. E. G. Mattison affidavit in response to complaint of J. O. Wyatt, April 5, 1961, folder 33, box 7, Kruse Papers.

33. Win LeSueur affidavit, April 19, 1961, folder 35, box 7, Kruse Papers.

34. Ibid.

35. Mattison affidavit in response to Wyatt.

36. Feild interview; Gordon, interview by Scott and Patton. The general story of Lockheed's negotiations with the PCEEO and the development of the quasi-voluntary Plans for Progress program has already been relatively well explored from a variety of perspectives: see Anderson, *Pursuit of Fairness*, 64–65; Delton, *Racial Integration in Corporate America*, 177–79; Dobbin, *Inventing Equal Opportunity*, 14–15; Graham, *Civil Rights and the Presidency*, 43–47; MacLean, *Freedom Is Not Enough*, 44, 70–71.

37. Peter Braestrup, "Lockheed Signs Equal Jobs Pact," *NYT*, May 26, 1961, 20.

38. *LSS*, June 2, 1961, 1. Although Gordon recalled in his 2009 interview with Scott and Patton that the personnel department had provided a two-page insert for the *Southern Star*'s announcement of the plan, no such insert has been found.

39. Delton, *Racial Integration in Corporate America*, 177–90.

40. Dobbin, *Inventing Equal Opportunity*, 6–10; Delton, *Racial Integration in Corporate America*, 180–82.

41. Troutman interview; "Statistics: Elections," *American Presidency Project*, https://www.presidency.ucsb.edu/statistics/elections.

42. Roche, *Restructured Resistance*, 176–77.

43. "Civil Rights Maverick: Robert Battey Troutman, Jr.," *NYT*, June 23, 1962, 21; Gordon, interview by Scott and Patton.

44. Feild Oral History; Troutman Oral History.

45. "Civil Rights Maverick: Robert Battey Troutman, Jr.," *NYT*, June 23, 1962, 21.

46. Peter Braestrup, "Javits Questions Troutman's Role," *NYT*, June 20, 1962, 16; Peter Braestrup, "U.S. Panel Split over Negro Jobs," *NYT*, June 18, 1962, 1.

47. Peter Braestrup, "White House Urged to Use Compulsion in Negro Job Drive," *NYT*, August 19, 1962, 1; "Troutman Leaves Johnson's Group," *NYT*, August 24, 1962, 11.

48. Taylor interview.

49. Delton, *Racial Integration in Corporate America*, 188.

50. Taylor interview.

51. "He Shaped Up and Wasn't Shipped Out," *NYT*, July 12, 1968, F3; "Program Finds Jobs for 100,000 Negroes," *Detroit Free Press*, August 27, 1965, 18. Miller went on to serve as chair of the Federal Reserve and Treasury Secretary under President Jimmy Carter.

52. Anderson, *Pursuit of Fairness*, 64–65. For an even bleaker assessment, see MacLean, *Freedom Is Not Enough*, 44.

53. Delton, *Racial Integration in Corporate America*, 190; Dobbin, *Inventing Equal Opportunity*, 48–49.

54. Delton, *Racial Integration in Corporate America*, 190; Gelber, *Black Men and Businessmen*, 207.

55. "Integration Has a Quiet Side, Too," *NYT*, April 7, 1963, 60.

56. Ibid.; *St. Joseph News-Press*, April 7, 1963, 5A.

57. Hudson, "Don't Stand behind the Fan," 61; McLendon interview.

58. Hudson, "Don't Stand behind the Fan," 70; McLendon interview.

59. Ibid.; *San Francisco Chronicle*, January 20, 2013. After a year of college and seven years with Dun and Bradstreet, Rieke, an Iowa native, had joined Lockheed as a purchasing clerk in 1941, rising to the position of executive vice president of the corporation and president of one of its subsidiaries prior to his 1980 retirement.

60. Hudson, "Don't Stand behind the Fan," 71.

61. Ibid.

62. Ibid.

63. Ibid., 69–70.

64. Ibid., 71.

65. Ibid.

66. Hudson, "Don't Stand behind the Fan," 70.

Chapter 5. "Build the People"

1. Holland, *Under One Roof*, 73–74; Sinkfield interview.

2. Holland, *Under One Roof*, 73–74. About 43 percent of Lockheed-Georgia employees participated in the survey, and no information on their demographics is available.

3. Holland, *Under One Roof*, 54.

4. R. H. Hudson to Mike Biddle, "Status of Hard Core Training Program," September 19, 1969, folder 30, box 2, Gordon Papers.

5. Holzer, "Work Force Development Programs," Kindle loc. 2904–21.

6. Ibid.

7. Sugrue, *Sweet Land of Liberty*, Kindle loc. 6729–65.

8. R. H. Hudson, "Industrial Pre-Employment Training Program (Hard Core)," September 19, 1969, "Lockheed-Georgia Hard Core Training 1968 Year End Report, both in folder 30, box 2, Gordon Papers.

9. R. H. Hudson, "Industrial Pre-Employment Training Program (Hard Core)," September 19, 1969, folder 30, box 2, Gordon Papers.

10. Ibid.

11. Ibid.

12. C. A. Jenkins to President's Staff, January 31, 1969, "Lockheed-Georgia Hard Core Training 1968 Year End Report," both in folder 30, box 2, Gordon Papers.

13. "Lockheed-Georgia Hard Core Training 1968 Year End Report, folder 30, box 2, Gordon Papers.

14. Ibid.

15. Ibid.
16. *NYT*, January 24, 1968, 24; Holzer, "Work Force Development Programs," Kindle loc. 2925.
17. Hugh Gordon, "Training," notes for panel discussion for "Employers' Seminar on Employing the Hard Core," June 26, 1968, Georgia Power Company Auditorium, Atlanta, folder 30, box 2, Gordon Papers.
18. Hugh Gordon to C. A. Jenkins, "Employee Discipline," February 12, 1969, folder 27, box 2, Gordon Papers.
19. Ibid.
20. Hugh Gordon to C. A. Jenkins, "Evaluation of Equal Employment Opportunity," June 27, 1969, folder 27, box 2, Gordon Papers.
21. Ibid.
22. Ibid.
23. Ibid.
24. Ibid.
25. Ibid.
26. Ibid.
27. Ibid.
28. Hugh Gordon, "Review of McDonnell-Douglas Corporation Affirmative Action Plan (AAP)," [early 1970?], folder 28, box 2, Gordon Papers.
29. Ibid.
30. Ibid.
31. Ibid.
32. "HLG's EEO Speech to Gelac President's Staff," n.d., probably March–April 1970, folder 28, box 2, Gordon Papers.
33. Ibid.
34. Ibid.
35. Ibid.; McCrudden, *Buying Social Justice*, 147–48.
36. "HLG's EEO Speech to Gelac President's Staff."
37. Ibid.
38. Ibid.
39. Ibid.
40. Ibid.
41. Ibid.
42. *Build the People: A Manager's Guide*, 1, folder 6, box 3, Gordon Papers.
43. Ibid.
44. Dobbin, *Inventing Equal Opportunity*, 101–31.
45. *Build the People: A Manager's Guide*, 13.
46. Ibid., 2.
47. Ibid., 3.
48. Ibid., 5.
49. *Build the People: A Manager's Guide*, 20.
50. Ibid., 21.
51. Ibid.
52. Ibid.
53. Ibid., 27–28.

54. Ibid., 26.
55. Ibid.
56. Boyle, "Inside a Segregationist," 53; Cohen, "Los Angeles Riot Study." See also Farley, "Politics of Colorlined Space," 120–21.
57. *Build the People: A Manager's Guide*, 29.
58. Ibid.
59. Ibid.

Chapter 6. "The Competitive Economic Advantages of Having an Excellent Minority Hiring Record"

1. *Banks v. Lockheed-Georgia*, NAACP Case Files.
2. Equal Employment Opportunity Commission decision, Frank Adair, Ralph Banks, et al., charging parties, December 12, 1967, NAACP Case Files.
3. Ibid.
4. Ibid., 9.
5. Ibid.
6. Ibid., 11.
7. Ibid., 25; EEO-1 Form, July 16, 1966, Banks Case File, NAACP Papers.
8. Minchin, "Making Best Use," 702, 690.
9. Keith McDonald, "Final Investigation Report," November 6, 1967, 11–12, NAACP Case Files.
10. Ibid., 12–13.
11. Ibid., 14.
12. Ibid.
13. Ibid., 3.
14. Ibid., 4–5.
15. Ibid., 11–13.
16. Ibid., 9.
17. *LSS*, January 5, 1967, 1.
18. Ibid.
19. Ibid., 4.
20. Ibid., 5; *Michigan Alumnus*, October 24, 1959, 46; Elkins Affidavit.
21. Hames, "Jumping into History"; Alexa Mills, "A Lynching Kept out of Sight," *Washington Post*, September 2, 2016; *ADW*, December 12, 1996, 1.
22. *ADW*, December 12, 1996, 1.
23. *LSS*, July 18, 1968, 8.
24. "Eight Charge Lockheed with Bias," *AC*, March 22, 1968, 37; "Negro Sues Lockheed on Alleged Race Bias," *AC*, June 15, 1968, 19.
25. Hugh Gordon to Dwight Zook, July 25, 1969, folder 28, box 2, Gordon Papers.
26. "Blacks Charge Lockheed Bias," *AC*, April 5, 1970, 2A; "Early Efforts," *Equal Employment Opportunity Commission*, https://www.eeoc.gov/eeoc/history/35th/1965-71/early_enforcement.html.
27. "Rights Groups Pledge Aid to Blacks' Lockheed Fight," *AC*, May 3, 1970, 8C.
28. Goodman, "Lockheed Racism."
29. Boyne, *Beyond the Horizons*, 338–39.

30. Ibid., 331, 340.

31. Dan Haughton to All Members of Supervision, "Our Legal and Contractual Requirements in Equal Employment Opportunity," June 16, 1972, folder 29, box 2, Gordon Papers.

32. E. G. Mattison, "New Developments in Equal Employment Opportunity, Midyear Performance Meeting," July 7, 1972, folder 29, box 2, Gordon Papers.

33. Ibid.

34. Ibid.

35. Ibid.

36. Ibid.; Gordon, interview by Scott and Patton.

37. Thomas O'Toole and Leon Dash, "How Space Shuttle Contract Was Won," *Washington Post*, reprinted in *Atlanta Journal-Constitution*, October 8, 1972, clipping in folder 29, box 2, Gordon Papers.

38. E. G. Mattison to L. O. Kitchen et al., November 3, 1972, folder 29, box 2, Gordon Papers. North American employed significant numbers of Mexican Americans, Asian Americans, and Native Americans as a consequence of the demographics of its California location; Atlanta did not yet have a substantial Latino population.

39. Hugh Gordon to Dwight Zook, July 25, 1969, folder 28, box 2, Gordon Papers.

40. Hugh Gordon to W. P. Key, August 29, 1972, "Outline of Program: Dissemination of Affirmative Action Policy Program," folder 29, box 2, Gordon Papers.

41. L. O. Kitchen, "Management Responsibility for EEO Compliance," October 1972, folder 29, box 2, Gordon Papers.

42. Ibid.

43. Ibid.

44. *Banks v. Lockheed-Georgia Co.*, 53 F.R.D. 283 (N.D. Ga. 1971); Hartstein and McCabe, "Weighing the Risks and Benefits," 670–71.

45. On the *Griggs* case, see Smith, *Race, Labor, and Civil Rights*.

46. Testimony of Hugh L. Gordon, December 14, 1971, NAACP Case Files.

47. Minchin and Salmond, *After the Dream*, 78–79.

48. Larry Kitchen to All Salaried Employees, "Gelac's Future," November 1, 1972, NAACP Case Files.

49. Settlement Agreement, signed by Roy Wilkins, January 17, 1973, NAACP Case Files.

50. Ibid.

51. Ibid.

52. C. W. Hill to Isabelle Gates Webster, December 14, 1972, NAACP Case Files.

53. Minchin and Salmond, *After the Dream*, 196.

Chapter 7. "Atlanta Will Be a Problem"

1. On national-level PFP-related efforts, see, for example, Delton, *Racial Integration in Corporate America*; Dobbin, *Inventing Equal Opportunity*; MacLean, *Freedom Is Not Enough*; Anderson, *Pursuit of Fairness*. On the nature of such public-private partnerships, see Delton, *Racial Integration in Corporate America*, 188. On the NAB's formation, see Califano, *Triumph and Tragedy*, 222–26.

2. Cobb, *Georgia Odyssey*, 81–82.

3. Hugh L. Gordon, "The Formation of Atlanta Merit Employment Association," January 25, 1967, paper presented at Fifth Annual Plans for Progress National Conference, Washington, D.C., folder 8, box 10, Gordon Papers.

4. "Employment Problems of Disadvantaged Youth in the City of Atlanta," July 19–30, 1965, Georgia State College, Atlanta, folder 2, box 8, Gordon Papers.

5. Minchin, *Hiring the Black Worker*; Gelber, *Black Men and Businessmen*, 92–95; Sugrue, *Sweet Land of Liberty*, 122.

6. "Minutes of Merit Employment Coordinating Committee, January 23, 1962," folder 2, box 37, AUL Papers; "Merit Employment Discussion Today at Hungry Club," *ADW*, February 14, 1962, 4.

7. Gordon, "Formation of Atlanta Merit Employment Association."

8. "Living Witness Program to Embrace 11,000 Youth," *ADW*, April 17, 1970, 8; John H. Patterson, "MEA and Youth Motivation Day: A Summary, 1966–1985," [late 1985–early 1986], folder 10, box 2, Gordon Papers.

9. Olivia Boggs, "The Impact of the Atlanta Youth Motivation Program," folder 9, box 2, Gordon Papers.

10. Ibid.

11. Hugh Gordon presentation to the Atlanta MEA Advisory Council on the twentieth anniversary, 1986, folder 2, box 8, Gordon Papers.

12. Gordon quoted in *New Orleans Times-Picayune*, November 11, 1966, clipping in folder 3, box 15, Gordon Papers.

13. Hugh Gordon presentation to Richmond, Va., business leaders, February 19, 1967, folder 2, box 8, Gordon Papers.

14. E. G. Mattison to Hugh Gordon, April 8, 1968, folder 24, box 1, Gordon Papers. Poore added the handwritten comment to a copy of the memo.

15. Hall, "Long Civil Rights Movement," 1258–59.

16. Drabant interview.

17. Ibid.

18. Ibid.

19. Helen Fogel, "Open Housing Making Gains?" *Detroit Free Press*, December 8, 1969, 28.

20. Drabant interview.

21. Ibid.

22. Ibid.

23. Ibid.

24. Conlan, *From New Federalism to Devolution*, 165–66.

25. Kruse, *White Flight Atlanta*, 5, 234; B. Drummond Ayers, "Atlanta Strikes Integration Bargain," *NYT*, April 25, 1973, 89. On Jackson's election, see Davies, *Mainstreaming Black Power*, chap. 4; Stone, *Regime Politics*; Keiser, *Subordination or Empowerment?*

26. See Kruse, *White Flight Atlanta*.

27. Joel Smith, "Massell Asks Help for Slowing White Flight to Suburbs," *ADW*, October 8, 1971, 1.

28. Davies, *Mainstreaming Black Power*, Kindle loc. 3671–77.

29. Ibid., 3658–64.

30. Ibid., Kindle loc. 4162–68, 4181.
31. Ibid., 4351.
32. *NYT*, August 14, 1979, B16; Gordon, interview by Scott and Patton.
33. Gordon, interview by Scott and Patton; *ADW*, August 14, 1977, 1, May 5, 1978, 1.
34. *ADW*, March 17, 1978, 1. In 2013, Turpeau remained convinced that CETA had been a boon to the community and lamented the Obama administration's inability/unwillingness to push for even larger-scale public works during the recent Great Recession (Turpeau interview) Tate, "Our Art Itself," explores the cultural significance of the Bureau/Office of Cultural Affairs and one of its signature early programs, the Neighborhood Arts Center, highlighting CETA employees' contributions to the city's cultural life.
35. Montgomery, "Private Sector Initiative Program." Card and Sullivan, "Measuring the Effect," for example, finds that "participation in CETA had a small to moderately large positive impact on the post-training employment probabilities of the 1976 cohort of adult male trainees" (526). In addition, classroom training provided significantly larger positive benefits than did on-the-job training, though the net effects of both were positive.
36. Stone, *Regime Politics*, 77–89.
37. "Private Sector Initiative Program (PSIP) Charter, Fiscal Year 1979," attached to Matthew Coffey to Robert Ormsby, March 20, 1978, folder 4, box 4, Gordon Papers.
38. Gordon, interview by Scott and Patton; Gordon, "My Story."
39. "PSIP Charter."
40. Hugh Gordon to Robert Ormsby, March 20, 1978, folder 4, box 4, Gordon Papers.
41. Montgomery, "Private Sector Initiative Program," 16–17.
42. Ibid., 14.
43. Ibid., 15.
44. Ibid., 16.
45. Ibid., 16.
46. Ibid., 16–17.
47. Austin Scott, "Sanitation Workers Strike in Atlanta Loaded with Ironies," *Washington Post*, April 17, 1977, 6; Davies, *Mainstreaming Black Power*, Kindle loc. 4383.
48. Austin Scott, "Sanitation Workers Strike in Atlanta Loaded with Ironies," *Washington Post*, April 17, 1977, 6.
49. Turpeau interview; Gordon, interview by Scott and Patton.
50. LaLonde, "Employment and Training Programs," 539; Holzer, "Work Force Development Programs," Kindle loc. 2972–3003.
51. Gordon, interview by Scott and Patton.
52. Stein, *Pivotal Decade*, Kindle loc. 3512; Stone, *Regime Politics*, chapter 7; Jennings, *Politics of Black Empowerment*, 29–30.
53. Holzer, "Work Force Development Programs," Kindle Loc. 3267–78, 3216.
54. White House Press Release, "Southern Regional Economic Conference, Session III," Emory University, Atlanta, March 29, 1995, Clinton Presidential Materials

Project, National Archives and Records Administration, http://clinton6.nara.gov/1995/03/1995-03-29-session-three-of-southern-economic-conference.html.

55. Jesse Jackson Address to Democratic National Convention, July 19, 1988, *American Rhetoric: Top 100 Speeches*, http://www.americanrhetoric.com/speeches/jessejackson1988dnc.htm.

56. Turpeau interview; *Atlanta Journal-Constitution*, August 17, 2009, A6.

57. See Dobbin, *Inventing Equal Opportunity*.

Conclusion

1. Harvey, *Enigma of Capital*, 10.
2. Delton, *Racial Integration in Corporate America*, 280–82; Stainback and Tomaskovic-Devey, *Documenting Desegregation*, Kindle loc. 4947–56.
3. Data for these tables come from a variety of sources, principally documents found in the Gordon Papers and the NAACP Case Files as well as *The Crisis* and Holland, *Under One Roof*, 33–34. The data are not comprehensive.
4. Gordon, interview by Scott and Patton; Taylor interview.
5. Delton, *Racial Integration*, 151–53.
6. Ibid., 152; Honey and Ciscel, "Race and Labor in Memphis," 241.
7. See Marable, *Race, Reform, and Rebellion*; Eskew, *But for Birmingham*; Wright, *Sharing the Prize*.
8. Sutton and Dobbin, "Two Faces of Governance," 808.
9. Wright, *Sharing the Prize*, Kindle loc. 3951.
10. Piketty, *Capital in the Twenty-First Century*, 1–38; Scheidel, *Great Leveler*, especially chaps. 3, 5. On the reductions in EEOC and OFCC funding, staff, and enthusiasm for enforcement, see Dobbin, *Inventing Equal Opportunity*, 136–39; Stainback and Tomaskovic-Devey, *Documenting Desegregation*, Kindle loc. 3009–3013; Wood, "Does Politics Make a Difference?"
11. Davies, *Mainstreaming Black Power*; Hobson, *Legend of the Black Mecca*.

Epilogue

1. Jade Jackson, "New Lockheed Executive Is Not Result of Bias Suits, Official Says," *ADW*, May 10, 2000, 1.
2. Ibid.
3. Sinkfield interview.
4. Ibid.
5. Ibid.
6. Ibid.
7. Ibid.
8. Cynthia Post, "Concerned Black Clergy Supports Lockheed Martin Workers in Discrimination Lawsuit," *ADW*, September 14, 2000, 8.
9. Bobby White, "Class-Action Status Denied," *Atlanta Journal-Constitution*, August 4, 2001, F1.
10. *Reid et al. v. Lockheed Martin*, August 2, 2001, 205 F.R.D. 655 (U.S. District Court, N.D. Georgia, Atlanta Division).
11. Ibid.; *Reid v. Lockheed Martin Aeronautics Co., Civil Rights Clearinghouse*, https://www.clearinghouse.net/detail.php?id=9440; Sinkfield interview.

12. Watkins, *Black O*, 202–4; Levit, "Megacases, Diversity."
13. Hudson, "Don't Stand behind the Fan," 127.
14. Ibid.; Frank, *Success and Luck*.
15. Hudson, "Don't Stand behind the Fan," 169.
16. Ibid.
17. Estlund, *Working Together*, Kindle loc. 2707–9.
18. Hugh Gordon to C. A. Jenkins, October 7, 1970, folder 30, box 2, Gordon Papers.
19. Ross interview; "High Tribute Paid John H. Patterson Here," *ADW*, December 15, 1996, 1.

BIBLIOGRAPHY

Archival Collections

Atlanta Urban League Papers, Woodruff Library, Atlanta University Center, Atlanta.
Hugh L. Gordon Papers. Gordon, Kruse, Wentzel Collection, Kennesaw State University Archives, Kennesaw, Ga.
Government Contract Compliance Case Files, Record Group 325, National Archives and Records Administration, Washington, D.C.
Hudson, Harry. "Don't Stand behind the Fan (Jet, That Is)." Kennesaw State University Archives, Kennesaw, Ga.
Joseph Kruse Papers, Gordon, Kruse, Wentzel Collection, Kennesaw State University Archives, Kennesaw, Ga.
Legal Department Case Files, 1960–1972, Section II, Series A, Supplement to Part 23, Papers of the National Association for the Advancement of Colored People, microfilm edition.
Fred Wentzel Papers. Gordon, Kruse, Wentzel Collection, Kennesaw State University Archives, Kennesaw, Ga.

Newspapers

Atlanta Constitution
Atlanta Daily World
Los Angeles Times
Marietta Daily Journal
New York Times
Washington Post

Interviews

Unless otherwise noted, all interviews are housed at Kennesaw State University Archives, Kennesaw, Ga., and are available via Scholarly Online Access Repository (SOAR).

Sue Dominy, interview by Hugh Gordon, April 15, 2003.
Richard Drabant, interview by Hugh Gordon, March 4, 2004.
John G. Feild, interview by John F. Stewart, January 16, 1967, John F. Kennedy Library Oral History Program, Boston.
Charles Ferguson, interview by Brent Ragsdale, November 17, 2007, Bell/Lockheed Oral History Series, Kennesaw State University, Kennesaw, Ga.
Joe B. Gabriel, interview by Thomas A. Scott, October 23, 2000.
Hugh Gordon, interview by Stephen Briggs and John McKay, November 6, 2009.
Hugh Gordon, interview by Randall Patton, September 10, 2005.

Hugh Gordon, interview by Thomas Scott and Randall Patton, October 19, November 9, 2009.
Harry Hudson Jr., interview by Randall Patton, August 6, 2013. In possession of the author.
Alonza Jones, interview by James Newberry, December 11, 2014.
Gordon Kemp, interview by Hugh Gordon and Randall Patton, March 12, 2004.
Reginald Kemp, interview by Stephen Briggs and John McKay, October 31, 2009.
William Layburn, interview by Hugh Gordon, March 21, 2002.
Sherman Martin, interview by Hugh Gordon, August 12, 2002.
Jack McLendon, interview by Hugh Gordon, November 2, 2002.
Jim Mercer, interview by Hugh Gordon, March 21, 2003.
Harold Mintz, interview by Thomas Scott, August 10, 2000.
Wade Mitchell, interview by Hugh Gordon, January 23, 2006.
H. Wynn Montgomery, interview by Randall Patton, May 29, 2012.
Victor Priebe, interview by Hugh Gordon, March 3, 2003.
Ernest "Pappy" Ross, interview by Hugh Gordon, February 12, 2004.
Clarence Sinkfield, interview by Hugh Gordon and Randall Patton, March 10, 2004.
J. Edward Stahl, interview by Hugh Gordon, July 10, 2006.
Hobart Taylor Jr., interview by John Stewart, January 11, 1967, John F. Kennedy Library Oral History Program, Boston.
Robert Battey Troutman Jr., interview by David Powers, February 2, 1965, John F. Kennedy Library Oral History Program, Boston.
Aaron Turpeau, interview by Randall Patton, May 23, 2012, September 10, 2013.
Charlie Webb Jr., interview by Stephen Briggs, November 16, 2009.

Books, Articles, and Dissertations

Abel, Joseph. "African Americans, Labor Unions, and the Struggle for Fair Employment in the Aircraft Manufacturing Industry of Texas, 1941–1945." *Journal of Southern History* 77, 3 (August 2011): 595–638.
Anderson, Terry. *The Pursuit of Fairness: A History of Affirmative Action.* New York: Oxford University Press, 2004.
Bartley, Numan V. *The Creation of Modern Georgia.* 2nd ed. Athens: University of Georgia Press, 1990.
———. *The New South: The Story of the South's Modernization, 1945–1980.* Rev. ed. Baton Rouge: Louisiana State University Press, 1996.
Biddle, Wayne. *Barons of the Sky.* 1991; Baltimore: Johns Hopkins University Press, 2001.
Boston, Michael R., Jr. *Labor, Civil Rights, and Hughes Tool Company.* College Station: Texas A&M University Press, 2005.
Boyle, Sarah Patton. "Inside a Segregationist." *Ebony*, June 1963, 53–58.
Boyne, Walter J. *Beyond the Horizons: The Story of Lockheed.* New York: Dunne, 1998.
Branch, Taylor. *At Canaan's Edge: America in the King Years, 1965–68.* New York: Simon and Schuster, 2007.
———. *Parting the Waters: America in the King Years 1954–63.* New York: Simon and Schuster, 1989.

Breen, William J. "Social Science and State Policy in World War II: Human Relations, Pedagogy, and Industrial Training, 1940–1945." *Business History Review* 76, 2 (2002): 233–66.
Brown-Nagin, Tomika. *The Courage to Dissent: Atlanta and the Long History of the Civil Rights Movement*. New York: Oxford University Press, 2012.
Bullock, Charles S., Scott E. Buchanan, and Ronald Keith Gaddie. *The Three Governors Controversy: Skullduggery, Machinations, and the Decline of Georgia's Progressive Politics*. Athens: University of Georgia Press, 2015.
Califano, Joseph. *The Triumph and Tragedy of Lyndon Johnson*. New York: Simon and Schuster, 1991.
Capparell, Stephanie. *The Real Pepsi Challenge: How One Pioneering Company Broke Color Barriers in 1940s American Business*. New York: Simon and Schuster, 2007.
Card, David, and Daniel Sullivan. "Measuring the Effect of Subsidized Training Programs on Movements in and out of Employment." *Econometrica* 56, 3 (May 1988): 497–530.
Carrington, M. H. "Skill to Order." *Flying*, July 3, 1940, 42–43, 56.
Chambers, Jason. *Madison Avenue and the Color Line: African-Americans in the Advertising Industry*. Philadelphia: University of Pennsylvania Press, 2011.
Cobb, James C. *Georgia Odyssey*. Athens: University of Georgia Press, 2008.
Cohen, Nathan. "The Los Angeles Riot Study." *Social Work* 12, 4 (October 1967): 14–21.
Collins, William J. "Race, Roosevelt and Wartime Production: Fair Employment in World War II Labor Markets." *American Economic Review* 91 (March 2001): 272–86.
Conlan, Timothy. *From New Federalism to Devolution: Twenty-Five Years of Intergovernmental Reform*. Washington, D.C.: Brookings Institution, 1998.
Conrad, Cecilia, and George Scherer. "From the New Deal to the Great Society: The Economic Activism of Robert C. Weaver." In *A Different Vision: African-American Economic Thought*, ed. Thomas Boston, 290–301. New York: Routledge, 1997.
Covington, Floyd. "Democracy at Work." *Opportunity* 12, 4 (Fall 1944): 162–64.
Daniels, Maurice. *Saving the Soul of Georgia: Donald L. Hollowell and the Struggle for Civil Rights*. Athens: University of Georgia Press, 2013.
Davies, Tom Adam. *Mainstreaming Black Power*. Oakland: University of California Press, 2017.
Deadspin staff. "Russell Wilson: The Curse of the 'Good Negro.'" *Deadspin*, February 12, 2014. https://deadspin.com/the-big-book-of-black-quarterbacks-1517763742/1521506522.
Delton, Jennifer. *Racial Integration in Corporate America, 1940–1990*. New York: Cambridge University Press, 2009.
———. *Rethinking the 1950s: How Anticommunism and the Cold War Made America Liberal*. New York: Cambridge University Press, 2013.
Dewey, Donald. "Negro Employment in Southern Industry." *Journal of Political Economy* 60, 4 (August 1952): 279–93.
Dinero, Donald. *Training within Industry: The Foundation of Lean*. New York: Productivity, 2005.

Dobbin, Frank. *Inventing Equal Opportunity*. Princeton: Princeton University Press, 2009.

Dorn, Richard D. "Investing in Human Capital: The Origins of Federal Job Training Programs, 1900–1945. PhD diss., Ohio State University, 2007.

Eskew, Glenn. *But for Birmingham: The Local and National Movements in the Civil Rights Struggle*. Chapel Hill: University of North Carolina Press, 1997.

Estlund, Cynthia. *Working Together: How Workplace Bonds Strengthen a Diverse Democracy*. New York: Oxford University Press, 2003.

Farley, Anthony Paul. "The Politics of Colorlined Space." In *Crossroads, Directions, and a New Critical Race Theory*, ed. Francisco Valdes, Jerome McCristal Culp, and Angela P. Harris, 97–158. Philadelphia: Temple University Press, 2002.

Flamming, Douglas. *Bound for Freedom: Black Los Angeles in Jim Crow America*. Berkeley: University of California Press, 2005.

Frank, Robert. *Success and Luck: Good Fortune and the Myth of Meritocracy*. Princeton: Princeton University Press, 2017.

Gelber, Steven M. *Black Men and Businessmen: The Growing Awareness of a Social Responsibility*. Port Washington, N.Y.: Kennikat, 1974.

Golland, David Hamilton. *Constructing Affirmative Action: The Struggle for Equal Employment Opportunity*. Lexington: University Press of Kentucky, 2011.

Goodman, Bob. "Lockheed Racism." *The Great Speckled Bird*, June 29, 1970, 11. http://wcadatadashboard.iac.gatech.edu/library/files/original/257945db4e82bd53eac5a8ee32946dc4.pdf.

Graham, Hugh D. *Civil Rights and the Presidency: Race and Gender in American Politics, 1960–1972*. New York: Oxford University Press, 1992.

Hall, Jacquelyn Dowd. "The Long Civil Rights Movement and the Political Uses of the Past." *Journal of American History* 91, 4 (March 2005): 1233–63.

Hames, Jaqueline. "Jumping into History: The Army's First African-American Paratroopers." *Soldiers*, November 15, 2013. http://soldiers.dodlive.mil/2014/02/jumping-into-history-the-armys-first-african-american-paratroopers/.

Hartstein, Barry, and Kathleen McCabe. "Weighing the Risks and Benefits of Voluntary Equal Employment Audits—Are They Really Worth It?" *Employee Relations Law Journal* 18 (Spring 1993): 669–79.

Hartung, William. *Prophets of War: Lockheed Martin and the Military-Industrial Complex*. New York: Nation Books, 2011.

Harvey, David. *The Enigma of Capital and the Crises of Capitalism*. New York: Oxford University Press, 2010.

Hatfield, Edward. "Atlanta Sit-Ins." In *New Georgia Encyclopedia*, June 6, 2017. https://www.georgiaencyclopedia.org/articles/history-archaeology/atlanta-sit-ins.

Henderson, Harold P. "M. E. Thompson and the Politics of Succession." In *Georgia Governors in an Age of Change*, ed. Harold P. Henderson and Gary Roberts, 49–65. Athens: University of Georgia Press, 1988.

Hill, Herbert. *Black Labor and the American Legal System*. Madison: University of Wisconsin Press, 1985.

———. "Status of Negro Workers at Lockheed Aircraft Corporation." *The Crisis*, March 1957, 146–48.

Hill, Walter B., Jr. "Finding Place for the Negro: Robert C. Weaver and the Groundwork for the Civil Rights Movement." *Prologue Magazine* 37, 1 (Spring 2005). https://www.archives.gov/publications/prologue/2005/spring/weaver.html.
The History Factory. *Innovation with Purpose: Lockheed Martin's First 100 Years*. Bethesda, Md.: Lockheed Martin, 2013.
Hobson, Maurice J. *The Legend of the Black Mecca: Politics and Class in the Making of Modern Atlanta*. Chapel Hill: University of North Carolina Press, 2017.
Hodgson, Godfrey. *America in Our Time: From World War II to Nixon—What Happened and Why*. New York: Vintage, 1978.
Holland, Jeffrey. *Under One Roof: The Story of Air Force Plant 6*. Wright-Patterson Air Force Base, Ohio: Aeronautical Systems Center, 2006.
Holzer, Harry. "Work Force Development Programs." In *Legacies of the War on Poverty*, ed. Martha J. Bailey and Sheldon Danziger, 121–50. New York: Sage, 2013.
Honey, Michael. *Going Down Jericho Road: The Memphis Strike, Martin Luther King's Last Campaign*. New York: Norton, 2007.
Honey, Michael, and David Ciscel. "Race and Labor in Memphis since the King Assassination." In *Life and Labor in the New South*, 236–57. Gainesville: University Press of Florida, 2012.
Hudson, Harry L. *Working for Equality: The Narrative of Harry Hudson*. Ed. Randall L. Patton. Athens: University of Georgia Press, 2015.
Huff, Christopher Allen. "Sibley Commission." In *New Georgia Encyclopedia*, May 17, 2016. https://www.georgiaencyclopedia.org/articles/education/sibley-commission.
Hunter, Floyd. *Community Power Succession: Atlanta's Policy-Makers Revisited*. Chapel Hill: University of North Carolina Press, 1980.
Irwin, R. Randall. "Experience with Negro Workers in Aircraft Factories." In *The Howard University Studies in the Social Sciences, Papers and Proceedings of the Eighth Annual Conference, October 18–20, 1944*, 65–72. Washington, D.C.: Howard University Press, 1945.
Jennings, James. *The Politics of Black Empowerment: The Transformation of Black Activism in Urban America*. Detroit: Wayne State University Press, 2001.
Katznelson, Ira. *When Affirmative Action Was White: An Untold History of Racial Inequality in Twentieth-Century America*. New York: Norton, 2005.
Keiser, Richard. *Subordination or Empowerment? African American Leadership and the Struggle for Political Power*. New York: Oxford University Press, 1997.
Kofsky, Frank. *Harry Truman and the War Scare of 1948*. New York: St. Martin's, 1995.
Kotz, Nicholas. *Lyndon Baines Johnson, Martin Luther King Jr., and the Laws That Changed America*. New York: Houghton Mifflin, 2005.
Kruse, Kevin M. *White Flight Atlanta and the Making of Modern Conservatism*. Princeton: Princeton University Press, 2007.
Laird, Pamela. *Pull: Networking and Success since Benjamin Franklin*. Cambridge: Harvard University Press, 2006.
LaLonde, Robert J. "Employment and Training Programs." In *Means-Tested Transfer Programs in the United States*, ed. Robert Moffitt, 517–88. Chicago: University of Chicago Press, 2003.

Leonard, Kevin Allen. *The Battle for Los Angeles: Racial Ideology and World War II.* Albuquerque: University of New Mexico Press, 2006.

Levit, Nancy. "Megacases, Diversity, and the Elusive Goal of Workplace Reform." *Boston College Law Review* 49 (2008): 367–429. https://www.bc.edu/content/dam/files/schools/law/bclawreview/pdf/49_2/02_levit.pdf.

Lockheed Corporation. "Lockheed Electra-Fies the Airlines." In *Of Men and Stars: A History of the Lockheed Aircraft Corporation*, June 1957. http://www.mbmcdaniel.com/burbankia/of_men_and_stars_4.pdf.

MacLean, Nancy. *Freedom Is Not Enough: The Opening of the American Workplace.* Cambridge: Harvard University Press, 2006.

Mangum, Kimberly, and Lisa M. Parcell. "The Pet Milk Company 'Happy Family' Advertising Campaign." *Journalism History* 40 (Summer 2014): 68–76.

Marable, Manning. *Race, Reform, and Rebellion: The Second Reconstruction and beyond in Black America, 1945–2006.* 3rd ed. New York: Oxford University Press, 2007.

McLaury, Judson. "President Kennedy's E.O. 10925: Seedbed of Affirmative Action." *Federal History Online* (2010): 42–57. http://fd.valenciacollege.edu/file/ftua/History%20of%20EO%2010925%20and%20Affirmative%20Action.pdf.

McLean, Nancy. *Freedom Is Not Enough: The Opening of the American Workplace.* Cambridge: Harvard University Press, 2008.

McCrudden, Christopher. *Buying Social Justice: Equality, Government Procurement, and Legal Change.* New York: Oxford University Press, 2007.

McQuaid, Kim. *Uneasy Partners: Big Business in American Politics, 1945–1990.* Baltimore: Johns Hopkins University Press, 1993.

Minchin, Timothy J. *Hiring the Black Worker: The Racial Integration of the Southern Textile Industry, 1960–1980.* Chapel Hill: University of North Carolina Press, 1999.

———. "Making Best Use of the New Laws: The NAACP and the Fight for Civil Rights in the South, 1965–1975." *Journal of Southern History* 74, 3 (August 2008): 669–702.

Minchin, Timothy J., and John A. Salmond. *After the Dream: Black and White Southerners since 1965.* Lexington: University Press of Kentucky, 2011.

Mixon, Gregory. "'Good Negro—Bad Negro': The Dynamics of Race and Class in Atlanta during the Era of the 1906 Riot." *Georgia Historical Quarterly* 81, 3 (Fall 1997): 593–621.

Montgomery, H. Wynn. "The Private Sector Initiative Program (PSIP): A Critical Analysis." Paper prepared for Georgia State University, ca. late 1980s, Georgia Department of Labor Library, Atlanta.

Northrup, Herbert. "The Negro in Aerospace Work." *California Management Review* 11, 4 (Summer 1969): 11–26.

Onkst, David. "'First a Negro . . . Incidentally a Veteran': Black World War Two Veterans and the G.I. Bill of Rights in the Deep South, 1944–1948." *Journal of Social History* 31, 3 (Spring 1998): 517–43.

Piketty, Thomas. *Capital in the Twenty-First Century.* Cambridge: Harvard University Press, 2014.

Putney, B. *Revival of Apprenticeship.* Washington, D.C.: Congressional Quar-

terly Press, 1940. https://library.cqpress.com/cqresearcher/document.php?id
=cqresrre1940122300.

Rae, John B. "Financial Problems of the American Aircraft Industry, 1906–1940." *Business History Review* 39 (Spring 1965): 99–114.

Reed, Merl. "Bell Aircraft Comes South: The Struggle by Atlanta Blacks for Jobs during World War II." In *Labor in the Modern South*, ed. Glenn Eskew, 102–34. Athens: University of Georgia Press, 2001.

Reed, Susan. *The Diversity Index: The Alarming Truth about Diversity in Corporate America . . . and What Can Be Done about It*. New York: American Management Association, 2011.

Roche, Jeff. *Restructured Resistance: The Sibley Commission and the Politics of Desegregation in Georgia*. Athens: University of Georgia Press, 1998.

Rockefeller Brothers Fund. *The Challenge to America: Its Economic and Social Aspects*. Garden City, N.Y.: Doubleday, 1958.

Roediger, David, and Elizabeth Esch. *The Production of Difference: Race and the Management of Labor in U.S. History*. New York: Oxford University Press, 2014.

Rubio, Philip F. *A History of Affirmative Action, 1619–2000*. Jackson: University Press of Mississippi, 2001.

Scheidel, Walter. *The Great Leveler: Violence and the History of Inequality from the Stone Age to the Twenty-First Century*. Princeton: Princeton University Press, 2017.

Scott, Thomas A. *Cobb County, Georgia, and the Origins of the Suburban South*. Marietta, Ga.: Cobb Landmarks and Historical Society, 2003.

———. "Impact of Bell and Lockheed on the Culture of Cobb County during the Civil Rights Era." Paper presented at the Georgia Association of Historians Annual Meeting, April 6, 2007.

———. "James V. Carmichael (1910–1972)." In *New Georgia Encyclopedia*, May 16, 2016. https://www.georgiaencyclopedia.org/articles/business-economy/james-v-carmichael-1910-1972.

Skrentny, John D. *The Ironies of Affirmative Action*. Chicago: University of Chicago Press, 1996.

Smith, Robert Samuel. *Race, Labor, and Civil Rights: Griggs versus Duke Power and the Struggle for Equal Employment Opportunity*. Baton Rouge: Louisiana State University Press, 2008.

Stainback, Kevin, and Donald Tomaskovic-Devey. *Documenting Desegregation: Racial and Gender Segregation in Private Sector Employment since the Civil Rights Act*. New York: Sage, 2012.

Stone, Clarence. *Regime Politics: Governing Atlanta, 1946–1988*. Lawrence: University Press of Kansas, 1989.

Sugrue, Thomas. *Sweet Land of Liberty: The Forgotten Struggle for Civil Rights in the North*. New York: Random House, 2008.

Sutton, John, and Frank Dobbin. "The Two Faces of Governance: Responses to Legal Uncertainty in U.S. Firms, 1955 to 1985." *American Sociological Review* 61, 5 (October 1996): 794–811.

Sverdik, Alan. "Atlanta Daily World." In *New Georgia Encyclopedia*, November 1, 2018, https://www.georgiaencyclopedia.org/articles/arts-culture/atlanta-daily-world.

Tate, Rachanice Candy Patrice. "'Our Art Itself Was Our Activism': Atlanta's Neighborhood Arts Center, 1975–1990." PhD diss., Clark Atlanta University, 2012.

Teel, Leonard Ray. *Ralph Emerson McGill, Voice of the Southern Conscience*. Knoxville: University of Tennessee Press, 2001.

———. "Ralph McGill (1898–1969)." In *New Georgia Encyclopedia*, December 7, 2015. https://www.georgiaencyclopedia.org/articles/arts-culture/ralph-mcgill-1898-1969.

The Training within Industry Report, 1940–1945. Washington, D.C.: U.S. Government Printing Office, 1945.

Turner, Sarah, and John Bound. "Closing the Gap or Widening the Divide: The Effects of the G.I. Bill and World War II on the Educational Outcomes of Black Americans." *Journal of Economic History* 63, 1 (March 2003): 145–77.

Vander Meulen, Jacob. *West Coast Aircraft Labor and an American Military-Industrial Complex, 1935–1941*. Seattle: University of Washington, 1996.

Wallerstein, Immanuel. "1968, Revolution in the World System." *Theory and Society* 18, 4 (July 1989): 431–49.

Watkins, Steve. *The Black O: Racism and Redemption in an American Corporate Empire*. Athens: University of Georgia Press, 1997.

Weaver, Robert C. "Negro Employment in the Aircraft Industry." *Quarterly Journal of Economics* 59 (August 1945): 597–625.

———. "Recent Developments in Negro Union Relationships." *Journal of Political Economy* 52, 3 (September 1944): 234–49.

Wilson, Francine Rusille. *The Segregated Scholars: Black Social Scientists and the Creation of Black Labor Studies, 1890–1950*. Charlottesville: University of Virginia Press, 2006.

Wood, Dan. "Does Politics Make a Difference at the EEOC?" *American Journal of Political Science* 34, 2 (May 1990): 503–30.

Wright, Gavin. *Sharing the Prize: The Economics of the Civil Rights Revolution in the South*. Cambridge: Belknap Press of Harvard University Press, 2013.

Zieger, Robert. *For Jobs and Freedom: Race and Labor in America since 1865*. Lexington: University Press of Kentucky, 2010.

INDEX

Abel, Joseph, 19
ads, blacks in, 72–73
Aeronautical Chamber of Commerce of America, 26
affirmative action: in Executive Order 10925, 11, 80, 90, 146; studies of, 3–4. *See also* Lockheed-Georgia
AFL (American Federation of Labor), 18, 19
Afro Magazine, 49
AFSC (American Friends Service Committee), 144
Air Force Plant 6: Lockheed reopening of, xi, 9, 34, 35, 83, 125; tunnel access to, 1; in World War II, 30, 39. *See also* Lockheed-Georgia
Alco Hydro-Aeroplane Company, 17
Allen, Ivan, Jr., 78, 150
Alston, Harry, 58–61
American Bakeries, 47
American Federation of Labor (AFL), 18, 19
American Friends Service Committee (AFSC), 144
American Steel and Wire Company, 61
Anaconda Wire and Cable, 45
Anderson, Terry, 3, 7, 95
Andrews, G. H., 68
Anti-Defamation League, 144
apprenticeships, 20–21, 71, 85, 88, 140
Arnall, Ellis, 39, 143
Arnold, Harold, 96
Association of Federal, State, County, and Municipal Employees, 157–58
Atlanta, Ga.: black political power in, 13, 141, 154, 160; business community of, 13, 94, 142, 144, 146, 147, 153, 157, 160, 163, 168; Jackson as mayor of, 12, 13, 150–52, 153–54, 155, 157, 158, 160, 161; in late 1970s, 150–58; Massell as mayor of, 150–52, 158; sanitation workers' strike in, 157–58; school desegregation in, 76–79, 143
Atlanta Area Voluntary Merit Employment Association, 12, 102, 130, 144, 147

Atlanta Bureau of Cultural Affairs, 153
Atlanta Chamber of Commerce, 153, 155
Atlanta Constitution, 36–37, 78, 79, 82, 131, 151
Atlanta Daily World: anonymous "already here" quote in, 82; on B-47 project, 49; on C-141 contract, 78; on Carmichael, 37, 41, 42; on Haughton, 50; Holmes's letter in, 67; Hudson as first black supervisor noted by, 51, 58; Lockheed-Georgia's third birthday noted in, 58; Massell's "Think White" statement and, 150, 151; on merit employment, 144; on Observatory Council, 81; politics of, 37–38; as source for book, 3; on Troutman, 91
Atlanta Merit Employment Coordinating Committee, 144
Atlanta Police Department, 64–65, 153
Atlanta public schools, 76–79, 150, 153, 161
Atlanta Urban League, 30, 69, 131; on area job gains, 95; hiring discussions with, 45, 47; Lydon meeting with, 44; merit employment and, 144. *See also* National Urban League

B-1 bomber, 1
B-29 Superfortress, 9, 30, 38, 39, 45, 83
B-47 Stratojet, 49, 84; aft section crew for, 10, 48, 63, 71; nose section crew for, 48, 50–51, 65; production levels of, 61, 70
badge, as source of pride, 101, 167
"bad Negro"/"good Negro" dichotomy, 56, 96, 119–20, 127, 151
Baldwin, William H., Jr., 33
Banks, Ralph, 125–27, 130
Banks et al. v. Lockheed, 3, 134, 138–41, 174; settlement of, 139–41
Bell, Tartt, 144
Bell Aircraft: at Air Force Plant 6, 9, 29–30, 38, 39, 45; former employees of, 38, 53, 63, 83–84; in Texas, 46
BellSouth, 161
B. F. Goodrich, 46

215

Biddle, Wayne, 19
Bird, Joseph, 35
Black Lockheed Employees, 131–32
Black Power movement, 115, 119
Blair, Rip, 29
Boeing, 30, 77, 85, 164, 177
Booker T. Washington High School, 87, 129
Boyle, Sarah Patton, 120
Boyne, Walter, 15–16, 132
Brown v. Board of Education, 60
Build the People, 11, 111, 115–21
Build the People (guidebook), 116–19
Burbage, Tom, 173
Business Advisory Council, 167
Butler Street YMCA, 79, 130, 144

C-5A transport, 147, 174; blacks as percentage of workers on, 114, 183; cost overruns with, 132–33; phasing out of, 139; production set up for, 105, 108–9, 114, 182
C-130 Hercules transport, 52, 139; contracts for, 10, 61, 69, 75, 77, 195n35; crew integration, 174–75; crew segregation, 70, 72; crews formed for, 70, 71, 72; demand for, 61, 75, 76
C-130B transport, 75
C-141 Starlifter, 11, 15, 16, 97, 174; contract for, 77–78
cafeterias, segregation of, 15, 65, 66, 81, 93
California Eagle, 24
Canada, Benjamin, 161
Carmichael, James V., 50, 56, 195n35; background of, 39; at Bell Aircraft, 38, 39, 45; C-141 contract and school desegregation linked by, 78–79; hiring of, 9; hiring plan of, 45; at Hollowell meetings, 69, 70, 81; local economy promoted by, 29–30, 40; NAACP criticism of, 41; patriotism evoked by, 38; political career of, 39–40; "qualified or can be trained" statement of, 41–42, 56; as racial moderate, 39–40; segregation maintained by, 36–37, 41–42, 43–44; selected to head Lockheed-Georgia, 40; "southern tradition" accepted by, 6, 36, 41, 42, 43; on training of black employees, 63
Carter, Jimmy, CETA and, 12, 152, 153, 154, 155, 157, 158, 159
Carver High School, 87
Casey, Paul, 62

CEA (Council of Economic Advisers), 102–3, 160
Center for International Policy, 31
CETA. *See* Comprehensive Employment and Training Act
Chamberlain, Kendrick, 125, 127–28, 130, 139
Chance-Vaught, 84, 164
Chandler, Betty, 40
Chappellet, Cyril, 20, 23
Chomsky, Noam, 79–80
Christmas parties, 50, 87, 88, 96
Chrysler, 95, 148–49
CIO (Congress of Industrial Organizations), 18, 19
Civil Rights Act (1964), 8, 11, 90, 91, 92, 103, 109, 122; EEOC created by, 6; EEO data mandated by, 6–7; IAM and, 125; merit employment and, 146; NAACP and, 125; right to sue in, 131; ruling on class-action suits and, 176; testing and, 138. *See also* Equal Employment Opportunity Commission
Civil Rights Commission, U.S., 111
civil rights movement, 8, 9, 35, 39, 103; assessment of, 170; caution urged on, 37–38; corporate response to, 13; in Detroit, 148; education and, 41; in Great Depression, 22; labor movement and, 18–19; in late 1960s, 147–48; legislation and, 40–41; literature on, 5–6; PCEEO and, 93; personnel departments and, 91; protest in, 37–38, 79
Clay, Lucius, 29
Clendenin, John, 161
Clinton, Bill, 161
Cobb, James, 143
Cobb County, Ga.: C-141 contract and, 78; school desegregation in, 77; U.S. decision for plant in, 29–30. *See also* Lockheed-Georgia
Cobb County Board of Education, 85–87
Coca-Cola, 40, 143, 175, 177
Coffey, Matthew, 155
Cohen, Nathan, 120
Cold War, 31, 32, 38, 43–44
Collins, William J., 22, 96
Comprehensive Employment and Training Act (CETA; 1973), 12–13, 150, 152–60; assessments of, 168, 203n34; as federal/state and local hybrid, 159; Jesse Jackson on,

161; public employment aspect of, 12–13, 152, 153, 154, 158–59, 160, 161
Congress of Industrial Organizations (CIO), 18, 19
Consolidated Air, 46
Consolidated Vultee Aircraft (Convair), 46, 77
constructive action, 146–47
Container Corporation of America, 45
Council of Economic Advisers (CEA), 102–3, 160
Covington, Floyd, 25–26
Crisis, 19

Dash, Leon, 135
Davies, Tom Adam, 171
Delta Airlines, 78
Delton, Jennifer, 80, 91; on diversity, 163; on International Harvester, 42, 169; on Lockheed, 169; overview of work of, 3, 5, 7; on PCGC, 59; on PfP, 94, 95
desegregation: in Atlanta schools, 76–79; four periods of, 6–9. *See also* Lockheed-Georgia
Detroit riot (1967), 106, 147
DeWester, Lloyd, 47–48
Dewey, Donald, 33
diversity, 163, 168
Dobbin, Frank, 3, 4–5, 91, 95, 169, 170
Dodson, Henry, 151
Dooley, Channing, 26–27
Douglas, Donald, 31
Douglas Aircraft, 24, 46, 77
Drabant, Richard, 148–49, 150
drinking fountains, segregation of, 15, 50, 65
Du Bois, W. E. B., 19
Duke Power, 4, 138
Duke University, 58

Earhart, Amelia, 17
Ebony, 120
education and schools, 33, 35, 41; Atlanta school desegregation, 76–79; Atlanta's growing black population and, 150; *Brown v. Board of Education*, 60; discriminatory requirements for, 47, 49, 66, 85, 123; guidance counselors, 129, 143; inequality ascribed to differences in, 83, 86, 87; recruitment, 47, 61, 87, 94, 129, 140, 143, 145, 146; Youth Motivation Day and, 145
EEO Action Committee, 130, 187

EEOC. *See* Equal Employment Opportunity Commission
Eisenhower, Dwight D., 10, 59, 84
Elkins, Willie T., 4, 69, 71; background and career of, 64–66; EEO complaint of, 122; 1961 complaint affidavit of, 64–66, 67, 68, 129, 194n25
Emory University, 40, 151, 161
Eppert, Kenneth, 138
Equal Employment Opportunity Commission (EEOC), 11, 69, 109, 122, 125–31, 138; amended regulations of, 133; Banks suit and, 125–27, 130, 139, 141; Black Lockheed Employees and, 131; creation of, 6, 8; data from, 3; Kitchen and Gordon's emphasis on compliance with, 140; lawsuit subsequent to complaints to, 130; Lockheed conciliation agreement with, 114, 130, 136, 186; performance reviews and, 116; promotions and, 113; under Reagan, 8, 177; Reid suit and, 175
Eskew, Glenn, 13, 170
Estlund, Cynthia, 178–79
Evans, James, 60
Evans, Leonard, 73
Executive Order 8802 (1941), 7, 22; Lockheed response to, 9, 16, 23, 24, 27
Executive Order 10210 (1951), 41, 44
Executive Order 10308 (1951), 9–10
Executive Order 10925 (1961), 7, 10; "affirmative action" required in, 11, 80, 90, 146; Lockheed and, 80, 82–83, 88, 90, 142; National Association of Manufacturers and, 91

F-15 fighter, 111
Fair Employment Practices Committee (FEPC), 16, 22, 24, 30
Fair Labor Standards Act (1938), 36
Faubus, Orval, 41
Feild, John G., 83, 89, 92
FEPC (Fair Employment Practices Committee), 16, 22, 24, 30
Ferguson, Charles, 51–52, 55
Firestone Tire and Rubber, 46, 169
Fisher (inspector), 52–53
Fitzgerald Act (1937), 20–21
Fitzpatrick, Jack, 155
Ford, 47, 148, 150
Ford, Gerald R., 160

Forest Service, U.S., 129–30
Forrester, J. Owen, 175, 176
Frank, Robert, 177–78
Freedom Budget, 103–4, 147
Fuhrman, Robert, 132–33
Fulton County, Ga., school desegregation in, 77
Fultz quadruplets, 73

Gaines, Marion, 78
Gelber, Steven, 95
General Cable, 47
General Electric, 46
General Motors, 42, 150
Georgia, University of, 77
Georgia Chamber of Commerce, 78, 102
Georgia Department of Education, 146
Georgia Department of Vocational Education, 86
Georgia Power, 175
Georgia State Employment Service, 102
Georgia Tech, 85, 101, 174
GI Bill, 36
Golland, David Hamilton, 4
"good Negro"/"bad Negro" dichotomy, 56, 96, 119–20, 127, 151
Goodyear Tire and Rubber, 95
Gordon, Hugh, 5, 11, 13, 46–47, 69, 82, 89, 120, 125, 128, 135, 161–62; on additional training for blacks, 63; assessments of role of, 169, 170, 171; Atlanta black political power and, 141, 142; Atlanta Merit Employment Association and, 12, 130; background of, 2; Banks lawsuit and, 138, 139–40; on Build the People, 115; CETA and, 152–53, 154; culture change and, 124; dismissal numbers of, 108, 110, 120, 181–82, 185; Dobbin on, 6; as equal employment specialist, 91; excerpts of documents by, 181–87; hiring of, 1–2; historical research of, 178–79; Kitchen video and, 137; MEAs and, 142–147; with NAB, 12, 142–47, 152, 154, 155, 157, 158, 159; necessity of affirmative action and, 163–64; 1970 EEO report of, 112–13; North American Rockwell advised by, 136; PCGC assessed by, 59; as politically conservative, 167; research and interviews by, 2; on training and affirmative action, 107–11, 121, 168; on voluntarism, 179; on work area segregation, 64

Gore, Al, 161
Government Aircraft Plant 6: Lockheed reopening of, xi, 9, 34, 35, 83, 125; tunnel access to, 1; in World War II, 30, 39. See also Lockheed-Georgia
Great Britain, 20
Great Migration, 36
Great Recession, 161, 171, 203n34
Great Speckled Bird, 132
Greenlea, C. W., 43, 44
Griffin, Marvin, 41
Griggs v. Duke Power Company, 138, 140
Grizzle, Sam, 173
Gross, Courtlandt, 15, 89, 128
Gross, Robert: background of, 17–18; Build the People and, 115; at congressional hearings, 31–32; on government-industry relations, 31–32; integration instructions of, 15; labor unions and, 19; NAACP letter to, 44; New Deal as viewed by, 18; on peak wartime production, 30–31
Grumman, 135
guidance counselors, 129, 143

Hale, Paul, 98
Hall, Felix, 130
Hamall, Tom, 155
Hamilton, Grace Towns, 44
Hampton Institute, 174
Harper, C. L., 43, 44
Hartsfield, William B., 79, 150
Hartung, William, 31
Haughton, Dan, 15, 69; arrival at Lockheed-Georgia, 49–50; C-130 line and, 70–71; equal employment memo of, 133; labor relations philosophy of, 50
Head Start, 103
Hibbard, Hal, 18
high schools. *See* education and schools
Hill, C. W., 140
Hill, Herbert: EEO complaints and, 125; 1957 Lockheed investigation of, 71; PCEEO and, 92, 93; pre–World War II work of, 21; on segregated unions, 67
Hill, Jesse, 155
Hinds, T. W., 65–66
Hire First program, 149
Hobson, Maurice, 171
Hodgson, Godfrey, 80
Hollowell, Donald Lee, 69–70, 81, 195n35; as EEOC office head, 122

Holmes, Alfred "Tup," 4, 67–68
Holzer, Harry, 102–3, 160–61
Housing and Urban Development, U.S. Department of, 23
Howard University, 26
Hudson, Edith, 72–73
Hudson, Harry, 4, 42, 72, 177, 179; assistant manager post sought by, 74, 98, 147; buyer position of, 97–100; on Carmichael, 38; early Lockheed career of, 47–57; on excessive training, 85; expanded supervisory role of, 54; Fisher's relationship with, 52–53; inspector's discrimination against, 48; memoir of, 2–3; Mintz's conflict with, 53–55; mixed crew managed by, 73–74; National Management Association and, 96; in Pet Milk ad, 72–73; Poore's relationship with, 56; progress seen by, 167; promoted to supervisor, 10, 51, 52, 58, 96; raise received by, 74; recruitment of, 10, 47; on retirement, 178; travel denied to, 99; unequal education requirements noted by, 123; unjust performance reviews of, 54–55; workers recommended by, 50–51
Hudson, Harry, Jr., 2
Hudson, Robert H., 5, 85–87, 102, 105
Hudson MK1, 20
human resources. *See* personnel departments
Humphrey, Hubert, 128, 167
Hungry Club, 144, 150

International Association of Machinists (IAM): as AFL member, 18, 19; desegregation efforts at, 67–68; discrimination and elections of, 124; Lockheed recognition of, 39; segregated lodges of, 65, 88; segregation perpetuated by, 10, 66–69, 71, 88, 124–25
International Harvester, 42–43, 55, 88, 169
International Shoe Factory, 45–46
Irwin, R. Randall: early Lockheed career of, 20; on hiring procedures for black workers, 27–29; Howard University presentation of, 26; on integration, 24, 25; Training within Industry and, 27

Jackson, Jesse, 161
Jackson, Maynard: as Atlanta's first black mayor, 12, 150; business community and, 13, 154, 157, 158, 160; on CETA, 161; election of, 151–52, 153–54; as outsider, 153; PIC and, 155, 157; sanitation workers' strike and, 157–58
Javits, Jacob, 92, 93
Jenkins, C. A., 105, 181, 182
Jennings, James, 160
Jet, 51
Job Corps, 103
Job Opportunities in the Business Sector program, 154
Job Training Partnership Act (JTPA; 1982), 158, 159, 161
Johnson, Kelly, 18
Johnson, Lyndon B., 12, 143, 167; Council of Economic Advisers of, 160; Kerner Commission and, 147; Lockheed affirmative action and, 89; as PCEEO chair, 80–83, 92, 94; policy tensions under, 102–3, 107; training programs under, 103–7; War on Poverty of, 147; Weaver appointed by, 23
Johnson, Napoleon, 61
Jones, Joseph, 124
Jones, Reginald L., 25–26
JTPA (Job Training Partnership Act; 1982), 158, 159, 161

Katznelson, Ira, 4, 6, 36
Kelly, Gilbert L., 96
Kemp, Reginald, 1–2, 52, 85
Kennedy, John F., 75; equal employment emphasized by, 64, 80; Executive Order 10925 of, 7, 10, 11, 80, 82–83, 88, 90, 91, 142, 146; Lockheed affirmative action and, 89
Kennedy, Robert, 5, 92
Kennesaw State University, 55
Kennon, Robert S., 61, 64; departure of, 194n25; Elkin's meeting with, 65; hiring of, 46–47, 75; recruiting trips of, 47
Kerner Commission, 147–48
Kheel, Theodore, 93–94
King, Martin Luther, Jr., 147
Kinoch, John, 24
Kitchen, Larry, 132–33, 136; Banks suit and, 139–40; EEO video of, 137–38; reduced workforce announced by, 139
Korean War, 2, 9, 32, 34, 38; end of, 44, 61
Krone, Robert C., 111–12
Kruse, Joseph, 92, 95
Ku Klux Klan, 50, 93

INDEX   219

Labor Department, U.S., 21, 113; CETA and, 152, 155, 156, 157; MDTA and, 104, 105–6
Labor Market Advisory Committee, 156
labor unions: apprenticeships and, 20–21; civil rights movement and, 18–19; corporate efforts against, 169; in Great Depression, 18. *See also* International Association of Machinists; *and other specific unions*
Laird, Pamela, 51
Land O' Lakes Creamery, 46
Lawman, J. T., 128
LeSueur, Win, 65, 87, 130
Lewis, John, 151, 175
Lincoln Airplane and Flying School, 56
Lindbergh, Charles, 17, 56
Little Rock school desegregation, 41
Livermore, Charles, 60
Living Witness program, 145
Lockheed Aircraft: apprentice program of, 21; bankruptcy and reorganization of, 17–18; Boyne's history of, 15–16; *Brown's* effect on, 60; California integration record of, 9, 15, 16, 23, 24, 35, 44, 46, 49, 65, 89–90, 137, 168; commercial versus defense sectors of, 32; early history of, 17; in Great Depression, 17–25; initial affirmative action plan of, 11; as integration leader, 16, 24, 29, 35, 112; as military organization, 50; name of, xi, 17; in postwar years, 31–32; in World War II, 24–31, 35. *See also* Lockheed-Georgia
Lockheed Electra, 18
Lockheed Electronics, 133
Lockheed Employees Recreation Club, 87–88
Lockheed-Georgia: alleged favoritism of blacks at, 108, 109, 110, 113, 120, 184, 185; Alston's assessment of integration at, 58–61; attitudes of blacks monitored at, 66; badge of, as source of pride, 101, 167; black skepticism of, 38; blacks underrepresented in skilled jobs at, 1, 2, 44, 46, 48, 49, 57, 71, 75, 166; black workers moved to problem areas at, 63; boom-bust cycle of, 75; cafeteria protest at, 81; civil rights leader skepticism of, 43; dismissal numbers at, 108, 110, 120, 181–82, 185; early affirmative action efforts at, 76–100; in early 1950s, 35–57; in early 1960s, 76–100; in early 1970s, 115–21, 131–41; EEO assessment of, 163–71; EEO dissemination plan of, 136–37; employment numbers at, 42, 61, 71, 75, 84, 102, 108–9, 110, 114, 122–23, 137, 139, 164, 165, 166, 182, 183; existing mores blamed for discrimination at, 11, 82, 84; first affirmative action plan of, 89–90; first black head of, 173; first black skilled workers at, 47; first black supervisor at, 51; initial years of, 35–57; as integration leader, 16, 112; labor relations philosophy at, 50; in late 1950s, 58–75; in late 1960s, 101–15, 122–31, 142–45, 146–49; plant reopened by, xi, 9, 34, 35, 83, 125; production problems at, 132–33; psychologists' survey of, 101–2; recreational segregation at, 87–88; residence of employees of, 4; satisfaction levels at, 101–2; segregated tunnel access to, 1; social versus work integration at, 52, 62; undercover promotion at, 174; white managers' "bad attitudes" at, 69; work area segregation maintained at, 36–37, 41–42, 43–44, 63–64, 70, 72, 84, 88
Lockheed Management Club, 96
Lockheed Martin Aeronautics Company: merger of, xi, 176; 2000 class-action lawsuit against, 173–77
Lockheed Missiles and Space, 132
Lockheed Southern Star, 3, 40, 128; affirmative action plan in, 89–90; on C-141 contract, 78; EEO coordinator announced in, 129; Haughton's praise of, 50; Hudson's promotion in, 51; inaugural issue of, 38–39
Lockheed Star, 20, 24
Lockheed Vega, 17, 23–25
Lockheed-Vega Plant, 23–25, 50
Lockheed-Vega Star, 24
Lockwood, Howard, 82, 91, 94
Los Angeles riots (1965), 120
Loughead, Allan, 17
Loughead, Malcolm, 17
Lydon, James P., 9; affirmative action plan finalized by, 89; background of, 44; hiring plan of, 45; limited black worker opportunities seen by, 59–60; transferred to Burbank, 83; transferred to Georgia, 9; Urban League meeting of, 44

Mabry, John B., 54, 66, 69, 71, 85
MacLean, Nancy, 3, 7
Maddox, Lester, 143

Management Development and Selection Department, 123, 124
Management Test Battery, 139
"manifesto of grievances," 131–32
Manpower Development and Training Act (MDTA; 1962), 102, 103, 104, 106, 159
Marable, Manning, 13, 170
Margo, Robert, 33
Martin, Glenn L., 17
Martin Marietta, 176
Massell, Sam, 150–52, 158; "Think White" comment of, 150–51
massive resistance, 41, 76, 77
Mattison, Eugene G., 9, 82, 89, 98, 194n25; assessment of role of, 170, 171; background of, 83; discrimination as "already here" and, 11, 82; equal employment assessment of, 133–35, 136; at Hollowell-mediated meetings, 69, 81; on Humphrey, 167; MEAS and, 147; North American Rockwell and, 136; with Plans for Progress, 91, 94, 143; segregation justified by, 83–84; on training discrimination, 85
McArthur, Douglas, 2
McCollum, Herbert, 78
McCormick, Fowler, 43
McDonnell Aircraft, 84
McDonnell-Douglas, 111–12, 113, 134, 135
McGill, Ralph, 37
McKinney, Cynthia, 175
McLendon, Jack, 55–56
McNamara, Robert, 93
MDTA. *See* Manpower Development and Training Act
Mead, 143
merit employers' associations (MEAS), 12, 142–47; equal employment compared with, 144
Metropolitan Atlanta Summit Leadership Conference, 131
Michigan, University of, 130, 148
middle class, black, 5, 13, 25, 73, 130
Miller, G. William, 94–95
Milton, Lorimer, 69
Minchin, Timothy, 4, 125
minority set-asides, 158, 160
Mintz, Harold, 53–54; background of, 53; C-130 line and, 70–71, 72
Montgomery, H. Wynn, 153, 155, 156
Morehouse College, 46, 47, 63, 64, 73
Morris Brown College, 61

Motorola Research Laboratories, 45
Moynihan, Daniel Patrick, 5, 102, 104, 107, 161
Murphy, Beatrice, 49

NAACP. *See* National Association for the Advancement of Colored People
NAB. *See* National Alliance of Businessmen
National Advisory Commission on Civil Disorders, 147–48
National Alliance of Businessmen (National Alliance of Business; NAB), 102, 106–7, 138; black political power and, 142, 160; CETA and, 153, 154; Gordon's work with, 12, 142–47, 152, 154, 155, 157, 158, 159; Hire First program of, 149; metros organized by, 12, 142, 148, 149, 155, 156; Youth Motivation Day studied by, 145–46
National Association for the Advancement of Colored People (NAACP), 10, 44, 69; Banks lawsuit and, 3, 134, 138–41; black job seekers encouraged by, 43; black Lockheed Employees and, 131; Carmichael criticized by, 41; EEO complaints and, 125, 130, 184; 1957 investigation by, 67, 71; 1961 letter to PCEEO from, 81–82, 83, 89; PfP and, 92; in pre–World War II years, 21, 22; on Troutman, 93; Vultee Aircraft and, 29; Wagner Act opposed by, 18–19; on white flight, 150
National Association of Manufacturers, 32, 91
National Carbide, 46
National Labor Relations Act (1935), 18
National Management Association, 96
National Urban League, 10, 22, 25, 40; Alston's report for, 58–61; employment opportunity survey of, 45–46; Lockheed hiring aided by, 27; Lockheed preference for, 44; merit employment and, 144; 1954 report of, 36; on PfP, 95; "southern tradition" comment and, 43; Wagner Act opposed by, 18. *See also* Atlanta Urban League
neoliberalism, 13, 142, 160, 163, 171
new federalism, 159
New York Times, 96
Nixon, Richard M., 37, 107, 113, 159, 160
North American Aviation, 21, 24, 46
North American Rockwell, 11, 135–36, 137, 186
North Carolina, 33
Northrop Aircraft, 46, 134
Northrup, Herbert, 33, 68

Obama, Barack, 13, 167, 203n34
Observatory Committee on Race Relations, 69, 81
Observatory Council on Discrimination, 81
Occupational Information Center for Business and Industry, 146
Office of Federal Contract Compliance, 8, 11, 111, 136, 140
Office of Production Management, 22, 25
O'Kelly, William, 138
Opportunity, 25
optimum objectivity, 183–84
organizational theory, 7–8
Ormsby, Robert, 12, 155
O'Toole, Thomas, 135

P-38 plane, 20, 30
Patterson, Frederick Douglass, 35
Patterson, John H. "Pat," 4, 65, 129–30, 179
PCEEO. *See* President's Committee on Equal Employment Opportunity
PCGC. *See* President's Committee on Government Contracts
Pepsi, 73
performance reviews, 116–19; explicit standards required in, 119; nonderogatory language in, 118–19; in promotions, 123
performance standards, 109, 115–19, 132
"Personnel Awareness" training program, 111
personnel departments (human resources), 64–66, 71, 90–91, 146, 184; Black Lockheed Employees and, 131; diversity and, 163; Drabant and, 148–49; equal employment embraced by, 5–6, 167–68; performance reviews and, 116–19, 123
Peters, James, 77
Pet Milk Company, 72–73
PfP. *See* Plans for Progress
PICs (private industry councils), 154–56, 158
Piketty, Thomas, 171
Plans for Progress (PfP), 15, 16, 90–96, 107, 138, 154; assessments of, 95; Atlanta Merit Employment Association and, 12, 130; conservative advisory council for, 167; Lockheed amendment to, 122, 128–29; merit employers' associations in, 12, 142–47; origin of, 11
Poore, H. Lee, 56, 72, 147; on Hudson managing mixed crew, 73–74; on Hudson's assistant manager request, 74, 98, 147

Post, Wiley, 17
President's Committee on Equal Employment Opportunity (PCEEO), 80–82; contract cancellation power of, 11; Hudson's contact with, 99; Lockheed affirmative action and, 90; NAACP and, 81–82, 83, 89; Troutman with, 92–94; voluntary versus compulsory approach in, 92–93
President's Committee on Government Contracts (PCGC), 59, 60, 67, 69, 80, 84
Private Industry Council of Atlanta, 157
private industry councils (PICs), 154–56, 158
Private Sector Initiative Program (PSIP), 154, 155, 156, 157
promotions and upgrades: Banks lawsuit and, 138, 139, 140; discrimination in, 30, 67, 82, 84, 89, 95, 101, 122–31; EEOC emphasis on, 113; Lockheed procedures for, 123–24; Mattison on, 135; Sinkfield and, 177; vague criteria for, 124. *See also* Hudson, Harry
PSIP (Private Sector Initiative Program), 154, 155, 156, 157
public employment, 163; CETA and, 12–13, 152, 153, 154, 158–59, 160, 161
public schools. *See* education and schools
Pulver, W. A. "Dick," 15, 69, 75, 78

racial sensitivity training, 11, 42–43, 115–21
Ramsey, Ted, 72
Randolph, A. Philip, 104
Reagan, Ronald, 8, 157, 159, 177
Reconstruction Finance Corporation, 18
recreation, 50; segregation in, 87–88
recruitment, 20, 26, 44, 45, 46–47, 182; Banks suit and, 140; at black colleges, 47, 61, 140; at high schools, 87, 94, 129, 140, 143, 145, 146; summer youth employment initiatives, 129
Reid v. Lockheed Martin, 175–76
restrooms, segregation of, 15, 50, 65, 66, 81, 93
Reynolds Metals, 46
Rhyant, Lee, 13, 173
Rich's, 143
Rickenbacker Field, 30
Rieke, Bill, 97
right-to-work laws, 39, 68
R. J. Reynolds, 47
Rochester, Jack "Roc," 72, 97–98
Rockefeller Brothers Fund, 80

222 INDEX

Rogers, Lee, 49
Rolls-Royce Aerospace, 173
Roosevelt, Franklin D., 17, 18, 59, 91; Executive Order 8802 of, 7, 9, 16, 22, 23, 24, 27; FEPC established by, 16, 22
Rosenwald Fund, 33
Ross, Ernest "Pappy," 61–62, 69, 85, 122, 195n35
Rubio, Philip J., 3–4, 6
Russell, Richard, 79, 93

Salmond, John, 4
Sanders, Carl, 143
sanitation workers' strike (1970), 157–58
Scheidel, Walter, 171
schools. See education and schools
Scott, C. A., 37
Scott, Tom, 29, 40
Scripto Pen, 40, 50
self-evaluative privilege, 138
set-asides, minority, 158, 160
Shoney's, 4, 176–77
Sibley, John, 77, 92
Sibley Commission, 77, 92
Simpson, O. J., 175
Sinkfield, Clarence, 101, 167, 173–77
Skrentny, Philip, 4, 6
Smith, Robert S., 4
SNCC (Student Nonviolent Coordinating Committee), 151
Social Security, 36
Southall, Sarah, 42, 43
Southern Bell, 143
Southern Cement Company, 78
Southern Regional Council, 95
Southern Regional Economic Conference, 161
Southern Star. See *Lockheed Southern Star*
Southern Technical Institute, 55
space shuttle, 135, 137, 141
Stainback, Kevin, 6–9, 163
Stein, Judith, 159
Stevens, J. P., 141
Stevenson, Adlai, 92
St. Joseph News-Press, 96
Stone, Clarence, 13
Strode, Woody, 65
Student Nonviolent Coordinating Committee (SNCC), 151
supervisors: age of, 182–83; black, 15–16, 69, 70, 96, 114, 135, 137, 164, 165, 166, 174, 175; discipline problems and, 108, 181–82, 184; first black, 10, 51, 52, 58, 96; minority, 134; training for, 115–21
Supervisory Awareness Manual, 115–16
Sutton, John, 170

Talmadge, Eugene, 30, 39, 40
Talmadge, Herman: as governor, 40–41, 59; as senator, 77, 78, 79, 91, 93
Taylor, Hobart, 94, 143–44, 167
Taylor Aircraft, 56
Temco, 48
testing, discrimination and, 28, 126, 138, 139, 140, 174
Texaco, 177
Textron, 95
Thomas, Clarence, 8
Thomas, Julius, 45
time clocks, segregation of, 65, 66, 82
Tomaskovic-Devey, Donald, 6–9, 163
trade unions. See labor unions; *and specific unions*
training programs, 12, 20, 21, 26–27, 45–46, 47–48, 49, 85–87, 163; apprenticeships, 20–21, 71, 85, 88, 140; Build the People, 11, 111, 115–21; Carmichael's statement on, 41–42, 56; CETA and, 150, 152–59; at Chrysler, 149; "close monitoring" in, 105–6; Gordon on affirmative action and, 107–11, 121, 168; for "hard-core" unemployed, 102, 103, 106–8, 110, 114–15, 121, 129, 142, 148, 149, 154; Johnson efforts for, 103–4; at McDonnell-Douglas, 112; NAB and, 142; at off-site facility, 104–7; in PfP amendment, 129; plant reopening and, 83; psychodrama sessions in, 106; in racial awareness, 11, 42–43, 115–21; statistics on, 106; unequal access to, 127; viewed as excessive, 10, 63, 85–86; in World War II, 25, 30
Training within Industry, 15, 26–27
Trans World Airlines, 32
Troutman, Robert Battey, Jr., 90–94; Kennedy's relationship with, 91–92; Plans for Progress originated by, 11; resignation from PCEEO, 94
Truman, Harry S., 9–10, 41, 50, 59
Trust Company of Georgia Bank, 143
Turner, David, 125, 126
Turpeau, Aaron, 153, 157, 158, 160, 161, 203n34
Tuskegee Institute, 35

UAW (United Automobile Workers), 19, 169
unemployment, 12, 13; "hard-core," training and, 102, 103, 106–8, 110, 114–15, 121, 129, 142, 148, 149, 154
unions. *See* labor unions; *and specific unions*
United Automobile Workers (UAW), 19, 169
University of California at Los Angeles, 83
University of Georgia, 77
upgrades. *See* promotions and upgrades
Urban League. *See* Atlanta Urban League; National Urban League
U.S. Conference of Mayors, 156

Vander Meulen, Jacob, 19–20
Vandiver, Ernest, 41, 76–77, 92
Vinson, Carl, 79, 93
vocational guidance counselors, 129, 143
Voting Rights Act (1965), 4
Vultee Aircraft, 21, 29, 46, 53

Wade, Lyndon, 131
Wagner Act (1935), 18
Wallerstein, Immanuel, 13
War Manpower Commission, 27
War on Poverty, 147
Washington Afro-American, 73
Washington High School, 87, 129
Washington Post, 135, 158
Watkins, Steve, 4
Weaver, Robert C., 96, 168–69; career overview of, 22–23; on World War II integration, 23, 24, 26, 27, 29, 31
Webster, Isabelle Gates, 140

Weinke, Clint, 51
Westbrook, Harold, 125, 126–27
Western Electric, 95
Westinghouse, 95
white flight, 150
Whitfield, Smokey, 28–29
wildcat strikes, against integration, 42
Wilkins, Roy, 81–82, 150
Williams, Samuel, 82
Wirtz, Willard, 103, 107
women: black, 8, 59, 132; gender bias and, 7, 59, 132, 134, 168, 177; white, 8; workplace progress of, 8, 9, 12, 16, 135, 137
women's movement, 9, 13–14
Wonderlic test, 139, 140
Woodruff, Robert, 40
Woods, James, 131
Woods, Lincoln, 139
Workers Against Discrimination, 175
World War II, 2, 16, 19, 22–23, 129; Bell Aircraft in, 9, 29–30, 38, 39, 45; Lockheed in, 24–31, 35
Wright, Gavin, 3, 7, 13, 36, 170–71
Wyatt, J. O., 64, 131

Yates, Clayton, 69
YMCA (Young Men's Christian Association), 79, 130, 144
Young, Whitney, 95, 131
Youth Motivation Day, 144–45

Zook, Dwight, 136, 186

www.ingramcontent.com/pod-product-compliance
Lightning Source LLC
Chambersburg PA
CBHW011755220426
43672CB00018B/2975